Lines Were Drawn

Lines Were Drawn

Remembering Court-Ordered Integration at a Mississippi High School ■ *Edited by*

TEENA F. HORN, ALAN HUFFMAN, *and* JOHN GRIFFIN JONES

University Press of Mississippi / Jackson

www.upress.state.ms.us

The University Press of Mississippi is a member
of the Association of American University Presses.

First printing 2016

∞

Library of Congress Cataloging-in-Publication Data

Names: Horn, Teena F. | Huffman, Alan. | Jones, John Griffin.
Title: Lines were drawn : remembering court-ordered integration at a
Mississippi high school / edited by Teena Freeman Horn, Alan Huffman, and
John Griffin Jones.
Description: Jackson : University Press of Mississippi, 2016. | Includes
index.
Identifiers: LCCN 2015024068 (print) | LCCN 2015040216 (ebook) | ISBN
9781628462319 (hardback) | ISBN 9781626746640 (ebook)
Subjects: LCSH: School integration—Mississippi—Jackson. | Murrah High
School (Jackson, Miss.) | High school students—Mississippi—Jackson. |
Discrimination in education—Mississippi—Jackson. | Jackson (Miss.)—Race
relations. | School integration—United States—History. | Discrimination
in education—United States—History. | BISAC: SOCIAL SCIENCE /
Discrimination & Race Relations. | EDUCATION / History.
Classification: LCC LC214.23.J34 L56 2016 (print) | LCC LC214.23.J34 (ebook)
| DDC 379.2/630976251—dc23
LC record available at http://lccn.loc.gov/2015024068

British Library Cataloging-in-Publication Data available

Contents

Authors' Note

When we began compiling recollections of our fellow classmates about their experiences at Murrah between 1971 and 1973, our goal was to create as complete a record as possible of a unique experience—being part of one of the first public schools in the United States to be integrated under court order. Our class was the first at Murrah to graduate whose entire high-school experience was integrated, though there were two classes ahead of us, and other, smaller integrated classes elsewhere in Mississippi, including in Greenville and Hattiesburg.

We knew going in that not everyone in our class would be interested in participating in our documentary effort, so "complete" would be a relative term; in reality, the most we could hope for was a representative sampling. And it wasn't just a matter of ensuring that both races were represented; race, though obviously the defining force at work, was only one of our defining characteristics. We had our own personalities and cultural identities, some of which were tied to economic status. We had different attitudes about high school. Did we feel "school spirit" and cheer at pep rallies? Were we more interested in sports, theater, art, the band, the school newspaper, academic excellence (of all things!), or certain unsanctioned extracurricular activities? Such factors not only influenced our time at Murrah—they have also influenced our lives since, including whether or not we care to think back on our high-school experience now.

What we ended up with was a voluminous, self-selecting, partial—and, we hope, representative—record of a complex social experiment that involved hundreds of teenagers, forty years after the fact. It may not be complete, but it's telling. As Freddie Funches sagely observed, "It is what it is."

Readers may note that the recollections vary in presentation. Some appear more thoughtful than others, while some seem abbreviated, even curt. In most cases, this is a result of the method of response. We asked our classmates to submit their memories in essay form, but gave them the option of filling out a questionnaire. In a few cases, we conducted interviews. Then we drew from those and organized the comments according to theme. In some cases we did minor editing to delete repetitive filler words such as "uh" and "like," but we did so sparingly, according to standard editing practices, not wanting to diminish anyone's voice nor excise meaningful words or passages; when necessary we paraphrased or cited partial passages, as indicated in the text by the placement of quotation marks and ellipses.

Because we received far more material than could fit into one book, we had no choice but to excerpt, and if we left anything out, we apologize. Again, we labored under the assumption that a partial, representative record is far better than no record at all—assuming that "partial" does not imply partiality. The latter possibility was always on our minds, and we sought to minimize our feelings of individual partiality toward friends, favorite teachers, treasured memories, and historical interpretations. We believe, and fervently hope, that the resulting book is an accurate and illuminating record of coming to terms with the injustices that stem from institutionalized partiality.

We have deleted a few names, mostly in cases where we had no way (or at least didn't know a way) to get in touch with a person who was named in a potentially sensitive story offered by someone else. We did not give anyone the opportunity to rebut the accounts of others nor to revise their stories after the fact. Our goal was to create a truthful record, even if it occasionally made some of us uneasy.

Preface

If you have picked up or been given this book, you may very well be thinking: Please, no, not another book about race and Mississippi. I understand exactly.

Surely it depresses everyone, as it depresses me, that this state and country continue to be so race obsessed. Don't you often think: when are we going to get past this? Didn't we all expect that by now the issue of race would have faded, perhaps literally, from black and white to, at least, beige? Here we are, after having elected a black president, continuing to fret over race, debating it, worrying about the role it plays in all manner of things. This ranges from the tragic—why did George Zimmerman kill Trayvon Martin?—to the ridiculous—did television chef Paula Deen use the N-word?—to the consequential—the Supreme Court's Voting Rights Act decision removing Justice Department oversight from elections in Mississippi and elsewhere. Are we really still thinking about all of this, consumed by it, haunted by it? Apparently so.

Forty-four years ago, forced integration/desegregation—"busing" in the vernacular—occurred in the Jackson public schools. In *Alexander v. Holmes County School District*, handed down in 1969, the Supreme Court superseded *Brown v. Board of Education*'s desultory, quasi-deferential "all deliberate speed" (interpreted by Mississippi's white leaders as "all deliberate sloth") with the angry, trumpeting "terminate all dual systems *at once*" (emphasis mine). Thirty-three Mississippi school districts—including Jackson's—were ordered to integrate immediately, and so, one day in midyear 1970, yellow school buses full of black children pulled up at Bailey Junior High School on North State Street, and cars full of white children fled in the opposite direction down Riverside Drive. But some white children stayed. Thus, this book.

This book comprises a revisiting by black and white adults of their adolescent experiences—never an easy task, even for the most insightful and gifted writer. But these essayists have the advantage of working with good, meaty material. They knew at the time that they were in the middle of something important. Caught up in a social struggle that must have been incomprehensible to many of them except in the most superficial of ways, it nevertheless suffices that they appreciated what was right in front of their eyes: yesterday they went to school with people of their color and experience; today they are going to school with people of a different color who are largely suspect. And, as accurately as one can resurrect a forty-year-old emotion, these essays reflect what those days and times felt like. These reflections have a fresh, you-are-there quality. Joy and anger and sadness come through, after all these years. Their parents had no doubt sat them down and had talked and explained and answered questions, but, when it came right down to it, these children had to deal with this turmoil at a very emotional level, and the emotions come through loud and clear. This must have been very difficult for all of them. The insecurities of adolescence are tough enough under the best of circumstances; try layering massive integration and "social experimentation" into the mix. Those who stayed deserve great credit for the grace with which they handled it, by and large. To my knowledge, at Murrah and at the other Jackson schools, there were no massive fights, no riots, no vandalism, no public grandstanding—all of that was left to the adults. These kids picked up their books and Bic pens and went to school.

This is not a top-down or bottom-up view, or a chronology, or even a history. It is an inside-out remembrance of what it was like for seventeen- and eighteen-year-old Mississippi children (and a couple of teachers and other observers) to go to school every day as sometimes witting and sometimes unwitting instruments of equity. Wrongs had been committed for decades and centuries and now justice was turning in the lurching way that justice turns, and these children were the stagecraft.

Unfortunately, it seems that justice is one thing and humanity another. Because here we are, forty-plus years later, still debating and fretting, gnawing at ourselves like neurotic dogs, seemingly unable to shed the benighted, race-riddled reality that is Mississippi and the United States. At one level, forty years really isn't very long, in the big scheme, but at another level, one wonders if this comprises patent manifestation of the crippling human condition, the original sin of man's inhumanity to man, and that we will never fully shed our lamentable past, that the statute of limitations will never run out, and that wearying racism or at least racial preoccupation is as woven into our Mississippi DNA as the triple helix. This is part of what Pulitzer-Prize winner Richard Ford—Murrah graduate, class of 1962—meant by our being "complicatedly lucky" to have been born in Mississippi.

But at times, like at lunch today here in Oxford, a beautiful early summer day, when half the tables at Ajax Diner were mixed black and white, everyone talking and laughing as naturally as any people ever do, I think maybe it's just my generation, it's just me, the gimlet-eyed census-taking bastard in the corner. Time for new actors! Days like today give me hope that my children and grandchildren forty years from now won't give color a thought, but will only consider the worthier and deeper things about the person sitting across the table.

—Claiborne Barksdale

What We Did

As Teena and Johnny began their research into our class's experiences with integration, they hoped to find out how it had shaped everyone's lives in the years since, and why, in their view, the effort had ultimately failed. They were operating under two assumptions: That most everyone involved in the integration of Murrah cared about it, and that the effort had, in fact, failed. Beyond that was an assumption they didn't realize they were making: That it was possible for two white former students to adequately tell the story.

What soon became apparent was that not everyone cared; that most who did care agreed that integration as it had been originally intended had, in fact, failed over time, though not for us, personally; and that their own—Johnny's and Teena's—vantage points had limitations. Johnny, Teena, and I, once I came on board, were, after all, white. We represented half the equation, and could tell only half the story on our own.

Enlisting the participation of black classmates proved challenging, in part because the project inevitably came across as a white undertaking. White people have been writing American history from the outset, and many individuals and groups have been included in it without being given the opportunity to couch it in their own terms. Not surprisingly, many of those individuals and groups are naturally suspicious of the underlying agendas of those who seek to document their experiences. A quick review of the history textbooks we used at Murrah would illustrate why.

I ran into this problem when I was researching a book about the colonization of the West African nation of Liberia by freed American slaves, the largest group of which came from Mississippi: What right, many of the black people I interviewed asked, did I have to tell "their" story? It was actually our story, but I understood their misgivings. Try as I might to include their perspectives, the ultimate author of the book was going to be a white guy. So it went with the Murrah book. Johnny is liberal and Teena is conservative, which is actually a good place to start, in terms of representing both sides of the white vantage point. But, again, that was only part—technically, 35 to 40 percent—of the story. It wasn't just a matter of trying to include the black perspective out of fairness—that wasn't a favor for us to bestow. It was about telling the whole story, even if the idea had arisen in the minds of two people who happened to be white.

The problem was intrinsic to our experiences at Murrah. Whites were in the minority, but as one black classmate later pointed out, she still had the feeling that whites were in control. Why else were we required to pick one black and one white student for class officers, including co-student body presidents?

Now, here came two white alumni seeking to tell everyone's story. The odds were that the result would carry the unmistakable imprimatur of white people. So it was that Robert Kelly, one of our most outspoken, gregarious classmates, who is black, asked, when he heard Teena was trying to get in touch with him: Why should he talk to this white girl who rarely spoke to him in high school? Kelly, as everyone called him, eventually came around, but not everyone did. The result is that this book is heavy on white recollections, compared with those of former black students. Hopefully, it overcomes its own limitations, but that will be for the reader to decide.

Particularly after my experience with the book about Liberia, I am perhaps overly aware of the sometimes subliminal dominance of white people in telling multicultural stories. White people tend to dominate even when they don't realize they're doing it, because that is the world they were born into. We don't always recognize that even good intentions may be perceived as a kind of cultural slumming, or that they may be based on faulty assumptions, egocentric viewpoints, or hidden agendas. We tend to see ourselves as the controlling factor—that, ultimately, it's about us, and always has been. Even integration, from the white perspective, we initially saw as being about us, whether we participated because we were compelled to or because we felt it was our duty. Few of our white classmates thought much about what our black classmates were giving up. They were the impetus, but even in the best cases, were apt to be viewed as costars, like the poor black victims in the movie *Mississippi Burning*, who were essentially there to showcase the villainy and heroism of whites.

When reading an article in the *New York Times*, which purported to objectively report on the sad poverty of the Mississippi Delta, I couldn't help noticing a telling line about an "elderly black man" the reporter had viewed in passing, sitting on the porch of his decrepit shack. Would he have been identified as an "elderly white man" had that been the case? No. He would have just been an old man. He was identified as black because that represented something, for better or worse, and precisely what that was would be decided by the white observer. White was the norm. It was the same in the fictional book *The Help*, which was ostensibly about black maids in 1960s Jackson, but was really about a white lady who deigned to tell their stories, and was written in such a way that the black characters spoke in dialect while the white characters spoke the King's English. Again: Whites were the norm; blacks were "other." I can say from experience, *everyone* spoke in dialect in 1960s Jackson, and likewise, no one has a monopoly on the experience of integration, much less on its documentation for posterity. It's not enough to try to include everyone; the story has to ring true because it is complete. I will go ahead and say: It isn't. This book is not complete because not everyone chose to participate. But we have made every effort to tell the story as fully as is possible, given the tools at our disposal. And the process itself was revealing, even for those of us who thought we knew what happened at Murrah forty years ago, and who thought we knew ourselves, and each other.

Our task, if we were to overcome the obvious limitations, was to recognize our own biases and make every effort to relinquish control of the story, to the extent that is possible, so that everyone who had something to say could say it, without being subject to translation or interpretation. As William Faulkner once observed, everyone knows a piece of the truth, and sometimes those pieces conflict; the only way to arrive at even an approximation of what is true is to consider all those pieces, together—to create your own mosaic of the truth. It's an inexact process, but it's better than simply assuming that you alone know. In the end, Johnny, Teena, and I are the creators of this mosaic, and we have our own perspectives, but we have made every effort to ensure that our perspectives do not get in the way of those various, sometimes conflicting pieces of the story as a whole.

To ensure we got as wide participation as possible, Teena ran notices in a local weekly, the *Northside Sun*, the *Northeast Mississippi Daily Journal*, and Jackson's primary newspaper, the *Clarion-Ledger*, asking for members of the class of 1973 to submit their recollections for this book. She also sent out e-mail notices to everyone whose e-mail address she had. In all cases, the audience she reached was largely white. To get beyond that required convincing black classmates to vouch for the project, which was asking a lot. Still, many did, and in the end the book represents a broad array of perspectives, though perhaps not as broad as it would have had more black classmates been on board from the beginning.

White or black, we approached our classmates the same way: We asked them to submit an essay outlining their experiences; answer a questionnaire about those experiences (a transcript of which is provided elsewhere in this book); or allow one of us to interview them. We also enlisted members of the class who attended various reunions, and in one case conducted a sort of impromptu focus group at Johnny's office. Eventually, we included teachers and, in a few cases, members of the classes ahead of or behind us. The farther afield we got, the greater the risks that we would be exerting too much control on the raw data. So we were circumspect in that regard. That brought us back to the original problem: How to tell "our" story, ourselves, without distorting the experiences of others. The solution was to let those recollections drive the narrative, and to limit our own voices to an explanatory role, rather than an interpretive one, or, when it was appropriate, to include our own, clearly identified, subjective experiences. There was a need to fill in the blanks, to put the story into context, but not to reduce or pass judgment on the observations of others. If we overstepped our roles, I can only hope that it will be obvious, and that we will be called to task for it.

—Alan Huffman

Acknowledgments

We wish to thank the following individuals for their assistance with this project: Mary Alene Cobb Alford, Ken Allen, Laura G. King Ashley, Carole Sanders Bailey, Claiborne Barksdale, Katie Barwick-Snell, Debbie Horn Bondon, Michael Bounds, Lenda Taylor Brown, Velma Robinson Chisholm, Doug Clanton, Lindy Stevens Clement, Roslyn Allen Clopton, Susan Culbertson, Adrienne Day, Foster Dickard, Barry Dent, Bee Donley, Charles F. Ezelle, David Flanagan, Mark Flanagan, Freddie Funches, Robert L. Gibbs, Lele Winter Gillespie, Chryl Covington Grubbs, Robert L. Hand, Linda G. Hardy, Steven Jenkins, Jimmy Jones, Orsmond Jordan Jr., Robert Kelly, Freddie Lee, Williams G. Lewis, Pete Markow, Susan McBroom, James Merritt, Charles Davis Miller, Willie B. Miller, Doug Minor, Art Minton, John S. Mixon, Myra Stevens Myrick, Bill Patterson, Margie Cooper Pearson, Joy Kathryn (Wilson) Phillips, Owen Phillips, Greg Powell, Joseph T. Reiff, Reginald D. Rigsby, Randy Robertson, Cy Hart Rosenblatt, Debra Lindley Ruyle, Richard P. Sanders, George Schimmel, Fred J. Sheriff Jr., Betsy Grimes Triggs, Laurel Propst Ware, William F. Winter, Amelia Reagan Wright, and "Maverick" and "Wolf" wherever you are.

Lines Were Drawn

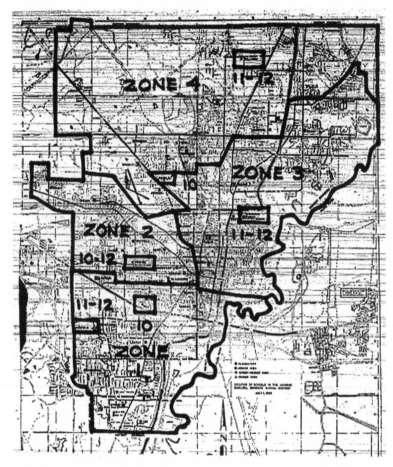

HIGH SCHOOL MAP — Four zones are provided in the Department of Health, Education and Welfare integration plan for the Jackson City Schools. This map, based on one contained in HEW Plan A, is one of three proposed for high schools. Wingfield (grades 11–12) would be paired with Hill (grade 10), while Provine (grades 10–11–12) would be in a zone to itself. Brinkley is designated as the school for 10th graders in Zones 3 and 4, with grades 11–12 going to Murrah in Zone 3 and to Callaway in Zone 4. Courtesy the *Clarion-Ledger*, January 8, 1970.

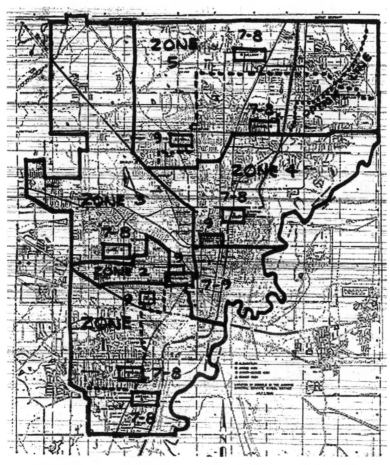

JUNIOR HIGH MAP — Five zones for junior high schools are provided under Plan A of the Department of Health, Education and Welfare integration plan for the Jackson Public Schools. Alternate maps (not shown) are drawn for Plan B and C. Under Plan A Peeples and Whitten Junior Highs would be paired with the Hill-Isable complex, with grades 7–8 going to Peeples and Whitten, and grade 9 going to Hill-Isable. In Zone 2 all students in grades 7–9 would go to Blackburn. In Zone 3 grades 7–8 would be at Hardy and grade 9 at Enochs. In Zone 4, grades 7–8 would be at Bailey and grade 9 at Rowan. In Zone 5 grades 7–8 would be at Chastain and Callaway, and grade 9 would be at Powell. This map is based on an artist's interpretation of the map contained in the HEW plan. The plan is subject to action and possible change by the court. Courtesy the *Clarion-Ledger*, January 8, 1970.

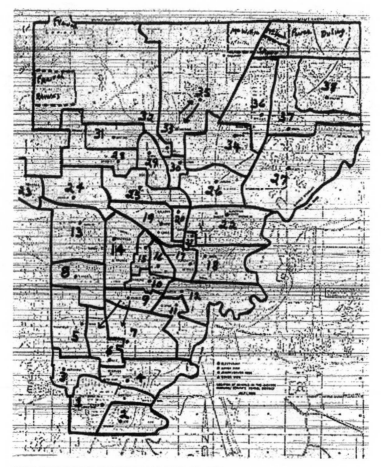

REPRODUCTION OF HEW MAP FOR COURT

ELEMENTARY SCHOOL MAP — This is the map showing elementary school zones contained in the Department of Health, Education and Welfare plan for the integration of the Jackson Municipal Separate School District. This organization of elementary school zones is provided in all three plans (A, B and C) submitted by HEW. The only exceptions to the zoning pattern would be that sixth graders in Isable would be assigned to Key and Lester Schools, while Green (grades 1–2) and Watkins (grades 3–6). Schools would be paired. The plan is under consideration by the US District Court. Courtesy the *Clarion-Ledger*, January 8, 1970.

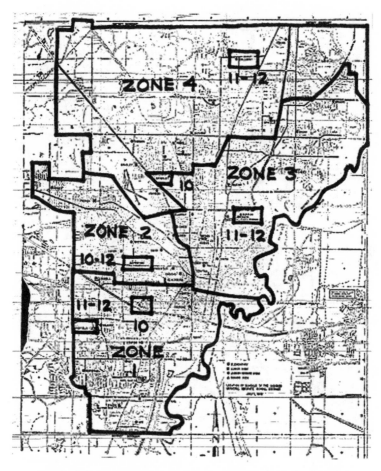

NEW HIGH SCHOOL ZONES — Four zones are provided in the new integration plan ordered in US District Court for the Jackson City Schools. This map is based on one contained in HEW Plan A, which was adopted by the court. The school district opposed all three secondary school plans submitted by HEW but raised more objections to Plans B and C. Under Plan A, Wingfield (grades 11–12) will be paired with Hill (grade 10). Provine (grades 10–12) will be in a zone to itself. Brinkley will draw 10th graders from Zones 3 and 4, with grades 11–12 going to Murrah in Zone 3 and to Callaway in Zone 4. Courtesy the *Clarion-Ledger*, June 16, 1970.

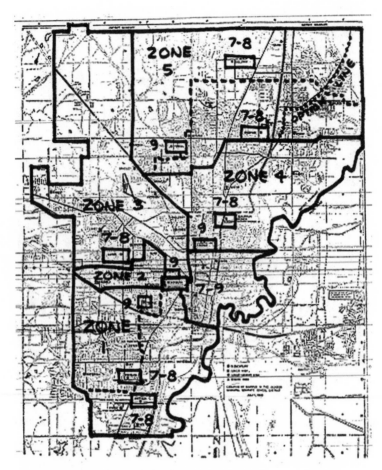

NEW JUNIOR HIGH ZONES — Five zones for junior high schools have been established in the new court plan for the Jackson City Schools. Peeples and Whitten Junior Highs will be paired with the Hill-Isable complex in Zone 1, with grades 7–8 assigned to Peeples and Whitten and grade 9 assigned to Hill-Isable. In Zone 2 all students in grades 7–9 are assigned to Blackburn. In Zone 3 grades 7–8 are assigned to Hardy and grade 9 to Knochs. In Zone 4, grades 7–8 are assigned to Bailey and grade 9 to Rowan. In Zone 5 grades 7–8 are assigned to Chastain and Callaway and grade 9 to Powell. This map is based on an HEW map, but the school district is allowed some flexibility in drawing exact zone lines. Courtesy the *Clarion-Ledger*, June 16, 1970.

Introduction: How This Book Came to Be

John Griffin (Johnny) Jones, Class of 1973

■

It started out as a small argument between us. Actually it was more of a "he said/she gasped" exchange, with Teena left to ponder whether, after fifty years of friendship, we'd lost each other completely. But it was common ground—our experiences during the earliest days of massive desegregation of the public schools in our hometown of Jackson, Mississippi—and among the better legacies of our youth is a shared understanding that every perspective is as worthy as the last, or should be. So, after I negligently challenged and Teena defended some of the core beliefs of her adult life, our e-mails skipped over politics and temporal gripes to what binds us and our African American classmates together across time: when we were guinea pigs in the grand social experiment of immediate desegregation of a large public school system in the Deep South by order of the federal courts, it worked. In the absence of precedent, leadership, even a plan from the federal courts, we made it work by turning to each other.

As we began the discussion in 2009, exactly forty years and most of our adult lives had passed since the beginning of the experiment of radical desegregation. We'd all grown up, more or less, settled into our families and work; most of us had raised our kids; and we'd mostly forgotten who we were back then. Whatever our differences, then and now, we agreed that the passage of time had only increased the significance of what we achieved together, black and white, in one of the unlikeliest places on earth: Murrah High School, located two miles north of the seat of state government in Mississippi's capital city. From the perspective of the dismal history that preceded the five years of the integration moment, the utter failure of school desegregation in Jackson since the mid-1970s, and, beginning in the early 1990s, the federal courts' abandonment of school desegregation as a means to correct the past and achieve the original goal of voluntary integration in every facet of life, it is as if our brief success never happened. But it did, and that's important. In the long struggle for authentic racial reconciliation and equality of treatment and opportunity, we came as close to reaching the millennium at Murrah as any group of Mississippians has ever come. There are no historical parallels to that success, only to the experiment's prolonged and tortured failure, for which there are too many.

Context is everything. In the critical period following the series of federal court orders handed down between December 1969 and August 1970, each more radical than its predecessor in adopting more the most disruptive methods imaginable, Jackson's majority-white community was almost unanimously opposed. White men occupying leadership positions in politics (except future governor William Winter, whose three girls were directly affected by the orders), or in education administration, business, and organized religion, all stayed silent and rode out the storm, or engaged in active efforts to undermine it. When aggressive opposition came from the usual southern loudmouths who profited then and profit now from racial division, very few spoke against them. In point of historical fact, the forces of massive resistance got more traction and gained more recruits in their opposition to school desegregation than in any other areas of their focus in those years: integration at Ole Miss in 1962; integration of public accommodations resulting from the passage of the Civil Rights Act of 1964; the long battles for and against voting rights culminating in the Voting Rights Act of 1965; indeed in all areas where today equal opportunity exists to an extent that we at least think we take it for granted. Those forces lost the early court battles, but they won the war here in Jackson.

In many if not most other cities with large inner-city black populations, north and south, massive desegregation "started out slow and then fizzled out altogether," to quote a leading voice from our youth: Neil Young. The reasons are neither uniform nor simple. Here, though, proponents of massive resistance were joined in opposition by the overwhelming majority of white people, including Jacksonians of "good will"—a term from the 1960s referring to grown-ups who, like most of our parents, believed in integration in the abstract and were willing to do something to change the state's racist image—who supported integration but not desegregation. Maybe it was because there really wasn't a coherent plan for massive desegregation underlying the early court orders. Maybe we had moved too far too fast by the late 1960s for white moderates to support any further assaults on our institutions. Without question it was because school desegregation touched white families in direct ways for which none had prepared in the least. And, as with all motivations, the strident opposition was the product of an unholy admixture of all these facts and more. Whatever predominated, the visceral response in those early days led to immediate abandonment of the entire school system, the creation of our apartheid system of secondary education in Jackson, and an overall retrenchment of the white community that has lasted to this very day.

Even the few moderates who had called for an end to the brutal resistance to change because it was counterproductive, bad for business and the state's image—the people who should have been counted on to maintain perspective and avoid hysterical responses to early integration methods—joined the opposition. They quite reasonably complained that the process selected by the federal courts to achieve desegregation virtually overnight violated fundamental rights of choice and autonomy. And they were right: radical desegregation did violate those rights. They asked how anything as reasonable and roundly democratic as "freedom of choice" (the approach replaced by radical desegregation in 1969–1970) could violate any principle grounded in the Constitution? What sins had been committed that could possibly lead to any federal court concluding that local school boards could not be trusted to follow the law? And, in a strange precursor to the arguments now embraced by our federal courts with calm reasonableness, the moderates asked when the Constitution was amended to guarantee racially balanced results classroom to classroom, or compelled the achievement of a ratio of whites to blacks in every school that mirrored the demographics of the entire community, or justified a desegregation plan that boiled down to hitting predetermined "quotas" from school to school. Even more fundamentally, they asked how things got so out of hand so quickly that the choices facing the federal courts by 1969–1970, and the methods of massive desegregation they selected, demanded maximum disruption of existing educational systems?

Context. In the revealed wisdom of *Brown v. Board of Education* (1954), the constitutionally protected interests at stake, at least initially, were the fundamental rights of black Americans to equal educational opportunities free from the inherently discriminatory effects of "separate but equal" systems. Recognition of those "rights" didn't require a leap in legal logic; the "rights" finally vindicated in *Brown I* were grounded in the very text of the Equal Protection Clause of the Fourteenth Amendment. The "separate but equal" legal fiction created in *Plessy v. Ferguson* in 1896 was a dodge; for fifty-eight years the doctrine was relied upon to justify gross discrimination, up to and including legal lynching, of black Americans, particularly in the "Jim Crow" South where blacks endured a wretched reality. By the time the strategy of Thurgood Marshall and the NAACP Legal Defense and Educational Fund, Inc., to focus the challenge to "separate but equal" on the nation's education systems wended its way to the Supreme Court and the cases known as *Brown I* were argued in 1954, it was all but self-evident that the "separate but equal" fiction glossed over gross inequalities in educational funding and quality that violated the equal protection rights of every black student without arguable justification. And on a deeper level, *Brown I* also recognized that the system of Jim Crow drove deep a sense of inferiority among black children whose opportunities were more dismal than their facilities. By the middle of the twentieth century, it was clear to most people outside the old Confederacy that the whole "separate but equal" charade represented an anachronism that was fundamentally indefensible and had to go. There simply was no longer any way to rationalize segregation and freedom.

After the unanimous court sided with the black plaintiffs and enforced the equal protection rights of black students against the fiction of "separate but equal," the next question was how to translate recognition of those gross inequalities and vindication of fundamental rights into action? The "separate but equal" myth had regulated and contained race relations in the Deep South for almost sixty years. Now that it was gone as a defense to obviously discriminatory policies and practices, what would replace it, and on what timetable?

In the year most of the participants in this project were born, 1955, the Court issued its implementation decision, *Brown II*, and quite reasonably, or so it seemed, allowed consideration of local conditions from school board to school board across the South in deciding *when* the massive changes would take place. The slow pace of the Jackson Municipal Separate School District ("JPS") in accomplishing desegregation during the first ten years was partly a function of that allowance and hardly unique. We all remember the days of "token" integration, beginning with the first little black girl at Power Elementary School, so protected by hulking US marshals, and scared, that she never looked up. By junior high we had a few more black kids with us, but not enough to change anything, particularly for the black kids themselves. Token integration was slow, indifferently managed, undoubtedly painful for the black students planted among us, friendless and scorned, and very costly. By the time the federal courts turned their attention back to implementation in the late 1960s, the delays of the JPS administration were perceived, and punished, as sins.

More than that, though, the justification for school desegregation expanded hugely beyond the first focus on the equal protection rights of the black children in unequal facilities. By 1968–1969, immediate desegregation of the public schools was necessary to accomplish a mammoth purpose: overcoming the effects of intentional or *de jure* segregation across the board. School boards were ordered to take "whatever steps might be necessary to convert to a unitary system in which racial discrimination would be eliminated root and branch." With such noble ends in the minds of the judges deciding what must happen in Jackson, and when and how it was to happen, any and all means could be justified. By December 1969, all that was immediately clear was that no further delay in desegregating our schools would be tolerated.

At ages fourteen and fifteen we found ourselves between extremes on all sides, unsteady, trying to figure out where to go and what to do. No balance had been struck, least of all in the courts. Did "Equal Protection" of the laws mean that a black kid could go to Murrah if he or she chose, free from impediments and "intentional" discrimination by school administrators? Or did it mean more? That a white kid could be forced by those same school administrators to attend Brinkley against his or her will because attaining a racial balance in the JPS that reflected the community at large trumped individual school choice? Who knew? When the Fifth Circuit Court of Appeals handed down its series of rulings affecting the JPS in the *Singleton* case between December 1969 and July 1970, the interests of black students to equal educational opportunities long denied them by intransigent local authorities, and the obligations of white students to become full participants in righting past wrongs no one could deny, carried the day. Whatever legitimate and illegitimate objections to the methodology of desegregation there were, for that moment they weighed nothing in a balance that included a constitutional duty to address and correct the effects of historical racism. So the orders implementing radical desegregation came fast and furious (seven in six months), in response to which the overwhelming majority of white parents withdrew their children from the JPS and sent them first home, then away, anywhere, eventually to new "seg academies" operated by the white Citizens' Council or the just-formed Jackson Preparatory School. The response was set before the problem was fully understood. And that . . . was that.

Viewed from the political/social context of 1969–1970, the Fifth Circuit's orders creating and compelling radical desegregation seem not only justifiable but just. They came some fifteen years after *Brown* not only recognized but *held* that in the field of public education the "separate but equal" fiction was "inherently discriminatory" to black children. From that point on local officials owed at least some consideration to what black students in the JPS were facing if not a massive, top-to-bottom overhaul of the system. But in those years the JPS administration engaged in such resistance, obfuscation, dancing and dodging that offended federal judges advanced Jackson to the very front of the line when the final "Desegregate *NOW!*" remedies were mandated by the Supreme Court in 1968 and 1969. At that point, resistance in any form was regarded as malice-aforethought sinning by school administrators, and the remedies that were imposed matched that "finding" or view of the historical facts. In court, even reasonable objections based upon individual choice yielded to the vast historical imperatives then at stake. Within that context, during that time in that place, who can say that the federal courts were wrong? The answer is, of course, the federal courts themselves, in changing contexts by new judges viewing the same history from different perspectives. And that is exactly what happened.

From the uninformed perspective of those us on the ground when those orders were implemented, it just seemed like chaos. We weren't thinking about the justifications behind what the federal courts were doing in Jackson, nor did we realize that we were being asked to act as warriors or victims—it was hard to tell which—in the war against the unholy sins, untold in number, of our state and region toward black people. As usual, nothing nearly so noble was included in the manner in which the debate was framed for us, and if remedying the effects of past discrimination was the true goal of school desegregation, that glorious mission failed to motivate any heart or mind I knew. The dilemma for us was much more straightforward: to join the exodus of white kids fleeing to private schools so new they'd not yet been named, or stay. When, with the guidance of our parents, we declined to endorse centuries of warped southern stereotypes, the choice became much easier. Considering the continents of crap dumped on all of us, black and white, as we grew up in segregated Mississippi during the 1960s, our biggest surprise was finding that there were no differences between the races that really mattered. That was the most important lesson, and it stuck.

For most of us who were there, but not all, the experience at Murrah left us with a sense of confidence and hope in the shaky future that has carried us through life, sustaining us with an unscripted success story in the wretched history of race relations in the South and, as we later learned with some smugness, across the entire nation. We suspected then but know now that we were part of something that brought us as close to true racial reconciliation as the country ever experienced before or after those days, for those who followed the traditions and believed the myths knew that if reconciliation were ever to come it would appear first in Mississippi. Those experiences matter more to us with each passing year. Now it seems like a strange blessing to have been involved, not just because we survived and thrived in the upheaval of forced desegregation on such a scale but because, for two years in the early 1970s, at Murrah, we lived in the future.

It didn't last. Today's statistics are numbing. At the time of this writing, the JPS secondary schools are 97.61 percent African American, with Murrah 94 percent black in a student body of around fifteen hundred in grades nine through twelve. Over the last thirty years Murrah has lost white enrollment at the rate of some 2 percent per year until at least 2009, and though

the fractions have become minuscule the level of abandonment has continued unabated. In 1970, Jackson had a 60 percent white-majority population.
The latest figures indicate an African American majority of some 80 percent
within the city limits. Here we were at least a decade ahead of the general
pattern of resegregation of the public schools across the South as a result of
Supreme Court decisions from the early 1990s. What we are left with in Jackson is a "separate but [un]equal" educational system, a hushed form of racial
and class apartheid in the way we educate our children that today achieves
its finest expression in the vast differences between the JPS and the private
academies that continue to grow year by year. It has been so all-encompassing
that most whites still involved with the public schools have largely ceased all
attempts to attract other white parents; they focus now only on obtaining
the highest quality education available for their children within the system.
It is scary stuff, especially in view of the historical fact that long periods of
regression do not resolve themselves spontaneously. Whatever spin is placed
upon these facts, this is certain: Jackson was among the very first places in the
country to experience massive desegregation remedies, and the first place in
the country of which I'm aware to successfully defeat them.

Why? What strange collision of historical imperatives, coincidences, and
luck made integration work in our time but fail so profoundly? And fail not
within one generation but within one decade? In a wider context, is public
school integration the past or the future in this country? When we made it
work at Murrah we knew that we were experiencing the best hopes of that
time in microcosm. Most of us believed that school desegregation provided
a workable model for achieving the twentieth century's version of manifest
destiny: saving the country through programs that might finally deliver it
from the tortured past. For if black and white could come together in Jackson,
Mississippi, the rest should be a cinch. In our time, during the few years of
the integration moment, it all looked plausible. And then it crashed, leaving
cynicism and millions who told us so telling us so for the rest of time.

Cynicism about our past or the future we glimpsed at Murrah doesn't come
easily or naturally to us, though it is a deliciously seductive response to all the
contradictions in our experience. In gathering the contributions that make up
this volume we were surprised to find that all of the critical questions, hypocrisies, and failures, tempered always by hope and odd synchronicities, are still
at stake when we even dare to scratch the surface of the mammoth issue of
integration of the two predominant (for now anyway) races who aren't going
anywhere in this place where we cast our lot and that of our children. Did
school integration fail in Jackson because of its suddenness, the lack of leadership, the justice or injustice of the methods utilized to achieve it, or the

sustainability of integration over the long haul? Is there something inherent in the demographics of the city, or the character of its citizens, that doomed it to inevitable failure? And is it still important, at least to us, to try and find as many answers as we can? Who knows?

Fortunately, we have each other. The website for the Murrah class of 1973, and our almost yearly reunions in June (thanks to the constant efforts of our beloved classmate Art Minton), provide us with a forum to flirt with and curse one another, to share successes, babies and (now) grandbabies, memories good and bad, lament losses of classmates way too early, seethe over current events as they relate to race and integration, pass on observations about lessons learned and forgotten, all before a group of veterans who know that each of us has at least earned our perspective. So we reach out.

In this spirit, I sent a missive through the website in the late summer of 2009 reporting on a two-year-old decision of the United States Supreme Court that, in my quick judgment as a practicing lawyer, signaled an end to the concept that integration of the nation's public schools was mandated by the Constitution or was even, at that late date, a desirable social goal. I fussed and fumed:

> With a stroke of a Republican pen, this Court abandoned the basic principle that dominated our youth and determined our experiences: desegregation of the public schools was mandated by the Constitution and would be achieved immediately, meaning overnight, regardless of what it cost in educational quality, inconvenience to students and their parents (even to the punitive extent of ordering children bused across several school zones to previously one-race schools), and the legitimate expectations of all involved. The historic racism that led to *Brown v. Board of Education* might not be entirely cured and behind us here in the Deep South, but now, 40 years since the school desegregation struggle transformed our lives so dramatically, this Court is apparently convinced that fighting past discrimination is no longer worth the trouble in Seattle and elsewhere, and might just infringe upon the constitutional rights of white people. The political will to ensure equal opportunity to black Americans (or women or the disabled or ... you name it) just isn't there anymore. But one would expect the Court to understand the history behind its own rulings and its continuing duty to protect the rights of the minority, especially when the political will has so turned against them, regardless of where they live. But nope. It's like we've paid and suffered enough already for the historic mistreatment of the entire African American race and it's time to move on.

The strange thing is that the author of the opinion, Chief Justice John G. Roberts, was born, like most of us, in 1955. He graduated in 1973 from a boarding school called La Lumiere, in LaPorte, Indiana, which is pretty far from Murrah, and his experience obviously differed from ours hugely. I wonder, though, whether he confronted the issues that defined our existence at Murrah before he became a federal judge and had to. Whatever motivated the Court in this Seattle case, they were willing to use the clarion call of *Brown* that the doctrine of "separate but equal" was inherently discriminatory to black children, and that race should play no part in determining student placement in the public schools, to strike down efforts to *increase* integration. The Court implies that the legal analysis may be different for the old Confederate states, but it is hard to see how that matters as what the Court seems to be protecting are the interests of white students affected by integration as opposed to the benefits to all citizens that comes with real integration. What gets me is using the epoch-changing language of *Brown* and applying it to white kids anywhere, because with that language a unanimous Supreme Court finally recognized the history of locking blacks out of places that were theirs by reason of nothing more or less than their citizenship, and meant that for the very first time in the history of the country blacks were entitled to same treatment as whites, at least in the field of public education, which was a hell of a good place to start. The cynicism about integration seems unearned, but really it's not as troubling to me as the indifference to the history of race in this country, and that includes what happened to us and what we made of it.

Either integration is a worthy goal in this country, or it isn't. If it still is, as I strongly believe (especially since the days of white majorities in America are numbered), then we shouldn't use conservative objections to desegregation methods to get rid of the legacy and continuing goals of integration. It's like we were part of a wrong detour, and the road we were put on by the federal judges in our time deserves to be shut down and charged off as another liberal mistake. I disagree with that view. I think that what we were put through was not only justified in history but probably the best thing that could have happened to whites in terms of getting finally free of the gross errors of the racists and opportunists who ran things for so long. We were the first generation in the history of the South that was given a chance to move beyond race. Justice Roberts, who could have been in our class, and his friends think the gross errors were not in our history of depriving blacks of the basic rights of the democracy but in the steps taken to improve the lives of black people, which should improve the lives of whites as well, through equal access to a quality education. The focus on the form of the remedy instead of what needed to be remedied is unbelievable to me and, in the end, profoundly disappointing. Then again, what do I know?

But is that the way you feel? Is it the way we should feel? Wasn't our experience worth something beyond the typical nostalgia for old time dying? Is the spirit that motivated our parents, and us, to stick it out in 1969 irrelevant in 2009?

Were all those serious issues of race finally irreconcilable in the Deep South, or are they merely old news now? Were we, the students who were treated as guinea pigs for testing radical desegregation to achieve equality, and lived through it, the only people who saw value in it? What, in the end, did it all mean?

Teena responded quickly and basically said she had no idea what I was talking about, or maybe I didn't. She said over the course of a few e-mails:

> I must have missed a lot of information about the condition of Jackson schools while raising my children in a small north Mississippi town. Our Houston public schools are fully integrated and have the active support of African American, white, Hispanic parents and the local community. All my children went there and had great experiences. We do not have a separate private school system, like you do in Jackson, up here or in the other towns around us or among the schools we compete against in sports. Maybe the way integration worked outside of Jackson was the way it was supposed to work everywhere. If it has failed in Jackson since we graduated, the failure didn't affect everybody the same. I don't think integration was a failure statewide. But, like you, I wondered then and now what it meant for people in the larger cities. I don't agree with your "Republican pen" remark and may not get all the legal discussion, but I can tell you that for my family and many people outside of Jackson, the process of integration has evolved into something both positive and normal. I never liked the initial way that it was forced on us in 1969 in Jackson, but however flawed the process was, it opened my eyes and heart to a different view of society. I used that knowledge during my lifetime, and I've seen integration continue to take hold within the small community in which I reside. It may not have produced optimal results, but where it did work it created something hopeful.

That started the process. We disagreed on politics but didn't care except as our disagreement touched on the issue of integration, which it did not—a little factoid I found exceedingly strange. Over the next several months our rigorous but well-intentioned bow shots were replaced by longer disclosures covering history, personal memory, faith, family, our children above all. Teena's last two children, twin girls, and my oldest girl, all started college that fall of 2009, and Teena confessed to "empty nest" syndrome that prompted not only her exploration into our common past but the yeoman duties she took on without being asked. It didn't take us long to realize that we were on to something that deserved attention and closer analysis. Once we realized we had a tiger by the tail, we started looking around for somebody more qualified than an overworked dentist and liberal trial lawyer.

It didn't take long. Alan Huffman is one of my best friends in life, my roommate for a semester in one of Oxford's more posh trailer parks since replaced by estates for the landed gentry, groomsman in my wedding, closest friend of my wife, Mary, and me in our first year of marriage in Oxford, and another member of the Murrah class of 1973. He is also an accomplished journalist and writer of several well-received nonfiction works. He is by far the most accomplished and talented writer of our time and place, a dear friend to all since we first met at Murrah in September 1971. In early October 2009 Teena and I accosted him at his annual pig roast at Holly Grove—an antebellum mansion Alan dismantled in Jefferson County, Mississippi, and brought to his land in western Hinds County where, with the help of many friends (I held some lumber and cleaned up but because I'm a lawyer I wasn't allowed to use tools) he reconstructed by hand—and sprung this project on him. He was not given a chance to decline. Alan has been an active participant in the process of gathering the interviews and other information needed for this project, and coauthor with Teena and me of this volume. His reassuring and generous presence has guided us, and without him we would not have gotten very far.

Later that fall we approached Claiborne Barksdale, not just because of his many professional accomplishments but because he was our teacher at Murrah and a mentor to Alan and, to a much lesser extent, me during our college years. We bored him cross-eyed reading our postadolescent (and that's exaggerating the quality of my work but detracts from the quality of Alan's) short stories and poetry, all of which he handled with characteristic equanimity. As former head of the Barksdale Reading Institute in Oxford, an organization founded by Claiborne's brother and Mississippi's leading philanthropist Jim Barksdale, Claiborne dedicated his work to improving the reading skills of less fortunate children in Mississippi's public elementary schools by providing the very best teachers and facilities available and achieving remarkable if largely unheralded success, all the while pushing school administrators, principals, teachers, himself, and his staff to more creative ways to combat illiteracy and the uneven opportunities for learning that hold Mississippi's children, and therefore all of us, back.

Claiborne graduated from the "old" Murrah in 1968, got his BA in English in three years at Ole Miss, and came back to teach a year at Murrah before starting Law School. He was young and happy, had the look of the bashfully hip circa 1971—longish but not-too-long hair, wire-rim glasses, James-Taylorish suggestion of a wispy mustache—and was always inclusive and extremely patient with us. To the girls who swooned over him, and the guys who admired his ability to make the girls swoon as well as what he knew and could actually discuss about things that mattered to us, he was a new archetype for both races. I know he was the first teacher to actually write something on the blank slate of my mind. His method of drawing us out during class, black and white students alike, taught us a great deal about each other. We learned that, even in our more contemplative moments, we were more like our black contemporaries than we would have ever guessed. Of course Claiborne admits to none of this today. But he was open to the promise of this project from the beginning, contributed an essay that unfairly downplayed his significance as a teacher for that single year, and participated in many of the interviews that we conducted at my law office. We wanted Claiborne to take an even bigger role in the work, but he demurred and said it was about us, our classmates, and what we felt about integration then and now. Still, Claiborne is a major part of this work in more ways than he knows.

But from start to finish, the heart, soul, elbow grease, cheerleader, and most valuable player has been Dr. Teena. It would never have happened without her, and it would have stalled out in frustration or lack of interest many times had she not jerked us up and pointed out the significance of what we were doing, and then kicked us in the butt. Of equal importance was what she wrote. She had guts enough to submit the first essay to a pretty tough audience, and in it she set the tone of honest reflection without pointless harm that we've all tried to follow. How and why she committed so much to this I haven't a clue. I can say that Dr. Teena is guileless, and I know that she truly believes that what we went through was a worthy and underappreciated experience that accomplished more than today's statistics would indicate, and she always said it would make a great story. I for one am glad to be a part of her story then and now.

Our pointed e-mail exchange in the fall of 2009 led us to dare each other to expand on our ideas and beliefs and bluff and bluster by drafting essays or personal memoirs about our experiences during desegregation generally and Murrah specifically. We admitted to each other that we had intended to preserve our memories in writing for a long time, and Teena had already done some fairly extensive work that she wouldn't show me. I had nothing. When her finished essay came I was astonished at the depth of feeling the subject matter generated. Somehow, in her story honoring her earliest influences on treating people of all races with respect and humility, especially her late father, reflected her fundamental beliefs as probably nothing else could. Inspired, I wrote thirty-five pages over a weekend and sent it to Teena on Monday. Editing it later I began to understand that almost everything I felt about history, politics, and the obligations of citizenship was subsumed in what I experienced and still believe about integration in Jackson. If one carried faith through life, or relocated it after many years, or just discovered it, the similarities and odd coincidences jumped out. Judging not from the literary quality but from the emotions our writing had wrung out of us, Teena and I knew we were on to something.

Art Minton provided us with his list of e-mail addresses for our class of 1973 website, and in November we sent out a mass invitation to all to submit essays or respond to a questionnaire I prepared, which was intended to reach those who didn't have the time or inclination to write. Alan and Claiborne sent in short but wonderful pieces that upped the ante for all, followed by submissions from old friends and people I never knew or had completely forgotten. The responses ranged from a couple of minimalist "What's the big deal?" retorts to very touching personal memoirs to prayers for understanding and reconciliation. Two or three competed for the most jaded and cynical among us, but that didn't last very long. Those who tried to diminish what desegregation meant, then and now, couldn't carry their case very far, convinced no one, and quit. By the end of 2009 we had about thirty or forty responses, interviews and essays, the overwhelming majority of which shared our common denominator: the subject hit each of us square on, stirring deep emotions.

Nobody we communicated with had come to any final peace or derived lasting lessons from our experience with desegregation and what it meant for Jackson in the long run or for them personally. On the contrary, some of our classmates, including people we knew very well, suffered real violence or scary sexual encounters unmitigated by new friendships or great teachers, and to them looking back wasn't a merry or even an interesting skip down memory lane; yet they contributed their stories anyway. I had no idea that anybody carried lifelong bitterness in their hearts over their integration experience, or had lost the faith they had in those days, or reached lasting conclusions about race that differed so drastically from the rest. All of it opened a new door on the experience, and for the very first time I realized that for many the journey was not recalled with the mellow, usually sepia, tones of nostalgia covering up ugly details. But it wasn't easy then, and I was deluding myself to think that time and memory worked the same magic on all hearts. Perhaps most significantly, all of us who took the opportunity to write on integration at Murrah learned in the process that making sense of our experience is just as difficult now as it was then, only now we know that there was no happy ending. Everybody wrote with the knowledge that there is no promise of lasting success or peace at the end of the tale. But for Teena, Alan, and me, that makes the stories collected here closer to the truth and even more interesting, the picture that emerges darker but, for us at least, more in focus.

By the end of 2009 I thought we had enough in those thirty or forty submissions to start thinking about a form for sharing them with our classmates.

In all likelihood the project would have wrapped up then and there but for the drive of Dr. Teena. She goaded, pushed, prodded, complimented, and criticized, pointing out the rare value of an individual contribution while acknowledging the weaknesses in the process, especially the paucity of responses from our black classmates. That had to be remedied if we wanted to go further. Without being asked, Dr. Teena dedicated herself to transcribing the taped interviews and then organizing what we had in order to make it accessible. Again without being asked, and without asking for help, she designed the method and assumed the expense of a second assault on Murrah students who graduated between 1971 and 1975.

In January 2010 Teena paid to place ads in the Jackson papers likely to reach Murrah graduates: Jackson's *Clarion-Ledger* and *Northside Sun,* as well as Tupelo's *Daily Journal.* Set against a rearing Mustang (Murrah's fabled mascot) and signature Mustang horseshoes dotting the page, she called out: "Looking for Some Mustangs! Murrah High School Alumni. Attention Classes of 1972, '73, '74, '75. All are Invited to Participate in A MURRAH MEMORIES PROJECT!" She listed her contact information, which her male partners would not have done, and we waited for the onslaught. It didn't come. So Teena craftily edited the ad to include a picture of the 1972 Teena we all knew and loved, wearing her Murrah cheerleading uniform. That triggered immediate responses, albeit mostly from her old boyfriends who thought she looked mighty good and expressed surprise that she could find her old uniform and fit in it so fetchingly. Most respondents thought the ads were announcing a big party, but Teena used the communication to bring more of her fans into the project, which was valuable. Thanks to our dear friend and Murrah in-law Jimmye Sweat (married to Andy Sweat, class of 1970), an article on the project appeared in the March 18, 2010, issue of the *Northside Sun,* which again drew in new contributors. Teena also ran down e-mail addresses from sources Alan and I still don't know about, and followed her e-mails up with phone calls to our black classmates and others soliciting essays or interviews. This intensive effort rounded out the project to a much greater extent, and by the summer of 2010 we had more than enough for a book.

Two deficiencies were apparent from the get-go. We take full responsibility for them and for the impact of those deficiencies on this final product.

First, we knew that to tell the whole story we needed as much participation as we could get from our surviving teachers and coaches, administration, politicians, as well as present teachers and school board members and those involved in "Parents for Public Schools," an organization started in the 1980s in Jackson, which has grown to become a critically important voice for integration in the public schools, with chapters across the whole country.

Plus, many of our classmates and contemporaries simply didn't and don't live on the computer or rely on it as the chief means of communication like Teena, Alan, and I were required to do by the nature of our work. The obvious answer was face-to-face interviews. First we interviewed Governor William Winter, then Murrah principal in our time Mr. James Merritt and his wife, followed by a trip to Brookhaven to interview Coaches Doug Clanton and Freddie Lee, and, later in my office, Coach Orsmond Jordan. I interviewed Ms. Bee Donley, a great lady who was an English teacher and student favorite at Murrah for many years before being sent to Brinkley in the spring of 1970, a victim of the slapdash methods used in the early days to achieve immediate desegregation. Ms. Donley, however, refused to seize on the negative and enjoyed herself at Brinkley.

Teena then took it on herself to gather other interviews with present Murrah teachers and other alumni with unusual perspectives, including the bard of integration at Murrah, Freddie Funches, whose positive attitude energized all who knew him then and now. For the chapter on Murrah sports, I interviewed too many athletes, black and white, teammates of mine and otherwise, to list here, except to thank Pete Markow (class of '71, quarterback of the fabled '70 Mustangs) for finding me the old *Murrah Football Facts: Mustangs '69* and *'70*, and my brother Dr. Jimmy Jones (class of '71), who, like me, recalls the glory of Murrah football in the 1960s down to the numbers worn by players nobody else, probably even the players themselves, remembers.

Our most famous classmate is Cassandra Wilson (nee Fowlkes). Cassandra moved beyond her past as a cheerleader at Murrah and her few years at Millsaps College to become probably the most famous and acclaimed female jazz singer since Billie Holiday, winning Grammies and too many other awards to list here. A concrete, brick, and glass historical monument to Cassandra sits today in front of Brinkley Middle School (formerly Brinkley High School, which Cassandra and I and many others attended in the 1970–1971 academic year when it was a tenth-grade center), listing her accomplishments in gold lettering. It is my favorite monument to integration in the city; then again it may be the only monument to the integration moment in the city. In March 2010 Cassandra performed in concert on the campus at Ole Miss and many of us showed up, unprepared, and were absolutely blown away by our classmate's performance. We repaired to Guy and Lele's house in Oxford where we smothered Cassandra, talked up the project, and accepted pledges to contribute from everybody. That created another flurry of contributions that are invaluable to this final product.

The interviews were often rambling and disjointed, but somehow each of them provided us with something we would not have gotten from the cold

page. Teena, Alan, Claiborne, and I did most of the questioning in these interviews, together or in various combinations or alone, until Teena ran out of
patience with our scheduling conflicts and traveled to get key interviews on
her own. Except for Alan, we were without much experience, and it is clear
from some of the transcripts that we were too overbearing in directing the
conversation (especially me), or at least too prominent in the discussions,
and sometimes we missed what the interviewee was telling us completely.
For those errors we assume full responsibility and humbly ask for the reader's
indulgence and patience. The reader will need it. Later, at Teena's suggestion,
we even interviewed one another and were reminded that personal communication where the taping is ignored or forgotten produces the most honest,
or the least inhibited, responses. But it's tricky, too.

For our annual reunion in June 2010, we moved a rollicking party peaking
in revelry and group participation from Hal & Mal's (one of Jackson's better
bar-restaurants located downtown, as is our preference) a few blocks north to
my law office on North State Street so we could tape the pontificating and blus-
tering and humor for this project. Some clammed up or couldn't get a word in
edgewise, some yelled and yelled, some flirted, some waxed philosophical or
poetic or pathetic, and some kept drinking. Thus, some of what happened was,
and remains, unfortunate. Feelings were hurt, things were said that shouldn't
have been said, and in the process some of the gold-plated memories were
permanently tarnished. The participants involved in some of the most pointed
exchanges were provided, and took, the opportunity to veto our inclusion of
the transcription of that evening in my law office in this volume. We have honored, and some of us agreed with, their requests to excise that entire exchange.
Some of us do not. Although we hope the transcriptions that are included here
show that we were not interested only in the mellowing effect of long memory,
or in recording only the more generous professions of love and understanding
between us, we have no intention of aggravating old wounds that have never
healed. It is not our purpose to harm anybody, especially our classmates. Still,
it is important for us to acknowledge that some wounds cannot be healed no
matter how many class reunions we have, although I thought that night and
still think that some of the wilder accusations were uttered to let some of the
hot air of glossed-over sentimentalism out of that room. In the end, we were
talking that night about race in Mississippi and memories of old emotions
supplemented by forty years of intervening experience, and mixing it with
drink. The combination is frequently explosive.

The second deficiency is more obvious, and more important. The
authors are white. We tried hard to tell each story and address each issue
using a cross-section of black and white voices, but our black classmates are

underrepresented here relative to their 65 percent majority of the student body the year we graduated. We are aware that our collective efforts as writers and editors of a book on integration can and probably will be viewed as another bad example of white authors writing about the black experience without authority to do so. We accept and often share the criticism. But by definition the integration experience involved both races, and our intention throughout has been to tell the story of integration through the voices of those who experienced it with us, supplemented and surely influenced by our own individual perspectives. We believe that we have accomplished that much anyway, regardless of the objections or criticisms that can be fairly leveled at what each voice says. If we thought for an instant that the orientation or perspective we have brought to this project diminished or unfairly characterized the experience of our black classmates or the black community as a whole, we would have long since stopped, chucked it all, and retreated to the familiar comforts and repetitions of adult life.

Despite these deficiencies, Teena, Alan, and I believe that the story we have tried to tell is important enough to justify all the work and endure whatever just criticism may be directed at our contributions as authors and editors. It has not been told before. What was attempted during the five or so years of successful integration of Murrah had never been tried before, has not been tried since, and constitutes a unique glitch in Mississippi's long struggle with race when such disruptive legal remedies seemed, for the moment at least, to be not only justified but compelled by history. The story needs to be told.

What we learned at Murrah stuck. To earn respect you have to give respect. It is not enough to be able to quote the right lines condemning Mississippi's racist past or to exhibit genuine concern for the victims of racism. We came together in the early years of desegregation from such radically different contexts that all we really knew were broad conclusions or opinions, usually wrong, about black or white people as a race or culture. For us it was easy to be politically correct about black people as a race; in fact, for some it was downright fashionable in the early '70s. But it didn't help us get to know a single black person better and may have made it much harder. The patronizing attitude that was part of a superficial political liberalism set our black classmates' teeth on edge. Even if one's purposes were not racist, dealing in stereotypes or characterizing the motives or actions of an individual as common to the entire race or group was not only wrong, it was the meaning of racism.

At Murrah we learned that we had to give each black person the same right to his or her own individuality that we gave our white counterparts, and to avoid the tendency to think about people by the group of which they were a member. The huge benefit of desegregation is that we were around our black classmates and teachers enough to do that: establish one-on-one relationships based upon mutual respect. Our proximity to each other over those three and one-half years also made us the first generation of Mississippians to ever learn that there were no differences between us that really mattered. Much of what happened in Jackson was a result of the earlier intransigence of the JPS leadership and our politicians to accommodate even the first meaningful steps toward integration. It was like the JPS was serving some sort of punishment for contempt of the federal courts in the early years of integration, and the leaders responded accordingly. We were always fighting someone else's battle throughout high school, but that power struggle eclipsed all else. Something had to give because integration was upon us and would not wait for a better time or yield to practical considerations no matter how warranted. No matter how brutal, misguided, and/or unsupported by any coherent plan, the urgency that attends such massive disputes nonetheless achieved successful integration in those early years. We were simply around each other enough, in changing contexts and circumstances, that we could finally judge each other as individuals and, in many cases, earn lasting friendships. That consequence was unintended by the battling grown-ups, but putting us in close proximity was the key. It still is.

We thank the participants in this project for giving their time without stint or money, and for sharing their own perspectives with such honesty, candor, and grace. The participants who were adults at the time and played important roles in the desegregation wars of the '60s and early '70s long ago earned our deep gratitude for what they contributed to our lives, but we extend our special thanks for their participation in this project, and for their continuing lessons. Above all, we thank our classmates for what they did and who they are, then and now. This is for them.

Childhood Memories of Mississippi: We Knew Something Was Coming

Narrated by Teena Freeman Horn

■

We were post-WWII baby boomers who grew up in Mississippi in the 1950s, 1960s, and 1970s. White and black people lived in different parts of town back then, probably in every Mississippi town. It was a racially segregated time in the history of our state.

In this chapter, Murrah High School classmates, parents, and teachers reminisce with personal stories about that era. Some of the contributors to this record did not mention childhood experiences; others remembered the ambience of home, Mama's cooking in the kitchen, hanging out with friends, and some explored racial situations. In evidencing a few acts of racial inequality, many of us said that we knew something was coming—a feeling of a change that we could not predetermine. The varied collection of background information gathered here gives a glimpse into what some family life in Mississippi was like, before the 1969 massive integration of Jackson schools.

The year of my birth was 1955, the same year as most of my fellow 1973 Murrah High School graduates. In 1955, Dwight D. Eisenhower was the president of the United States and Hugh L. White was the governor of the state of Mississippi. The previous year, the Brown v. Board of Education *Court ruled against "separate but equal" in the schools; this case precipitated progress as well as challenges in society. The Mississippi legislature (in the 1950s and 1960s) tried to ignore this ruling to maintain a traditional divide between the white and black races. Powerful segregation groups, specifically the Citizens' Council, had great influence on legislative elections and decisions in Mississippi.*

Governor William Winter *went through the integration journey with us. His daughter Lele was our age. The parents, such as Governor and Mrs. Winter, are as much a part of our story as the students and teachers. Governor Winter shared background information with me and **Johnny Jones**, as to the prevailing atmosphere in the Mississippi government during the 1950s.*

Governor Winter: "In the [Hugh] White administration there were various proposals to avert the impact of the *Brown* decision including of course, the implementation of Minimum Foundation Education Program, which was funded at the 1955 special session of the White administration. Then the fever was rising every day and the force of massive resistance was dominating the political picture."

Governor Winter said that J. P. Coleman was elected governor later that year and took over in 1956.

Winter: "I had run for Speaker, was defeated, but served in that 1956 session. When the Coleman proposals were put for election, among those proposals, and let me interject here, Coleman's attitude was relatively moderate in the context of the times. He was very defensive of segregation, was a segregationist, but his thought was that we cannot confront the federal government. We have to be more resourceful on that and we are going to have to give some if we are going to avert a real confrontation."

Johnny: "Were there people back then, Governor, that would have gone to the streets with guns to fight over that?"

Winter: "No question about it. That is what some members of the legislature were doing. There was a no compromise; a line had been drawn in the sand. Not just in the sand, but on the concrete of the roads leading to a school that was going to be integrated, figuratively. So this is what Coleman, having a realistic understanding of the problem that we were confronted with, and the practical realities of handling it, tried to provide some cover for himself as well as those of us who agreed with him. Citizens' Council was a very forceful force in the state. They were very suspicious of Coleman, because they did not think he was deeply enough committed to the maintenance of segregation 'til the last dog died. Coleman proposed, among other things and perhaps most significant, the creation of an organization known as the Sovereignty Commission. His avowed stated purpose was to help us do everything we could to maintain segregation, but to do it without violence and without bloodshed and without unnecessary controversy. Part of that strategy was to help inform the rest of the country of our position that everybody in Mississippi didn't get up every morning wondering how many black folks they could kill. That we have a lot of reasonable people in this state who disagreed with the *Brown* decision and who did not want to see it implemented, but who understood that we had to take some measures to avert a catastrophe."

I asked Governor Winter to explain the Citizens' Council and its purpose.

Winter: "It started in Mississippi and spread across Louisiana, Alabama, and even over to Georgia ... to maintain segregation at every level and every situation. They would hold south-wide meetings and it became a huge political force in Mississippi."

Governor Winter stated, "It helped," to have the endorsement of the Citizens' Council for elections and was difficult for moderates on segregation to be elected to public office. Another term, "Dixiecrats," Winter explains, "The Dixiecrats were Democrats that were opposed to integration."

These were the events that we were born into, as part of the baby boomer generation; many of us were children of soldiers who fought in WWII. We were toddlers in the 1950s, elementary and junior high school children in the 1960s and high-school and college students in the 1970s. Kids don't think about solving the world's problems. Their realm is generally the neighborhood and the terrain therein. I recall dreaming about riding into the sunset on a golden palomino horse with Roy Rogers. That is all I could think about—campfires and a horse that would not fit in my backyard. My childhood began as what I felt was an idyllic start in a small south Mississippi town named Shubuta.

The smell of gardenia and magnolia blossoms, the white and pink spindly flowers of the mimosa tree I climbed in my backyard, and mockingbirds singing in the late afternoon are vivid memories of my childhood years in 1950s Mississippi. Hot summer Sundays sizzled with only cardboard fans to cool us in church, as Daddy preached an animated sermon in his black satin pulpit robe with a white stole around the neck. Pale-skinned ladies donned in pastel hats, white gloves, high heels, and waisted frocks that fell beneath the knee, sat with their men who rolled up their starched white shirts. All said, "Amen," to the determined orations of the lesson. I drew pictures and letters on white offering envelops that mostly said, "I love you," to my daddy. My mother, who placed the altar-flowers from her white or purple hydrangea bush, sat with the proper posture of a minister's wife. She would pinch my thigh when I moved around too much, as a four-year-old is prone to do. I can remember dinner-on-the-grounds held on occasion after church. Every family came with plenty of food to share during this time of special fellowship. There were white linen tablecloths adorned with vases of fresh flowers, and baskets full of fried chicken, chicken pot pie, many bowls of homegrown vegetables, deserts, biscuits with molasses and my mother's grape jelly. Ladies in aprons served the parishioners by making sure that platters were filled and supplied plenty of sweet iced tea with slices of lemon and sprigs of mint. Mrs. Patsy Toney, a church member, always showered my brother and me with love and acceptance, blueberry pie and blackberry jam. (Patsy still does; she just recently, in 2013, sent my yearly jar of her muscadine jelly, by way of my brother.) Patsy and Miss Mary Weems took me under their loving arms and showed me how Christian women can make a difference in the lives of others, even in a small town like Shubuta.

Miss Mary Weems, my Sunday School teacher, taught me at a young age to accept all races and people who looked different. She had her students sing for the congregation using little hand motions to songs like, "Jesus loves the little children, all the little children of the world. Red and yellow, black and white, they are precious in his sight, Jesus loves the little children of the world." Miss Mary was a silver-haired woman of means, a banker, who enjoyed traveling; she relished missions to Africa, where she taught the Bible to African children. "See no evil, speak no evil and hear no evil," was her mantra alluded to by three monkeys on the mantle of her home. She gave me a silver dollar every year for my birthday, and a little necklace with a mustard seed, quoting from the Bible that said, "If you have faith as small as a mustard seed," you can do anything. I only understood the value of her teachings when I became an adult and realized that acceptance of different races was not the norm of all society. In the fifties, our small-town church was all white. I remember some black people attending funerals and sitting together, but not coming to our regular services. The white and black churches were separate, but my father would never turn away any worshiper.

Murrah classmate, **Steve Jenkins,** had a different experience with his metropolitan church in Jackson. Steve wrote:

My family were Methodists turned Episcopalians. I remember switching churches when I was very young. I didn't really know why, except that my mother loves high church ritual and probably saw it as a break from her small-town upbringing in Pontotoc. (Much later I discovered that the triggering event was the decision by St. Luke's Methodist to turn away black worshippers. That made me proud.) At any rate, we were an unobtrusive, by-the-rules, walk-on-eggshells family. I believed I'd fit in just fine on the path that was laid out before me: Spann Elementary for six years; Chastain Junior High for three years; Murrah High for three glorious years. And except for being a bit of a smartass and figuring out that some junior high teachers are spectacularly dull-witted, I did. (I still remember the day a teacher who will remain unnamed lowered her voice to an ominous whisper and asked, in all seriousness, how we'd feel if we came to school one day and saw a "communist flag." Oooohhh, scary. Never mind that a communist takeover in Jackson, Mississippi, or the U.S. in general, was about as likely as Jackson State and Ole Miss merging and calling themselves Oreo State University. That's when I started to figure out that a lot of what they tell you in school is nonsense.)

You couldn't grow up in Jackson in the 1960s without understanding that race was the defining issue of our place and time. Even though I only ever heard the white establishment side of the debate in the media, it was clear to me that something was wrong. See, if you're a by-the-rules guy, you can't read the Constitution and find segregation, repression and violence. Sure, there was the three-fifths nonsense, but even the framers knew that didn't square with the fundamental principles of liberty and equality. And it damn sure didn't square with the Christian love and charity that I constantly heard proclaimed but rarely saw practiced. At some point you had to choose what side you were on, and for me it was easy. Ironically, it was the white leaders that made it easy ... I was born in Memphis and lived briefly in North Carolina and Tennessee again before my family returned to Mississippi in 1960.

"White only" signs were in various places. In my case, it was the Shubuta artesian well, which was a two-sided continuously flowing water fountain where I stopped and had a sip when walking downtown. My older brother, Howie, called "Bubba," and I would race from our house to that nearby natural "red water" spring, that was said to have health benefits. He would giggle at me, because I drank from the wrong side, the "colored" side. Bubba went to the "white" labeled area of the fountain and told me not to break the rules. As a four-year-old who could not read, I did not care, as the water tasted the same on both sides of the spouts. The pipes from the fountain drained down into a water trough from which the horses drank. I remember thinking that it was stupid to separate the water holes because of skin color, when no one else was waiting in line.

Doctors' offices had a colored waiting room and a white one. I found myself drawn to areas deemed "colored" and sensed, through the eyes of a child, that it just didn't feel right and perhaps something was coming to bring change. Not sure why I felt this when others did not, but we were singing that Jesus loves "all" the little children in church, so the separation signs evoked duplicity. The signs in Shubuta, Mississippi, are gone at present day, and there is only one water spout at the famous artesian well.

Lenda Taylor Brown remembered, "going to the Jackson Zoo and told my mama I wanted the colored water, did not think it was fair for me to get plain water—as you see I had no clue."

Fred Sheriff wrote:

Having been born in Jackson, Mississippi, and growing up here ... I remember the "Colored Only" signs. Even in elementary school, it seemed at the time that there were advantages to being white in Mississippi; the girls even seemed prettier. Then came the James Brown song "I'm Black and I'm Proud," and I was encouraged to be proud of who I was and not try to be someone else.

My family moved from Shubuta to the Jackson area when my father decided to make a career change and attend medical school. Jackson was/is a thriving

metropolitan hub that houses our state government, with all the support, lob-
bying, and partying that goes on behind the scenes when the legislators are in
session. It is a beautiful city, set amidst towering hardwood and pine trees, sur-
rounded by green and fertile agricultural areas. Additionally, Jackson is a center
for art, dance, theater, and culture. It is where women come shopping for unique
and unusual lines of clothing and produce.

As elementary school began during the 1960s, our area felt safe and secure.
Power Elementary (in centrally located Belhaven) was very orderly. It was a white
neighborhood school, with a few black classmates. Students obeyed the school
handbook mandates and dress codes. The Pledge of Allegiance was repeated
daily, followed by "The Star Spangled Banner" and other patriotic songs. Square
dancing was one of our exercises; it was funny to watch. My mother took me
to school each morning and typically picked me up in the afternoon. However,
sometimes I walked up the hill when school was dismissed to join my brother
who attended Bailey Junior High School, and we went home together. When the
final bell rang at Power, we walked outside in an orderly fashion to be directed
by the whistles of little white patrol boys in gloves and yellow vests, who were
responsible upper classmen. They made sure we crossed the street safely before
going up the hill. Safety was something I took for granted. I fearlessly rode my
bike, and skated up and down the hills around North State Street, Millsaps Col-
lege, and Riverside Drive with delight. (Now, as I revisit Jackson, I cannot believe
that I ever roller skated on those long steep hills.)

In the radius of a mile lay six great institutions, perhaps planned by Jack-
son educators of the distant past to be the ultimate educational hub: Power
Elementary, Bailey Junior High, Murrah High, Millsaps College, the University
of Mississippi Medical Center (which housed the medical school, nursing school,
health-related professions school and later the dental school), and the Veterans
Hospital. All schools lay within walking distance of our Belhaven home.

Johnny Jones best explains this educational area in an excerpt from his
essay:

The tract of 16th Section land on which Murrah, Bailey Junior High and Power
Elementary were built had once been the grounds of the Mississippi State Insane
Asylum. A *large* place. The first structure was Bailey, built in 1937 along the western slope of the Section facing North State Street. The exterior was featured in
Life magazine in 1938 when it was sleekly new and white, with lions and gargoyles
and art deco filigree cut right into the concrete that was the only construction
material used. By the time we got there 30 years later it looked more like Attica
Correctional Facility in New York, a graying fortress that was, and remains, for-
bidding. Power Elementary was a buff-brick, one-story warehouse plopped down

in the lowland between the upper schools. And Murrah? The utilitarian edifice rose majestically along the northeastern border of the Section atop one of the highest hills in Jackson. We were told that the entire area had been the northern crater wall of a volcano that has been dormant for 65 million years, or since the dinosaurs. More relevant to some of us was the fact that Murrah faced due north, away from the older parts of the city and in the direction all white Jackson was moving just as fast as it could get there. Still, in the pre-integration heyday of the neighborhood school, we could expect to start the first grade and graduate high school in that one large place. Our constant proximity to Murrah formed many of our expectations.

Johnny recalled the first years of integration:

> At Power there was one black student, a tiny girl a couple of years behind us who rode to and from school in a police car and was escorted everywhere she went by two huge officers. She was dressed in her white Sunday-school clothes with stiff undergarments and poofy skirts, bobby socks and black patent-leather shoes, small clips and things in her close-cropped hair, no color but her skin. She could have been the model for the Norman Rockwell painting titled (strangely I always thought) "The Problem We All Live With." And like that painting, the "problem" was only seen from the perspective of the viewer and not the viewed, which is one-sided if not patronizing anti-art. We didn't know what she looked like because she never raised her head. She was this miniature person who was clearly petrified by the attention and what she had been told might happen to her at the hands of the white people she saw everywhere all day long at school. I don't recall anybody telling us why she was treated like that; I don't think we asked. But it took no knowledge or curiosity to see how scared and thoroughly unhappy she was. It was wrong to put this little bitty baby in this setting, just as it was wrong to ask her to carry the weight of all that history and symbolism and emotion. I remember identifying with her, or wanting to.

Susan McBroom told us in an interview, "You see, I had been exposed to desegregation in Centerville, Mississippi, in 1966. I was in the sixth grade and I remember having big groups of police officers outside the school to escort this black family with three little girls into William Winas Attendance Center, the only school I knew of in Centerville. I remember being a little frightened at first, not of the little black child in my class, but of all the police outside. I will never forget her as long as I live. I felt so sorry for her, because all the boys in my class threw spit balls at her and laughed and called her names. They even tied her sash to the desk one day. We had to wear dresses back then. I was horrified at how cruel people were to this girl just because of the color of her skin. Then it got even worse when we found out she had just been passed along through the grades and had not been taught how to read."

Lenda Taylor Brown wrote:

Tolerance without pre-judging someone because of difference was taught to me and my sisters throughout life. We moved to Jackson, Mississippi, when I was five from Fort Worth, Texas, and I started first grade at Duling. I remember seeing Mexicans in Texas but I do not remember seeing blacks until we moved to Jackson. Most families had maids and I think the going rate was $21 a week—we never had a maid as my mama was lucky enough to stay home with her girls. I remember going to the old A&P and when ready for carry-out the front yelled OUT SIDE and a rather older black man came out of the back to carry the groceries outside! . . . We moved to Boston in the sixties; my daddy was at Harvard, and yes we were surrounded by liberal thinking people, our schools and neighborhoods were already integrated—no big deal. . . . We returned to Jackson, start of the seventh grade at Chastain. The public pools had already closed because of integration, but the schools were not forced for integration until the middle of my ninth grade.

Katie Barwick-Snell remembered,

Many of the white middle- and upper-class families in Mississippi had household help. I never asked my black friends if they did. Our family was able to afford a maid, Gertrude, once a week. She was my "other mother." Gertrude worked for us since I was a baby and stayed with me when my parents left town. She taught me how to make chocolate meringue pie and how to iron. She made me an apron from one of my old dresses and taught me how to hand sew. She also taught me that everyone has a story and not to judge people because of how they look but who they are inside. Gertrude represented the working black women in the 1950s and '60s that raised my generation with great love and decency. I feel many of these women helped my generation learn by example. She made sure I knew I could come to her house, down the street from Brinkley High School, if violence occurred or I was scared when I attended the tenth-grade center at Brinkley. She stopped coming to our house regularly when my mama started working full time but she kept in touch and she attended my high school graduation and gave me a beautiful gift.

As a young girl at Power Elementary, I remember being in the Monkees' Fan Club, dreaming about Peter Tork and listening to the Beatles on the radio. A good deal of extended family socialized more often in the 1950s and 1960s. At these gatherings I picked up the social mores of our clan . . . the military stories, discussions of service to the church, card-playing, observing the women cooking in the kitchen and preparing festive tables. Many women in Mississippi had a love for festivities, and dressing for them in their own unique feminine way; in the 1950s Mama and I wore a lot of hats. There was one family car. That was all that was needed; we traveled together. Without the distractions of multiple electronic devises, we socialized, talked, ate, and shared stories. The Belhaven area enjoyed a close community connection with the neighborhood schools. I recall how upset we were when they closed the pool at Riverside Park, because "black people" were to be allowed to swim there. It made me wonder what the big deal was. I just wanted to swim; it did not matter to me who was in the pool! Why were people so concerned about skin color and water in fountains and aquatic areas? My swimming lessons continued at the downtown YMCA. I cannot remember if this pool was integrated; I believe it was.

Robert Kelly: "You know most of us couldn't swim. Has anybody mentioned that? Most of the black kids in Jackson that were my age, you couldn't swim, because you good white folks closed the swimming pools down to the public, because you all didn't want us swimming with you. You all had these private pools. I remember driving by the zoo in Jackson, Mississippi, going to my grandmother's house and you would see the pool over there where all the white folks were swimming, jumping off diving boards and stuff. Hell, we couldn't swim . . . If I got in water, we would walk the railroad track to Lake Hiko, you know and got in the little dirty dangerous water. We didn't have swimming pools in our back yard . . . Yeah; we would have loved to have learned how to swim. But during that time, you good white folks said, 'Oh hell no! We are not gonna allow them to come over here and swim in our swimming pools.'"

As the years passed, I later went up the hill to Bailey Junior High School, as my brother moved on to the much-anticipated Murrah High School. I took for granted that I, too, would have my opportunity to attend Murrah. One of the favorite social experiences during my tenure at Bailey was the River Hills dance for junior-high-age students. River Hills was/is a private country club and tennis center in exclusive northeast Jackson. This club exuded class, and always included events for young people. The dance featured a lively band engendering young boys and girls to gather and celebrate Valentine's Day or some other holiday. It was sort of competitive seeing who could get the most taps on the shoulder to dance. Parents would drop us off and come back a few hours later.

We looked forward to these special socials. At that time it was a well-chaperoned private event. Again, I was not thinking about racial inequality or any other social issue other than wearing the perfect dress and dancing.

Johnny Jones described his early junior high school experience:

At Bailey the population of black students increased to about five or ten per grade level. To this day we remember their names because they were such an oddity to us. I don't remember anybody commenting on their presence in any mean or spiteful way; we just gawked at them. Those few who played sports with us on the Bailey teams had it harder than the others. The coaches threw a poor black player into the thick of every game and counted on him blossoming before their eyes into Willie Richardson or Oscar Robinson because surely it was in the blood of their race. We learned quickly that black athletes were more like us than not despite our expectations born of nothing more or less than the lowest form of stereotyping. We also learned that they were more like us than not in the classroom despite the stereotypes. Beyond those basic lessons we learned very little, not because of anything facially racist but because we had to invent a way of dealing with them with no help at all from adults. As I recall, no grown-up at the school said one thing to us about the black students. Certainly we were not encouraged to welcome them or include them in any school activities. Our black classmates didn't seem to care one way or another. They just stayed to themselves as if they understood that they were merely token presences, lab rats with no chance to escape from the cages and take over the lab. Communication was much improved after real integration was ordered, but in the days of token compliance with the law the black students were unhappy, even resentful. They didn't want to be there. It must have been awful for them playing off so many stupid white clichés, and many of them did not stay with us after the courts decided to make our school system the nation's test case for radical integration. Who could blame them?

It is useful and surprising to recall how little we knew about . . . anything . . . on the cusp of massive integration of our schools. Our ignorance extended beyond knowing nothing about the black half of Jackson's population to blindness to any other part of the city outside our protected northeast quadrant. My friends and I knew that white kids from the Capitol Street area near downtown went to old Jackson Central, those from west Jackson went to Provine, and those from south Jackson went to Wingfield, but that was it. Until we played Hardy and Peeples and Enochs in junior high school we had never been to those areas of town those schools served. I still don't know how to get to Forest Hill. We didn't know a soul from those places; to this day I know more people from Meridian than I do from west or south Jackson.

Mary Alene Cobb Alford, whom we called "Mary Al," communicated these thoughts:

My memories of my Jackson Public School education are positive aside from the serious school phobia I suffered in the first grade. For some unknown reason I thought I was supposed to be able to read when I started school. I ran and hid at neighbors' homes and caused my parents untold stress and concern and for this I apologize.

My parents, Alton and Mary Cobb, were progressive and liberal-minded individuals, although I don't recall realizing such distinctions as a child. My father grew up in rural Madison County in a very poor environment but excelled at Camden High School and Holmes Junior College. He attended Johns Hopkins Medical School where he met my mother, a nursing student from Waterloo, Iowa, attending Rosary College. After a short stint as a general practitioner in Pickens, Mississippi, he went on to earn a master's in Public Health from Tulane. Dad served the state as health officer from the year of our Murrah graduation, 1973, until his retirement in 1992. Mom was a public health nurse for thirty years and a very active member of St. Richard Catholic church. While both are retired, they maintain active lives as volunteers in northeast Jackson. Commitment to public service was a given in my family.

I grew up in an idyllic setting on Maywood Circle with my younger siblings Tommy and Susan. Early memories include riding my bicycle to the Tote-Sum store and sliding down the mountain of insulation while Maywood Mart was being constructed. The latter was not a good idea! Taylor Burgers, the first fast-food restaurant in Jackson, was located behind my home. Our only out-to-eat experiences occurred at Morrison's Cafeteria, however, as kids ate free on Tuesdays. Trips to my grandparents' farm near Camden were possible thanks to the Greyhound bus that amazingly came to a complete stop on I-55 and dropped me off so that I might cross the highway and return to my 221 Maywood Circle home. We watched little television (it was black and white, of course, and there were three channels) and instead played wonderful, creative, and dangerous games outdoors. Saturday mornings were spent at the Playpen racing miniature cars on the basement track or bowling at Larwil Lanes when we were a bit older. I walked to the neighborhood school, Spann Elementary, and suffered the ultimate humiliation when my public health nurse mom taught the fifth-grade sex education class.

I have very little memory of the tragic and violent events of the sixties. Of course, I do remember Mrs. Thigpen's tearful announcement in the third grade that President Kennedy had been assassinated and I especially remember my friend . . . jumping out of the desk in front of me proclaiming, "My mother will be so happy!" This was my first recollection of racism and political division. My parents were strong Kennedy supporters and I recall tearfully watching John-John's salute of his father's caisson as it progressed down Pennsylvania Avenue.

Chastain days were emotionally challenging, totally unrelated to the pending school upheaval. My good friend committed suicide in the seventh grade along with a next-door neighbor and a Chastain English teacher . . . These were obviously faith-testing events. As one of the few Catholic students at the school (remember those fish sticks every Friday that everyone complained about?), I acquired an empathy with the one or two black students present at Chastain. The Protestant prayers offered during daily devotionals were a source of spiritual tension for this good Catholic girl and I continue to be skeptical toward prayer in public schools.

Johnny Jones continued recalling his youthful experiences:

I have no Willie Morris stories about playing ball with incredibly gifted black athletes on dusty playgrounds down by the tracks. As a kid I was never introduced to a black man or woman, let alone a black person my age, and what we thought we knew about black people was warped and hardly representative.

Our information came from experiences around black domestics, or "maids," who worked for our families. They came from what grown-ups called "the quarter" or worse. That area of town had no defined location; it was just where black people lived. Occasionally we would ride with our mothers to "take the maid" and stare transfixed at the widespread poverty of their neighborhoods like we had come upon the poorer sections of Kingston or Capetown, certainly not Jackson. My favorite "maid" lived in a cardboard-and-tar shack by the railroad tracks in what is now called "Belhaven Heights," less than a mile from my present home. She lived with some twelve to fifteen people in that shack without electricity until my grandfather got it for them. My grandparents' old refrigerator/freezer and black-and-white TV became their living room furniture. I remember how the naked bulb hanging from the living room ceiling made everything look damp, pestilential, and so foreboding that it entered my dreams for the rest of time. There were, even then, nicer middle-class neighborhoods in northwest Jackson, but we never saw them. Like patronizing whites all across the South, especially in our literature, I loved my "maid," especially when she had a belt or two. She took it from my grandfather's bootlegged fifth of vodka and, with me as her accomplice, covered the theft with water and vigorous shaking so the amount in the bottle appeared as he left it. As much as she seemed to enjoy life, telling me stories that caused her to howl with laughter through her toothless mouth, nobody ever explained to me why she had to live that way—beyond poverty. It didn't take much understanding to know that something had to give in the lives of the black people I knew. The disparity in their lives and ours begged for some sort of justice. I just remember feeling that something was coming, and that it would affect us directly.

Myra Stevens Myrick answered some questions for us and commented,

Some memories of integration go back to fifth and sixth grade when we had school choice and at Boyd, we had a couple of black kids in our class. We thought it was the end of our world, but looking back on it, I wonder what it was like for the black kids that had to leave their schools and be the only black kid in the fifth grade.

Richard Sanders noted,

For what it's worth, I found it a wonderful story with some troubling characters and situations. I had never thought before of my aunt's or grandma's maids, who were always there for Thanksgiving or Christmas events, that they might want to be home with their own families. I, too, recall the occasional rides with Mom or Dad to take home some help who had missed the bus at the intersection of Southwood Road and Hickory Ridge. Many of their homes matched the one in our backyard.

I had never looked or treated them with anything other than a kind heart. But then, my perception of a kind heart might be received differently. I can remember two of them getting in trouble with Mom.

While Mom was gone one day, Sadie (I think it was her name) took a nap on the couch. I didn't think anything of it but Mom had a whole different prospective on it when she found out. Sadie was gone the next week.

I also remember another—the name fails me—who got in trouble for coloring with me one day. She was really good too! She was gone within a week or two. Mom never flinched to accuse the help of taking anything that was misplaced. Mom was a fine lady, but had trust and comfort issues with folks of color. Well, maybe with most folks, period.

Related to this was a small event in summer of the tenth grade. I was working at Bailey Brothers lumberyard. Ned, a very large and wonderfully hearted black truck driver, and I had made a delivery near our house. After some coercion on my part, he agreed to stop by our home for something to drink. We showed up and Mom was quite surprised but always the welcoming hostess, invited us in. Ned refused to come in our house. He was very nice about it and in reflection, Ned was doing the "Yes, Boss, shuffle" in our north Jackson carport. He understood about it. Mom never said anything to me beyond, "It was nice to meet your friend today." I think Dad must have gotten a kick out of it.

In an interview, Robert Kelly told me, "My daddy was not formally educated. Now he was the most educated man I ever met before in my life, but he did not have a high-school degree. My mother didn't finish high school; she worked in the factories. She was the help at different parts or times in her life. What was so amazing about that was, it was like we were always doing good. It wasn't like we were struggling because we had a steady paycheck coming in. My daddy was working a couple of jobs and then he ventured into entrepreneurship and right away I could see things getting a little bit better around the house."

Robert continued, "I love bacon. I love the smell of bacon and biscuits. My mama, every morning for years, would bake biscuits. Because you eat biscuits and syrup and I could tell you how many sops were in a gallon of syrup, like 385. [laughs] She would scramble some eggs and fry some green tomatoes for breakfast and hot biscuits—and that was breakfast. Now on weekends on Saturdays and Sundays we would have bacon. That was slab bacon, thick bacon you would cut, and she would always give me one piece of that bacon. I always said man if I ever get me some money, I am gone fry and eat all the bacon that I can find! When my daddy eased into entrepreneurship, things got a little better around the house. I will never forget, on a Tuesday morning, I was at Murrah then, we had bacon. My mama said, 'Go ahead and get another piece.' To this day I love the smell of bacon."

Robert's breakfast sounded really good to me. Robert and I laughed about this. Biscuits and bacon was/is a southern staple. Those biscuits of the old days that our mothers made from scratch were truly wonderful; there's an art to making these well. Mostly, I just wanted a bowl of extra sugary cereal before leaving for school. What we were eating was one economic indicator of how well we were doing. In the Deep South, good food is a language of its own that we all understand, especially biscuits, bacon, grits, and sweet tea.

Joseph T. Reiff shared,

My family moved to Jackson in 1960 when my father began teaching at Millsaps College. I attended first through fourth grades at Power Elementary School—still all white, of course. My parents were behind-the-scenes supporters of the civil rights movement, and I remember going out to the Tougaloo College campus a few times in 1963 and 1964; my parents were participating in gatherings for support and planning for the Jackson movement's Church Visits campaign, when interracial groups of students and visiting clergy went to various white Jackson churches in attempts to integrate their worship services. I knew enough not to mention these visits to my friends. We left Jackson in the summer of 1964 to live in Abilene, Texas. West Texas was enough different from the Deep South that I noticed. The schools were not integrated yet, but I competed in a track meet which included kids from the black school on the south side of town where I lived. That would not have happened in Jackson in the 1960s.

Joe continued,

We moved back to Jackson in 1965, settling in the northeast part of town in an area we called "Leftover," a play on the name Eastover, the wealthier section of that part of town. My first experience of "Freedom of Choice" school integration was in the seventh grade when a handful of blacks came to Bailey Junior High in 1966–67, including one male student, a ninth-grader named Sammy, I often got to school early, and I remember several cold mornings waiting with Sammy and several other kids in one of the large covered doorways before the building opened at 8:00. On more than one occasion, a couple of ninth-grade white guys peppered Sammy . . . with all kinds of verbal abuse, trying to get a response out of him and hoping, I guess, that he would talk back so they could escalate the bullying. He never responded, keeping his cool and succeeding in ignoring them. I wish I had had the courage to stand up for him in some way, though I am sure I would have suffered retaliation from those white guys if I had. I wonder what other abuses he endured—probably several much worse than what I observed. He possessed strength of character that I lacked at that age.

By ninth grade there were a few more black kids at Bailey, but still not many. I was not aware of any of them being treated badly on a day-to-day basis, though I would not be surprised if they were. Our Class Day dance in the spring of 1969 was privately sponsored and did not include our black classmates. A female friend told me how awkward she felt delivering a printed invitation to the dance to one of our white female classmates, with no corresponding invitation to give to the black friend sitting with her.

My family was out of step with the northeast Jackson elite culture. My dad drove a baby-blue 1954 Chevrolet then, and I rode to school with him most days. It seems ludicrous now, but because most of the kids I sought to impress were upper middle class and did not have fourteen-year-old cars in their families, I was ashamed of the car. And worse (in my view), my dad, who attended the 1968 Democratic Convention in Chicago as part of the inter-racial Mississippi delegation, put a Humphrey sticker on the back of that car (SURELY the only northeast

Jackson family to publicly declare that political allegiance!). So each morning when he dropped me off in the fall of 1968, I exited the car and walked back five steps to disassociate myself from it.

The kids I knew were for Nixon in that election, so I told my parents I was for Nixon, which now symbolizes to me the misguided desire in those years to be part of the "in crowd," a nebulous entity which may have existed more fully in my own mind than in reality, but which nonetheless had its power over me in those years. One illustration of this power: I spent a Saturday at Riverside Park with a junior high girlfriend whose family was much wealthier than mine. I had ridden the three miles from my house to the park on my bike to be with her, and upon arriving to take her daughter home, the girl's mother offered to put my bike in the back of their station wagon and give me a ride home. In spite of the attraction of spending more time with the girl, I declined, because at some level I was ashamed (absurdly) of our Leftover neighborhood and home.

Claiborne Barksdale, Alan Huffman, Johnny Jones, Margie Cooper Pearson, and I met at Johnny's office for an interview. Margie indicated that she had attended black elementary schools in solidly black Jackson neighborhoods. The demographic of those neighborhoods is still black, but looking back Margie noted that the community was "more solid, much nicer. Back then you had teachers who lived in your community. My teacher was a neighbor around the corner." She said her son hasn't really experienced anything like that, "and that was the difference in, I think, our growing up back in the day versus him today."

Claiborne Barksdale [to Margie]: "Did you even think about white folks?"

Margie, shaking her head, said, "My grandmother, who right now is at home and I'm there taking care of her, she was the person that came to your homes and cleaned . . . a domestic, or whatever . . . she would come home and tell her stories, so I had an impression through her eyes, and she is not an educated woman, of what . . . that world was like. But at the same time I read a lot . . . I had my own perception of things too, so I really didn't think about your world so much. I was living in my own world . . . And my own was pretty comfortable to me."

Claiborne asked what she read—was it black fiction?

Margie: "No—*Little Women*. I looked for black fiction, which was hard to find . . . But I remember finding a book and it was, I think, the name of it was *April*. It wasn't anything substantial or heavy duty, but I think I was probably eleventh grade then . . . It was just a little story about this young black girl, and it had illustrations in it. That was just exciting to me. But I mentioned that just because, no, I didn't read, per se, black novels, I just read a little bit of everything."

Claiborne: "Did you have any animosity toward white folks?"

Margie: "No, because I didn't really know any except for the ones that were brought into my world through my grandmother and through aunts whose work was to work in their homes. And a lot of these people that they worked for were very decent, good people. I mean my great-grandmother, even. She had worked for this family for years. I don't know what her job entailed, per se, but every Christmas, or around the holidays, they would come to get her to stay with them for a week or two, and they would just do all this baking. And I mean, when she came home, we were just jumping up and down. We were so excited because we knew we were going to get all kinds of homemade treats—divinity and nut rolls and red velvet cake—and all this stuff from her visiting there."

Alan: "Was this your great-grandmother or your grandmother?"

Margie: "This was my great-grandmother. And sometimes she would send clothes. A lot of times it wasn't stuff we wore, because we didn't wear the full skirts with the poodle kinda thing on it." [all laugh]

Claiborne: "Like you did, Teena." [all laugh]

Margie: "But still, it was . . ."

I said: "I don't remember that." [all laugh]

Margie: "But who said it was . . . [laughs] You don't remember that?"

I laughed: "No."

Margie: "Well, look now. This *was* the '50s and '60s. [all laugh] This was the '50s. So, 'cause she was much older and she would still go there, she would send home items of clothing, all of it with a gesture of sincerity and goodness . . . You know we loved this family. This lady loved my great-grandmother, and how could you not love that?"

Alan: "Do you know who they were?"

Margie: "I just remember her name was Ms. Billie. I'm sure my grand-mother could probably tell me her last name. And the same thing with my uncle—not an educated man, but he worked for a guy, I remember he was a welder, so I'm thinking this was the business this man was in. And they were close; they were good friends. So, a lot of the experiences I had were positive. I'm not gonna say they all were, but to me, most of my negative experiences happened after I got out of high school, as an adult. The first time I was ever called the N-word, I was an operator at South Central Bell, and it was some-body on the phone. And that just knocked me off my feet because that just had never happened to me before."

Johnny: "You never saw any evidence of white racism at Bailey or Brinkley or Murrah?"

Margie: "If I did, I really didn't."

Claiborne: "Didn't register?"

Margie: "No. I will tell you, I know that there are some things that happened, I can, and I don't know if you've heard this through some of the others. I want to say it happened more at Brinkley than I remember it being at Bailey. A few who saw, noticed that a couple of black kids seemed to be really chummy with the white kids and looked like that was all they were hanging out with."

Johnny: "Yeah."

Margie: "They started kind of, what's the word?"

Claiborne: "Shunning."

Margie: "Bad mouthing, shunning that person."

Johnny: "You mean a black person for hanging around the white kids?"

Margie: "Yes."

Claiborne Barksdale was a teacher in 1972–1973 and a 1968 Murrah graduate. He wrote:

> I had been reared in a large, largely apolitical, middle-class home in Jackson, on the Leftover side of Meadowbrook Road. My experience with black folks was similar to that of other white Jacksonians from my class and time: We had "maids," we had "yardmen," the "n-word" was absolutely verboten, but Katherine used a separate bathroom. My father was senior warden of the vestry at St. James' Episcopal Church when it was confronted in the mid-sixties with the question of attendance by black folks. Churches throughout "white" Jackson—First Presbyterian, First Baptist—the ones with the sprawling edifices and parking lots metastasizing throughout the better parts of town—were posting guards at the doors on Sunday mornings, arms crossed, blocking entrance by "outside agitators" and such, and some on the vestry at St. James' wanted a vote: Let 'em in or block 'em? My father said that there would be no vote and no sentries; anyone who wanted to worship at St. James' would be welcome. Period. End of discussion.
>
> My parents were horrified when the Meredith Crisis occurred, pacing the living room in front of the Zenith that Sunday night. They reviled Barnett, that redneck peckerwood.
>
> But, as I say, we had woefully paid "maids" and we had Caesar the yardman who couldn't read. In high school, I would give Jessie a ride home some nights—at first she would sit in the back seat until I finally made her sit up front with me—to her rough neighborhood, down Woodrow Wilson, near Hawkins Field

and the Glorioso Food Mart. She would get out and I could look down the entire length of her shotgun house. It was clean and it was pretty empty, there was one naked light bulb hanging there, and I knew exactly what she had and what she didn't have. And then I would get the hell out of there.

One rainy afternoon, when I was a freshman at Ole Miss, Jessie, waiting on the bus by the side of our house, waited too long in the rain, caught a cold, contracted pneumonia, and died about five days later.

(About the apostrophes around "maid": Apart from the obvious [such as *The Help* by Kathryn Stockett], this is an especially sensitive subject for me, with some history. When I was in the tenth grade, my father had what we thought was a heart attack—it turned out to be pericarditis and in some ways was the beginning of the end—while we were at an Ole Miss football game in Oxford. I came home—solo—and the next day went to the fair, ate too much Malone's taffy and such, this somehow morphed into appendicitis, had an appendectomy, then recuperated at home. Without doubt one of the best weeks of my life to that point. Ruby, who was working for us at the time, was so thoughtful and helpful to me. I wrote an essay about all this for Miss Meda Bonne Crawford's class, and at one point I referred to Ruby as "my maid." I read the essay to Ruby—I on the porch, she in the kitchen, I can see it clearly—and when I got to that passage, she glared at me and said: "I am *not* your maid!" She was not my maid, she was not our maid, she was not anybody's damn "maid." I was ashamed. Ashamed of my stupidity in throwing this in the face of someone who deserved infinitely better, but also ashamed because I had realized at an unspoken level before I read it to her that I was committing a serious offense by the condescension. In short, I knew better, but I thought it made the essay better, so I committed the offense in writing, then compounded it by reading it to Ruby. I believe that this latter offense was a sin.)

The Historical Context of Radical Desegregation in Jackson, Mississippi

John Griffin (Johnny) Jones, Class of 1973

■

Jackson, Mississippi, is a tough place. It always has been. We have the record to prove it, especially in the area of race relations. From the founding of the city in 1822 through the late 1980s (when white flight out of the city limits created a black voting-age majority and we elected our first black mayor), Jackson's history was remarkable for a consistent attitude, supplemented by occasional acts, of determined resistance by its white citizenry. When that historical attitude was challenged by identifiable outside influences, we never quit fighting; we just moved away. Examples of our successful resistance to change in the city abound in our history.

During the Civil War, there were three separate pitched battles for Jackson. Union forces actually occupied the town on five separate occasions through April 1865, the last occurring a week before the surrender of General Robert E. Lee and the Army of Northern Virginia at Appomattox. Through it all there was no accommodation, cooperation, or capitulation. Metaphorically speaking, white Jackson's response during the Civil War was but prelude to our response to the *Brown v. Board of Education* in 1954, the civil rights movement in general, and the most conspicuous legal consequence of the combination of these huge historical forces affecting our lives: desegregation of the public schools in Jackson.

In the first engagement alone—called the "Battle of Jackson" in the literature of the war, fought in May 1863 during Union general U. S. Grant's successful campaign to take Vicksburg—the Confederates lost 1,136 to the Union's 1,422 casualties, while property losses were estimated between $5 million to $10 million, all in fighting over a town of approximately 4,000 citizens. Many hotels, warehouses, and homes were burned to the ground following each major engagement, earning us our most descriptively accurate, even tasteful, nickname: "Chimneyville." But each and every time the federals destroyed our existing structures, we built them back even stronger than before.

Exactly a century later, this time during the civil rights movement, Jackson's resistance took forms that were just as determined but meaner, of ignoble purpose, unjustified . . . and much more successful. A few years before radical desegregation of the schools, Jackson's response to a renewed call for racial justice was symbolized best by the "Thompson Tank," a souped-up police paddy wagon fitted out with gun turrets and razor wire on the undercarriage to prevent overturning by "rioters," named for then-mayor Allen Thompson. The Freedom Riders ended their bus trips through the South in Jackson in 1961. A deal cut between Attorney General Robert Kennedy, Greyhound Bus Company, and state and city officials resulted in the Jackson Police Department protecting the Freedom Riders as they disembarked at the Greyhound station in downtown Jackson, but only so long as they walked through the "Whites Only" section of the station and straight into police paddy wagons, which took them directly to jail. For sins like disturbing the peace and demonstrating without a permit, our local judges sent many of the Freedom Riders to Parchman, the state penitentiary, where they served excessive sentences among the general prison population. And that largely ended the Freedom Rides, which was the point.

We were just getting started. Jackson's new brand of resistance, vintage 1963, included demeaning measures like refusing a formal request by the town's leading African American ministers and businessmen that black citizens be addressed in public as "Mister" and Miss" in place of common nicknames like "Leroy," or the much more common epithets, "Boy" and "Girl." We hurriedly built "camps" on the state fairgrounds to hold those arrested while demonstrating for such dignities and courtesies as well as the hiring of black police officers, firemen, and other city services workers not yet protected by Title VII of the Civil Rights Act of 1964. These "camps" were open-air pens surrounded by razor-wire fencing where demonstrators were held until the few black lawyers in Jackson, later aided by organizations like the Lawyers' Committee for Civil Rights under Law and some of the best legal minds in the nation, could raise the money, or pledge enough real or personal property among Jackson's black citizens, to bail them out. Nationally and across the world, Jackson's resistance is forever memorialized in TV footage of one professor and three students from nearby Tougaloo College sitting-in at the Woolworth's lunch counter on Capitol Street in May 1963, until the surrounding throng of white kids and seething old codgers poured condiments and sugar on their heads and then knocked them, males and females, off their stools and beat them viciously. The splotchy old film is still disturbing both because of the force of the beatings of those kids—they almost killed twenty-year-old Tougaloo student Memphis Norman—and because it occurred with increasing brutal insanity under the leering grins of uniformed police officers, who just stood around watching until those administering the beatings exhausted themselves.

Less than a month later, NAACP field secretary Medgar Evers was assassinated in the driveway of his home in Jackson on June 12, 1963. Among many cruel ironies, Evers was killed a few hours after the nationwide television broadcast of President Kennedy's first (and best) substantive speech on civil rights and the need for national legislation that would become his chief domestic-policy legacy: the Civil Rights Act of 1964. Evers was not murdered by a Jacksonian; he was back-shot by a white extremist from Greenwood, Byron de la Beckwith (though the *Jackson Clarion-Ledger* identified him as a "Californian" when he was first arrested). Beckwith was tried twice in Jackson for the murder in 1964, got off both times when all-white juries couldn't reach a verdict, but so proud of his deed that he could not keep from bragging about it in public over the next thirty years, earning him a final conviction for the murder in 1994 and a resulting life sentence to his death in 2001.

Following Evers's funeral, black citizens and others came together on Farish Street near the funeral home and the state NAACP headquarters where Evers had worked as Mississippi field secretary. It was an impromptu gathering, without organization, leadership, or design—just a mass of people sharing an angry sense of irreplaceable loss. Quickly, however, a line of Jackson policemen and auxiliary officers, armed and in riot gear and standing shoulder-to-shoulder, formed a line stretching across Farish Street and began moving toward the mourners. Whether the angriest among the mourners had weapons and were prepared to respond violently to such provocation by the police depends upon whom one asks, but all recall the scene with fearful apprehension. As the line of armed police approached, taunts and curses were hurled from the growing crowd. Some among the mourners stepped up and tried to disperse the crowd with calls for peace and calm or, at the very least, nonviolence, but nobody moved. At that point, just as the lines met and the tension reached critical mass, a white Justice Department attorney, the late John Doar, stepped out from the crowd of mourners and, turning to them, acknowledged their anger and frustration, said he shared it, but pleaded that, however justified, violence would surely follow armed confrontation with the police, and that violence in any form disserved Evers's memory. At that crucial point the mourners backed down and slowly walked off the line. But for those acts of personal courage in the face of intentional provocation by the riot cops, and the extraordinary restraint of those present to honor Evers, Jackson would have experienced an awful progression of racial violence just a month after the Birmingham demonstrations had drawn the attention of the nation. Even as the crowd dispersed, the police broke their line and waded into the crowd firing tear gas and busting heads with clubs, creating an ugly but brief confrontation in a period of our history full of them. Like so much of what happened here in the 1960s, we managed to avoid disaster by the narrowest of margins, and only because nobody fought back.

After that close call, the city was no longer the scene of serious confrontation or racial violence, even during the height of the movement's activities in Mississippi in 1964. What Medgar Evers, John Salter (a Tougaloo sociology professor who was beaten at the Woolworth lunch counter a month before Evers's assassination, dubbed "Mr. Mustard" by the white press because his brush-cut and face were covered with the stuff in the photos and film of the incident, and who was beaten again in the police riot after Evers's funeral), Reverend Ed King, and others had called the "Jackson Movement" did not recover from Evers's murder. Movement leaders wisely focused activities on other places in the state where defiance of federal law by local law enforcement was less lethal. When two young blacks were killed by gunfire from members of the Jackson Police Department (whether intentionally or by stray bullets is still an open question) during a demonstration on the campus of Jackson State University in May 1970, there was no organized, citywide response by any civil rights group or organization that I recall. We were in the first semester of radical desegregation when the events at Jackson State exploded in the press, and I specifically remember hysterical rumors running through the white community that armed blacks were marching in force from Jackson State into white neighborhoods to avenge the shootings. Nothing of the sort occurred. We just were ordered to stay home from school for two days. That was all the administrators knew to do. There was a shootout between Jackson cops and members of an organization called the Republic of New Africa in Jackson in 1971, but that was at best tangentially related to traditional "civil rights" activities or concerns such as school desegregation. Beyond that I recall no organized demonstrations or confrontation in Jackson during any of the tense years that followed Evers's murder through massive desegregation in early 1970. Other cities, north and south, burned or were the scenes of protest or organized demonstrations over issues of race and politics in the late 1960s and early 1970s, but not Jackson. Something traumatic occurred with the assassination of Medgar Evers and its aftermath that contributed to our long history of successful resistance. Its effects are everywhere.

In no context has Jackson's history of determined resistance been more successful, with more far-reaching effects, than in our response to massive desegregation of the public schools by federal court order. The backlash against desegregation has for over forty years now defined the demographics of the city. The traditional paths of white flight toward the northeast along the

Old Canton Road were followed until all the suburbs planned for in the 1950s and early 1960s were packed full, and then the paths extended beyond the city limits into Madison County to the north and Rankin County to the east. The outward-migration transformed small towns, villages really—Madison and Ridgeland in Madison County, Flowood (the site of Jackson Prep) and Pearl in Rankin County—into some of the fastest-growing communities in Mississippi. In terms of sheer numbers, it is the largest intrastate migration Mississippi has ever seen. As always, the results were mixed. Leaving aside the abandoned JPS, the exodus to escape desegregation had, and continues to have, a devastating adverse impact on Jackson's commercial, tax, and residential bases from which the city has never recovered. Yet, over time, those same forces managed to yield great public schools in the outlying counties: massive things that are fully integrated and hugely successful in every way that can be measured, especially against the JPS. Those splendid new public schools helped double the pace of the exodus: from an average of 10,000 white families moving out of Jackson per decade from 1960 through 1990 to 20,000 per decade from 1990 through 2010. Jackson, of course, is left with "separate but (un)equal" schools for blacks and whites—public for blacks, private for whites—in segregated circumstances that surpass anything we've seen in this city since the beginning of "token" integration of the JPS between 1964 and 1969. With Murrah now 97 percent black, and *still* losing white enrollment year by year, there remains little hope for the future we glimpsed at Murrah in the first years of desegregation of the JPS. There is a lot of shame in that.

"Radical" desegregation came to Jackson very early for a number of reasons, as well as timing and dumb luck. It was "radical" in the sense that the remedies imposed by the federal courts on the JPS were so sudden and so transformative of the entire system that it stunned the leadership to total ineffectiveness and, in the vast majority of whites, triggered the fight-or-flight response. Most flew. Even more than that, the timing of such a destructive effort to achieve social change was absolutely indispensable. It could only have happened in the late '60s and early '70s when, for better or worse, what the historian Arthur M. Schlesinger Jr. called in his *Cycles of American History* "the politics of public purpose over private interest" reached their high-water marks for the entire twentieth century. The methodology itself turned "radical" in late 1969 because none of the conservative-to-moderate steps taken by the federal courts to end active, ongoing segregation had worked, but also because the moral authority and popular acceptance of the whole civil rights agenda peaked around 1970. It was the only time in our lives when enough people were willing to finally do something about race, even sacrifice their own convenience and expectations, that for a brief moment the politics fell in line and massive strides were made. By that point many Mississippians, including my parents and their wide circle of friends, welcomed the changes, were proud that something was finally being done, and were willing to bet their children's futures on it.

All these historical and cultural forces, torqued up by the intransigence of the JPS administrators in moving from "token" to meaningful integration, came together at precisely the moment that the *Singleton v. Jackson Municipal Separate School District* case was before the Fifth Circuit Court of Appeals. When the court ruled on December 1, 1969, and then contradicted itself and ordered an even more extreme remedy in an order handed down on January 21, 1970, the integration moment in Jackson had reached critical mass.

The law led the way. It usually does. Our federal Constitution, like our Declaration of Independence, is a radically anti-majoritarian and, to use an old 1960s term, "anti-Establishment" document no matter who interprets it. Its mandates often have to be forced on people, many of whom violently disagree with protecting the rights of the minority or a single citizen against the wishes of the majority as expressed through our elected officials. But if the law retains the moral force of the constitutional and ethical principles that bring it into being out of need, the hearts and minds of the citizenry will usually follow. The last to fall in line, and the first to depart, is, of course, the political will, which tends toward fickleness in its support of anything affecting the majority of voters for which the politicians can't take credit. The tension between the will of the majority of voters and the constitutional rights of any minority or, indeed, a single individual, produced most of our concepts of personal liberty and "civil" rights, however hallowed or unhallowed they may be these days. And in no place has that tension been played out more dramatically, and with more traumatic yet lasting results, than in the decisions over school desegregation. To understand how fast and far we moved in our youth, and then to more fully grasp how far we've come in more recent times on the same issues, the best sources are the decisions and court orders themselves.

The Law

> We conclude that in the field of public education the doctrine of "separate but equal" has no place. Separate educational facilities are inherently unequal. Therefore, we hold that the plaintiffs and others similarly situated . . . are, by reason of the segregation complained of, deprived of equal protection of the laws guaranteed by the Fourteenth Amendment.
>
> Brown v. Board of Education (1954) (emphasis added)

The Constitution is not violated by racial imbalance in the schools, without more . . . The way to stop discrimination on the basis of race is to stop discriminating on the basis of race.

   Parents Involved in Community Schools v. Seattle School District No. 1 (2007) (Chief Justice John G. Roberts for 5–4 majority) (emphasis added)

If our history has taught us anything it has taught us to beware of elites bearing racial theories.

   Seattle School District No. 1 (Justice Clarence Thomas, concurring) (emphasis added)

The American historian Frances Fitzgerald wrote an article in *Esquire* in 1983 praising the significance of *Brown* and the achievement of Chief Justice Earl Warren in overcoming all odds to obtain a unanimous US Supreme Court behind the constitutional and moral principles that drove the result in 1954. Crediting philosopher Sir Isaiah Berlin, Fitzgerald wrote: "A great man is one who can turn a paradox into a platitude within his lifetime. That's what the Warren Court did" in *Brown*. In 2014, the more accurate observation is that *Brown* went from paradox to platitude to punch line within *our* lifetimes. Who could have predicted in 1955 when most of us were born, or 1973 when we graduated, or 1983 when Fitzgerald wrote her article and I was in Law School (fully three years into the Reagan revolution), that the Big Bang that shattered the "separate but equal" universe of legal segregation—for that is what *Brown* truly did—would end up being regarded with such cynicism verging on low sarcasm? As always, some context is essential.

In its first forty-odd years, *Brown* was American scripture. It was the original text for almost everything that followed in the area of civil rights, the *sine qua non* (a useful legal term meaning "without which there is nothing") case for the development of constitutional principles that protect the rights of individuals and minorities and ensure their open and fair participation in the democracy, and the best example we have of the Court placing the country on the path of righteousness when the executive and legislative branches were powerless to do so. At the Ole Miss Law School *Brown* was taught to us with great reverence: the finest example of the courage and majesty of the law ever to come from American courts. Standing alone, it still is. By providing the foundation for the radical desegregation of the JPS beginning in December 1969, *Brown* and the cases applying and expanding it through the early 1970s formed together the most significant external event of our youth. Had *Brown* been decided differently, or if the more conservative of current constitutional analyses were applied to the facts (many of which are remarkably unchanged after almost sixty years, or have returned after a thirty-year respite precisely because of the recent narrow victory of the conservative interpretations), our lives would have been vastly different.

In Mississippi in 1954, *Brown* was met with everything from *Black Monday,* a diatribe from Mississippi Supreme Court justice Tom Brady excoriating the Warren Court and providing the most extreme Chicken-Little predictions of its impact in the South, to the immediate actions of the Mississippi Legislature in repealing mandatory-attendance laws, closing public schools and reopening them as private schools using state funds, among other reactionary measures. *Brown* caused the creation of the white Citizens' Council, first in the Delta town of Indianola before moving to fancy offices in Jackson. By the 1959 election of the candidate endorsed by the Citizens' Council, Governor Ross R. Barnett, the organization had taken control of state politics, engaging in state-sanctioned spying and economic (and worse) terrorism against blacks and anybody who did not adhere to the orthodoxy of massive resistance, steamrolling anybody in public life that stood against them, and generally feeding an atmosphere of paranoia and fear not unlike the anticommunist witch hunt led by Wisconsin senator Joseph McCarthy in the early 1950s. Those stories are out there for anybody who wants to study the extreme lengths to which Mississippi whites in that period went in the warfare against *Brown* and the Warren Court. For our purposes, the more important story is how the integration mandate of *Brown* wended its way through, over, and under countless obstacles to become the radical desegregation orders of 1969-1970, and how the phenomena it undertook to remedy grew far beyond segregation in the schools.

Implementation of *Brown* occurred over a long period, each subsequent case extending its meaning and expanding its reach—until the federal courts called a halt to extensive desegregation efforts beginning in the early 1990s. In terms of what happened in Jackson generally, leading to what happened to us specifically beginning in December 1969 and thereafter until the integration "moment" ran out of momentum, the following chronology describes most of the significant chapters in the desegregation story:

- *Brown v. Board of Education* (1955) (*Brown II*): From *Plessy v. Ferguson* (1896) through *Brown I* in 1954, segregation was maintained by the fiction that schools for whites and blacks, and all that the schools needed from funding to facilities, would be "separate but equal." They weren't; by 1954 white students received 43 percent more of every dollar spent on education in the South. When the question of implementing the decision was argued and decided the next year in what is known as *Brown II*, the still-unanimous Court adopted a gradual approach: "Full implementation of these constitutional principles may require solution of varied local school problems," including "adjusting and reconciling public and private needs." Local federal district courts were directed to develop desegregation orders that took local problems into account under a timetable requiring public schools to open for admission "on a nondiscriminatory basis *with all deliberate speed*" (emphasis added). The chief justice had to compromise on the implementation issues to keep a unanimous court, and in doing so created a convenient escape hatch used by southern school boards to avoid integration as long as they could get away with it. Progress was slow to nonexistent for ten years.

- The Civil Rights Act of 1964. By the time of the assassination of President Kennedy on November 22, 1963, *Brown* had been reduced to an aspiration: only one percent of black students in the South were attending majority-white schools. There was not a single black student in the white schools of the JPS in the academic year 1962-63. The Kennedy brothers early on decided to defer "civil rights" enforcement until the second term, but of course things turned out differently. Three external events combined to make the radical changes *Brown* demanded politically viable: the loss of President Kennedy; the political radicalization of President Lyndon Johnson on civil rights issues following Kennedy's death; and public revulsion and outcry at the series of murders and beatings of blacks and a few whites working for civil rights in the South, dramatized in the televised police riots in Birmingham in the summer of 1963, which themselves encapsulated the confrontation between the forces of light represented by Reverend Martin Luther King Jr. and the forces of darkly violent resistance represented by Birmingham police chief Bull Connor. With the murders of the three civil rights workers, Schwerner, Chaney, and Goodman, in Philadelphia, Mississippi, in June 1964, and the successful strategy of the civil rights organizations (mainly the Student Nonviolent Coordinating Committee) in placing white college students with local people directly in harm's way, and harm followed as they knew it would, the nation was drawn into the story. By July 1964 President Johnson was able to utilize the nation's righteous indignation at the violence and the South's response to the simple dignities being requested by black people, along with his considerable skills at persuasion and legislation, to push through Congress what became the Civil Rights Act of 1964. Among other avenues of relief, the 1964 Act authorized the US Department of Justice to go to war against recalcitrant southern school districts in order to enforce *Brown*, which it did, almost never losing a case during the 1960s.

- The Elementary and Secondary Education Act of 1965. This legislation, originally aimed at high-poverty school districts, put federal money for education into the South, on the condition that the schools desegregate. Pocketbook persuasion.

- *Green v. New Kent County* (1968). A significantly more radicalized Warren Court announced that *Brown* meant more than granting "freedom of choice" to black students who desired to attend previously all-white schools, signaling the beginning of the end of the "freedom of choice" dodge to meaningful integration. Between opening up white schools to elective attendance by black students on one hand, and requiring wholesale transfers of faculty and students to achieve a balance that reflected the community's racial makeup in all schools on the other, lay fourteen years of avoidance and a quantum leap in understanding what the Constitution guaranteed after all. The recognized justification for swift judicial action on desegregation expanded beyond simply securing an individual's right to get the best education offered regardless of race, as *Brown* reasoned. The purpose and intended function of desegregation orders expanded to "remedying the effects of past intentional discrimination" because that was the legislative goal of the Fourteenth Amendment from the get-go. Those ends justify any means. In retrospect it may have been too much to load on the system of public education in this country; the Court chose to remedy the effects of our wretched history of discrimination by making our schools the proving grounds, with our children placed on the front line. *Green* expanded even this expansive constitutional interpretation, ordering the schools "to take whatever steps might be necessary to convert to a unitary system in which racial discrimination would be eliminated root and branch." The timetable of "all deliberate speed" was ignored as the schools were to "disestablish" the old dual system and "come forward with a plan that promises realistically to work, and promises realistically to work *now*." (Emphasis original.)

- *Alexander v. Holmes County Board of Education* (1969). The Court "sent the doctrine of deliberate speed to its final resting place." School districts "may no longer operate a dual school system based on race," and must "begin immediately to operate as unitary school systems within which no person is to be effectively excluded from any school because of race or color." "Immediately" meant "no delay may ensue because of the need for modification or hearing." The effect was to mandate desegregation "Now!" with no further delays allowed for the school districts to argue the "varied local school problems" allowed in *Brown II. Alexander* was the proverbial falling of the other shoe.

- *Singleton v. Jackson Municipal Separate School District.* There were actually seven decisions in this one case, all by the Fifth Circuit Court of Appeals, dealing with desegregation of the JPS, beginning in 1965 through the last in 1975. For our purposes the key decisions were:

  - *Singleton III* (December 1, 1969): Applying *Alexander,* the Fifth Circuit ordered that all faculty and other staff of the JPS should be transferred to schools within the district "so that the ratio of Negro [*sic*] to white teachers in each school, and the ratio of other staff in each, are substantially the same as . . . in the entire school system." The order was effective "not later than February 1, 1970," although the court was careful to note in several places that the JPS had no plan in existence whatever to deal with any of this. This was to be the first step, followed by complete desegregation of all students beginning in the fall of 1970.

  - *Singleton IV* (January 21, 1970): Relying on an intervening Supreme Court precedent, the court held that student transfers could not be delayed until the fall, overruling *Singleton III.* JPS was given ten days to accomplish all of it, so that by February 1, 1970, all students, black and white, were to be transferred to schools within the district until each school reflected the same ratio of black to white students "in the entire school system." Nobody was ready; in fact, when the decision came down we were still at home during the extended Christmas break that was a function of *Singleton III,* only now the JPS was ordered to extend the chaos to all students (not just faculty and staff), to draw the lines determining the new school assignments and get new administration and faculty and all support functions up and running for the reopening of all JPS schools by February 1. Again it was to be accomplished without any overall plan for school authorities to "steer by," as noted in the long dissents. The JPS was ordered to implement the broadest goal—immediate metamorphosis of the JPS into a "unitary" system in which every school would have the same ratio of black to white students as in the entire district—but provided no guidance on how to do it. So, the schools opened the first Monday following the tenth day, the panic set in, administrators and most teachers holed up in their offices and classrooms and tried to maintain some semblance of discipline, and enrollment and class rolls changed from day to day depending on how many white kids had pulled out—or, more accurately, had been pulled out by their parents. Of all the orders entered during the crisis, *Singleton IV* was by far the most important, the most transformative, the longest lasting. While the context helps explain why the court allowed no transition time or even explained itself in depth, the real legacy of that one key order, then and now, remains the creation of the private-academy system in Jackson.

- *Singleton V* (July 20, 1970): The January order begot more orders, including finally and belatedly what had always been lacking: a plan. Offered by the US Department of Health, Education and Welfare (a cabinet-level agency that no longer exists), the plan's methodology tried to focus on the size, location, transportation, history, and other issues particular for each school, and then attempted projections of long-term goals, needs, population trends, and other effects of implementing radical desegregation methods. The HEW planners got much more wrong than right, but what else could the federal courts do with the mandate from *Brown I* through *Alexander*? For our purposes, the order implementing the HEW plan closed formerly all-black Brinkley High School and made it a tenth-grade "center" for students in the Murrah and Callaway High School zones. We were allowed to attend eleventh and twelfth grades at Murrah and Callaway depending upon the zone of our residence, but the idea of a "center" for all kids in the same class was new . . . and stupid. Mercifully, it lasted only two years, affecting the Murrah and Callaway Classes of 1973 and 1974, before everybody involved recognized that it was unduly disruptive, doubled the transportation problems, and all but destroyed the top-performing black high school in the city. The opinion in *Singleton V* included HEW projections for enrollment at all JPS schools for the 1970-1971 academic year: Murrah was forecasted to have 529 whites and 406 blacks; Brinkley 507 whites and 475 blacks. The fact that the court obviously relied on these projections without considering the white flight that had already occurred in the spring 1970 semester reveals the vacuum in which the courts worked in a series of desegregation orders that were so flawed as to imply some intention that they not work. It helped no one and harmed most for the HEW and the court to project a perfect world of amicable adjustments to a unitary system without considering the actual costs of ordering immediate, wholesale transfer of students who, whether the court believed it or not, had other options or would make them. As a mere example, of the 507 white students projected to attend Brinkley in our tenth-grade year 1970-71, only 83 showed up.

The dissents in the key decision in *Singleton* are worthy of mention, not only because of the accuracy of their predictions but because of the clarity with which they expressed the position of white "moderates" in the very real world of Mississippi, 1970. They were both published with the one-paragraph opinion of the court's majority in *Singleton IV*, the January 1970 decision ordering student transfers all over the district within ten days. There were two separate dissents by the only two members of the Fifth Circuit Court of Appeals from Mississippi: Judge (and former Mississippi governor and attorney general) J. P. Coleman; and Judge Charles Clark, father of five wild Clark boys raised with us in north Jackson, including our friend and Murrah '73 classmate Jimmy Clark. Both correctly pointed out that, without a plan or a clear judicial expression of what was expected (what Coleman termed "a lighthouse in the new storm which is upon us"), proceeding to dismantle the dual school system would lead to "dismantling the schools as well." Judge Coleman compared the court's aggressive remedies to Samson, who "slew his enemies ... but he likewise destroyed the hall and liquidated himself." Coleman warned that the rush to inter the corpse of segregation, dead but unburied for fifteen years since *Brown I*, would end up "burying the schools in the same grave."

Judge Clark was less poetic but more direct. He had only been on the court for just over a year, and it took some guts to dissent over the application of constitutional-law principles to such a hot-button issue like school desegregation. More than that, Judge Clark had the distinct disadvantage (for a judge deciding any case based upon the facts and the law rather than his own experiences and certainly his own attitudes and opinions, as citizens have a right to expect of any judge) of having high personal stakes in the outcome of the court's decision. The immediate future of his family, which included our good friend and MHS '73 class cut-up Jimmy Clark, would be determined to a significant degree by the Fifth Circuit's opinion. Beyond his personal stake in the outcome, Judge Clark's dissent pretty clearly reflected his own tension in applying Supreme Court precedent that obviously exceeded his personal beliefs and judicial temperament. He struggled for an honorable balance.

Asserting that, to ever be effective, any plan of radical desegregation "must secure popular acceptance" in order to "bring about the result intended,"

Judge Clark zeroed in on the responses he anticipated from people he knew well: white Jacksonians he had worked beside or for over a lifetime as a practicing lawyer, community leader, and father. "If our remedy is so unreasoned and so abrupt that the non-Negro [*sic*] community exercises its freedom and withdraws its participation in and support for a public school or a public school system, then in the end we have remedied nothing in that school or district." As far as I can tell from researching this, Judge Clark's dissent was the first prediction that the white community wouldn't stand for it, that white kids and their parents were likely to quit the JPS in large numbers. "This is not specious speculation," he continued. "It is happening at this very moment in the districts before us today." The Citizens' Council schools, and other private schools dedicated to segregation and God, had existed in the far-right fringes since *Brown I* in 1954, but the January 21 order triggered the frenzy that followed as new schools were opened in metal buildings and church basements around Jackson and its outlying communities throughout the late winter of 1970. Seeing that immediate future clearly, in his concluding paragraphs Judge Clark tried to step back for a moment and offer his views of the larger, philosophical meaning of it all, ending with a warning: "When the clear, bright light of history illuminates what has been done, it is bound to show that too great a haste for 'equal' played a major role in destroying the protection we sought to provide," he predicted—accurately as it turns out. "There is more at stake here than the tremendously valuable rights that lie on the surface of this controversy. Much of the vitality of the rule of law hangs in the balance, for we here deal not only with a vast number of people but also with perhaps the most sensitive area to any citizen—the welfare of his children."

Absolutely right. There is probably no more direct statement of the tension between the constitutional rights at stake and the costs of enforcing them in the entire desegregation debate. That tension persists. Judge Clark just saw it clearly, not only with respect to the competing interests at stake in 1970 but what would happen in the long run on the whole struggle for school desegregation. The costs of achieving the Supreme Court's mandate to create a unitary school system and desegregate "*NOW!*" were too high in 1970. They still are. And in the end, the considerations Judge Clark urged in his dissent carried the day because it was good politics if questionable constitutional law.

And so on it came in a great rush. The stories of our classmates gathered here are better testaments to whether it was done correctly, or not, than any historical overview. It is important to understand that from the perspective of the federal courts the extreme remedies put in place during radical desegregation drew their justifications from prior acts of intentional, *de jure* segregation across the South and the old border states. With the entire wretched

history of mistreatment of black people, from slavery through legal segregation, to choose from in formulating a remedy that would bring whites and
blacks together in the public schools, it is little wonder that each new case
took radical desegregation to further extremes, like the infamous "busing"
decision, *Swann v. Charlotte-Mecklenburg School District* (1971), that became
the whipping boy for conservative objections to desegregation for the next
twenty years. Eventually those objections prevailed, as we shall see. The weight
of our history of racial injustice was just too much to ask any system of public
education to bear.

Let's face it: nobody likes being punished for wrongs they didn't commit.
The visceral objections of white people to the historical justification for radical desegregation have always been lamely straightforward: "I never owned
any slaves! Did you? Why should I, or my children . . ." and so on. For at least
the past forty-five years some version of this defense has been relied upon to
avoid all issues relating to race. And in a sense we were always fighting someone else's fight during desegregation. But by 1969-1970, something had to give.
Some generation of black and white students had to fight that fight, and the
consistent lesson offered here by those of us who did fight it is that it wasn't
that hard, and/or that the benefits far outweighed the difficulties we faced.
And given the choice between the perspectives we earned about each other
and ourselves and the world by sticking it out, and the perspectives that must
have come to those who ran from it for all the reasons that were and still are
offered, we remain proud of our choices and the success we were able to make
of it on the ground and person to person where it mattered most.

Within a year or two, however, even the moderate federal judges had had
enough. As early as 1973, a new conservative bloc on the Supreme Court
refused to hold that education was a "fundamental right" of anybody, meaning that school districts that had never practiced *de jure* segregation could be
liable only on proof of specific intent to discriminate (always a tough thing
to prove: nobody admits a bad motive, even to themselves), effectively ending
judicial remedies for segregation in the North. The hypocrisy of that false dis-
tinction is still galling to us in the South. That same year the Court held that
huge disparities that always exist between urban and suburban tax bases, and
the huge disparities in school funding that result, did not violate the Equal
Protection Clause. Concluding that inequality in funding is not inequality in
educational opportunity was a stretch in any context, but the reality of wealth
discrimination is anathema in American constitutional law. Then, in 1974, the
Court rejected an effort by the Detroit school district to develop a multidis-
trict remedy that would result (finally) in integration between inner-city and
suburban children, a sharing of tax revenues and thus school funding, and

perhaps an end to the grinding cycle of poverty in the historically isolated "quarters" which have existed in big cities forever and were themselves the products of *de facto* if not *de jure* segregation. That decision, *Millikin v. Bradley*, established white flight as the most effective legal method for avoiding school integration throughout the nation, and made certain that the large populations of inner-city blacks and Hispanics would attend "apartheid" schools. As a result, in large cities like today's Chicago the per-student expenditures for students at the "apartheid" schools are less than half of the expenditures for students in the suburban schools. With all the disruption that was forced on us in the old Confederacy in the name of retribution for our history of legal segregation, it is awfully regrettable that the Court never took a step to remedy the revolving legacy of poor academic performance, dropouts, crime, and hopelessness that characterizes those "quarters" in every large city in the United States, including Jackson. The Court threw up its hands at that problem first, making it increasingly difficult for even self-confessed moderates in the South to justify having desegregation rammed down our throats. The hypocrisy of selective application of desegregation remedies against the backdrop created by these early cases pulling back on the reach of *Brown* finally became too much for the federal courts themselves. Yet rather than searching for effective remedies for the ongoing constitutional violations north but especially south if *Brown* were still the measure, the Court in decision after decision allowed artificial lines around inner-city schools, in the process abandoning the children most in need of improved educational opportunities. By 1974 the integration "moment" was lost; it just took another twenty years or so for the federal courts to recognize it, and then another twenty years for compulsory integration programs to be abandoned as an acceptable constitutional remedy.

Back to the Future

What has actually happened in the federal courts over the last twenty years is at least as surprising as the sudden appearance of *Brown* in 1954: the federal courts have essentially abandoned the struggle. Forces work in pairs, but in law it is rare to see the force of constitutional interpretation work against itself so dramatically and, in the sweep of historical time, so quickly. Beginning in *Board of Education of Oklahoma City v. Dowell* (1991), followed quickly by two other decisions in 1992 and 1995, the Supreme Court allowed district courts to vacate desegregation orders so long as the reasons proffered by the school boards were educational, not racial. All three decisions came out of states where segregation was *de jure* prior to *Brown,* but that fact made a difference only in analysis, not result. Adopting the position of the Reagan/ Bush Justice Department, the Court held that desegregation was a means and not an end, and a temporary one at that. If the "end" is integration, then the Court failed to explain how to get there without some form of desegregation; then again, it is most probable that integration ceased being regarded as a constitutional mandate or goal in the 1973-1974 decisions, and, as Chief Justice Roberts recently indicated, has been replaced by a new interpretation of the Fourteenth Amendment as concerned with removing all racial classifications. The Equal Protection Clause is no longer understood to create a constitutional duty to achieve equality; rather, it is but a shield against race-based remedies aimed at increasing integration, diversity, or other vague societal goals. I think that Justice Roberts would agree with that characterization, especially the condemnation of using any decision to further or even directly address any "societal goal." I think he, and many other judges who face constitutional-law questions regularly, would say that his job is to interpret the Constitution in the manner in which its drafters intended, consistent with the original intent of the founding fathers (to oversimplify the concept somewhat, but not unfairly), and *not* to advocate any social or theoretical concepts that might be good for the largest number of people. I do not know the answer, but the question is at the heart of what we experienced in 1969 and what is happening today across the land.

Following *Dowell,* most federal courts wisely avoided such tortured semantics in favor of an "Enough already!" approach and began removing federal-court oversight and returning the schools to the control of local boards. Even when the local school boards expressed the positive desire to maintain "magnet" schools and other methods of fighting white flight and promoting community involvement in securing the best education for the broadest demographics, the courts wouldn't allow it. As a result, the South has undergone resegregation at a rate undreamed of during the first fifteen years after *Brown* declared segregation illegal yet change advanced at a glacial pace. The percentage of blacks in white-majority schools in the South has fallen over 25 percent since 1988, while the percentage of black and Latino students in "minority" schools reached 70 percent in 2000, with over half that number attending schools that were 90 percent to 100 percent minority, justifiably called "apartheid" schools. In the cities the percentage has risen to two-thirds of black and Latino students attending "apartheid" schools. The last thorough studies on these resegregation trends that I could find ended around 2005, before the *Seattle School District No. 1* case and at a time when resegregation was picking up speed each year. Newer statistics will doubtless show much more resegregation and many more "apartheid" schools across the South and inner-city schools the nation over.

In the end, the federal courts now regard desegregation as a means, not an end. If the methodology for achieving desegregation offends the rights of white students who are displaced or lose opportunities in the pursuit of any voluntary program to increase diversity in a school setting, then they are now regarded as victims of racial classification that itself offends equal protection. It is a strange turnabout on the theory of *Brown I* and the school desegregation cases through the 1960s that what was truly at stake was ending the effects of past, *de jure* or intentional discrimination. That goal is now regarded as beyond judicial remedy, and the "end" of all the efforts of the federal courts in our time at Murrah—to achieve integration in American life, starting in the South—unobtainable. Our experience at Murrah dealing with the series of increasingly disruptive orders from highly motivated federal courts is now just as anachronistic as the total segregation that preceded it. Both are regarded as mistakes in constitutional interpretation, replaced by the theory that no judicial remedy based upon any form of racial classification can stand. Sadly, the best proof that the historical justifications for radical desegregation are still with us, that we didn't truly get it then or now, is the return of segregation in our schools.

The JPS statistics are, again, off the charts in terms of resegregation. To be accurate, though, the resegregation trend in Jackson predated these recent court decisions by more than a decade; as stated, Jackson has set the curve in this area if no other. Worst of all, in all our research and discussions with a range of people in this project, including parents and teachers, present members of the JPS School Board and officers in the Parents for Public Schools who are still very much in the fight, not a single soul expects any change for the better in the foreseeable future.

For us, integration of the public schools was not an abstraction or a theoretical exercise in applied constitutional law. To us it was never about "elites bearing racial theories" because we had no elites in the JPS or anywhere else, and we knew no "racial theories" that were not flatly racist. In the earliest days it was about confrontation, not cooperation, and it's hard to be theoretical when people are really angry at you. In the first year of integration our black classmates didn't embrace us with open arms; I don't recall anybody ever crossing arms and holding hands to the strains of "We Shall Overcome." I doubt we white students were any more welcoming, and I know many of the white faculty weren't. The theoretical leap was much more subtle: a great many responsible people tacitly (this was still Mississippi, and no whites in positions of power could come forward for desegregation) agreed that the time had come to move beyond where we were in the embarrassing and debilitating stalemate over race, to at least try to overcome race as the defining factor in our lives as Mississippians. But those of us on the ground during radical desegregation would not have been able to move forward an inch by declaring that we had "stop[ped] discriminating on the basis of race." Those new classmates not doubled over with laughter at such a statement wouldn't have believed us anyway. It took real people dealing in real time with the flesh-and-blood realities of a person of another race, learning in the only way human beings really learn anything: up close, personal, tangibly, without filters or scripts. What we learned—that between us and our new classmates there were no differences that really mattered—was the most important lesson that could have been imparted to us on history, sociology, government, law, religion, philosophy, and all the sciences combined. I doubt that lesson could have been taught or learned as a theoretical notion; it had to be experienced. And the price we paid to learn it was worth what we went through in the massive social experiment to correct, even if only temporarily, the historical wrongs that were its focus and ultimate purpose.

Introduction to Integration:
December 1969 through May 1970

Narrated by Teena Freeman Horn

■

In December 1969, families were going about their everyday lives in Jackson, Mississippi. Parents were busy getting children up for breakfast and ready for school. Children often walked or rode their bike to the local neighborhood schools. Patrol boys, like mini policemen, directed us across the street toward the school. The order of the school systems kept the children safe, so parents did not have to worry much—on my side of town.

Laypeople, like my family, had little dealings with the legal and political ramblings that were going on behind the scenes in Mississippi government systems. We received a daily paper and had a couple of local channels on our television.

Politicians and groups like the Citizens' Council resisted other awakening changes that were sweeping the country in the 1960s. The black community wanted the same equal rights to the pursuit of happiness and freedom that the white community enjoyed. This included an equal education for their children. Many of the elected officials had agreed to education being equal, but they held on to the "separate" point. More money was being spent by our state on some schools than others.

Teacher **Linda Hardy** gave testimony about the poverty in a county school called West Side, where she began her career in the Jackson area. Mrs. Hardy told me that the school lacked some textbooks, had inadequate facilities, and the children were so poor that it was possible that the school meal was the only good one some had to eat all day. They had a "free lunch." She brought them "my husband's shirts," from her home, when needed and "did stockings for them," at Christmas.

Several court cases were going on behind the scenes of our daily lives, beckoning a change. The powers-that-be in our state would not take steps toward accommodating what was coming. The reason for the lack of reaction by our officials was beyond the ordinary person's control. The president of the United States was Lyndon B. Johnson until Richard M. Nixon took over in late January of 1969. John Bell Williams was the governor of Mississippi.

The federal government must have believed that the separation between the races in Mississippi had reached a critical point. Figuratively speaking—the lid blew off—anger that had been hidden below the surface in Jackson came forth with much vocal discontent when a court order was issued. Most of us did not understand what was happening. Our federal judicial system pushed its way into the traditional local and state educational system and took control, forever changing Jackson, our state capital. The initial moments of massive integration were the most profound; they were shocking/chaotic, whatever you want to call it. It was a bad deal for me, initially.

There was an abundance of chatter. Mothers gathered outside to talk with friends and neighbors, while children roller-skated or rode their bikes. No one knew in December of 1969 the transitions that lay ahead for our city.

The neighborhoods in Jackson during the sixties were either all white or all black. I remember seeing the black maids in uniform, waiting at a bus stop or the cooks in Primos restaurant making and serving our food, especially my Saturday treat: Primos awesome gingerbread man cookies, with raisins for eyes. We liked "Shorty," a smiling black man, at Mr. Jack Calhoun's "Dickerson's Service Station" on the corner of North State Street and Euclid, who regularly filled our car with gas, and provided mechanical services. But, in my remembrances of friendly relations between my white family and our black acquaintances, there was an absence of the black children. They did not play with us on Riverside Drive or swim and picnic at Riverside Park. We saw each other briefly, downtown on Capital Street, where I would tag along with mother as she shopped at Gus Mayer. There were a couple of black children in our schools, but when school was out, they went home to a neighborhood that was far away from mine. I really did not give these matters a second thought. My focus in the ninth grade was my hair-do, my clothes, and not being sent home by Mrs. Harris, a strict English teacher at Bailey Junior High School. She measured the girls' skirt length from our knee, with a ruler, to see if we were in compliance with a rigid dress code, which she vehemently enforced. I remember her starring at my legs when I gave a presentation in class. Then I was busted. Mrs. Harris embarrassed me in front of schoolmates, by measuring my dress and smugly sending me to the principal's office.

When the courts announced plans to move black and white children in Jackson to attend school together in massive numbers, at unfamiliar destinations, fervent chatter began. "Busing" was the new buzzword. We were feeling many things, mostly panic, anger, and fear of the unknown. What I found interesting in my research is that many of us had no real conception of whom, why, and what caused this turn of events. I thought it was "the Yankees"; Laura King Ashley called them, "middle-aged, pudgy political males." Rosalyn Allen Clopton said it was "the state of Mississippi." I don't think we fully understood the amount of federal influence that was pushing us to and fro.

At the William F. Winter Archives and History (MDAH) building in Jackson, Mississippi, I found an article by the Associated Press included in the January 7, 1970, *Clarion-Ledger* (Vol. 130, no. 237, p. 1):

> Mississippi moved deeper into desegregation Tuesday, but registration figures from some of the 30 public school districts ordered to integrate indicated there would be a mass exodus of white students.
>
> The 30 districts were ordered to totally and immediately desegregate by the U.S. Supreme Court. Meanwhile, the state legislature went into session Tuesday and was expected to consider some type of legislation for financing private schools, long an issue in the state.
>
> There were new private schools in almost all the affected districts. Estimates differed on the number of white pupils dropping out of public education . . . Some observers believed a more segregated system than before would come about because of the white exodus.
>
> Some white parents may keep their children out of school for the rest of the year or until private facilities are available. Mississippi does not have a compulsory attendance law.

In another article on the same page of the *Clarion—Ledger* by Billy Skelton: "A Jackson pupil desegregation plan based on zoning and to a lesser degree on pairing was filed Tuesday by the Department of Health, Education and Welfare in the U.S. District Court here. . . . Later Tuesday the Board of Trustees of the Jackson Municipal Separate School district—the state's largest—filed its desegregation plan. The plan would allow pupils to attend the school of their choice where space is available."

According to the paper, the board tried to make changes and modifications to a plan outlined by HEW. The US Supreme Court ordered, "the reassignment of faculty members must be implemented no later than Feb. 1 . . . to produce a 60 per cent white—40 per cent black ratio of teachers at each school," wrote Skelton. At first the teachers were to be moved according to a "lottery" system. "HEW said in its plan for the establishment of a unitary school system that 'Although total desegregation of every school system does not result in this plan it is the opinion of the evaluation team that the basic structure of the dual system has been disestablished.'"

Mr. Skelton's piece goes on to explain that since there was no wide busing system in play that the elementary schools were not changed initially, but movement began mostly "at the seventh grade level."

The Department of Health, Education and Welfare came up with three different plans (A, B, and C) for zoning Jackson City Schools. These plans are published as maps in the Thursday, January 8, 1970, *Clarion-Ledger*. A high-school map begins on page 4 followed by other pages of junior high and elementary zones. The elementary school map went to the US District Court.

My sister, Patricia, an elementary school student at the time, was able to remain at her neighborhood school, Power Elementary, to complete that year. My brother, Howie, completed his last two years at Murrah. I was moved.

The dialogue, of so many different voices, is very important—to me—in understanding the life-altering times in which we lived. How could I alone tell this story? My point of view is just one of many. Others may not remember events in the fashion or with the strong feelings or terms expressed here. It is not my intent for the narration to dominate the story, rather to transition from one segment to the next. My classmates and I were sent all over town and came through this with varied experiences and opinions. I loved learning from them all! Students', parents', and teachers' words help us to relive history from the time period of December 1969, through the spring semester of 1970 in Jackson, Mississippi. The following are clips of essays, questionnaires, or interviews. Also, I did not define the race of each participant. I allowed the participants to speak for themselves.

Kip Ezelle said in an interview:

"I grew up in the greatest neighborhood that has ever been developed, Belhaven. Johnny Jones has been my friend since we could talk . . . We had a neighborhood school, went to Power Elementary School. It was fabulous as a kid. We roamed the neighborhood from Northwest Street to the Pearl River, all the way past the university [the University of Mississippi Medical Center]. Nobody ever knew where you were. They didn't care. We came in when Grandmama Ezelle would whistle at night . . . I was student body president [Bailey Junior High] the first half of my ninth-grade year and then the schools changed . . . After that, I don't even know what I would call myself, because, I mean, we still had student council and things, but it really wasn't the same. I could have gone to Prep or any of those places, but I told my parents, 'heck with this, I'm not going out there with that bunch of northeast Jackson rich kids.' When the schools integrated . . . I had to move and change my address and have an apartment on Berkley, I believe it was . . . I would have had to go to Rowan in the ninth grade."

Art Minton:

After the Christmas break, federally mandated integration was initiated and Chastain seemed to be about half black/half white, students and teachers. Though I had lived in Mississippi my whole life, I don't remember knowing any black people in my age group prior to January 1969.

Velma Robinson:

I was fearful at first. It was clear on the first day of school that we were not wanted there from comments that we would overhear in class. I was sick for the first couple of weeks. The reality was we didn't have a choice and not everyone felt that we should be there. Now I can look back and say I am grateful for the experience because separate but equal was never going to be equal in education. I feel sometimes stigmatisms for white and black people were finally settled. But for some it will always be a black and white issue.

Robert Kelly said in an interview:

"I grew up in Shady Oaks and when they integrated schools, I was in the ninth grade. I remember that year we were sent to Bailey . . . I was thinking about that this morning. It was absolutely amazing, but on that day when I got to Bailey, we got dropped off by Ike's mama. Do you remember Mike Adams? His mother dropped us off and it was that day that I realized that I did not know one white person in the world, not one. Not one white person in the world. I remember that day, it was like, wow! Which was very weird in itself and also showed how segregated we were as a city and a community. To think about, what were we, fourteen to fifteen years old in the ninth grade? To be on the earth for fifteen years, living in Jackson, Mississippi, and you didn't know one white person. So I had lived for fifteen years just in my community with nothing but black people.

"I remember that day it was very uncomfortable for me, because I was very anxious and just didn't know what to expect. I also remember how it was when we first went to class. All the black kids would sit on this side and the white kids would sit on that side. We were all looking at each other, because it was just a new experience. Now looking back, I am so glad that I got a chance to experience that. I think it was not only good for our city, but it was good during that time for our entire country. Because we were just so separate, and although there were some things that made all of us at times feel a bit uncomfortable. I think being uncomfortable sometimes is good, because I think you end up growing and get a chance to develop more as a person.

"The other thing I remember about Bailey is they had a good lunch over there. The cafeteria was great! [laughs] I remember going to lunch that day and . . . Ohhh this is pretty good! Bailey—that experience just flew by, and then the next year we all went to Brinkley."

Johnny Jones account from his essay:

It happened in December 1969, when we were in the ninth grade at Bailey. We knew something was up that Christmas holiday because we were given two extra weeks of vacation, which had never happened before and never happened again. After the court decisions late in the fall of 1969, the rumors about what might happen to us drove great hysteria. My neighborhood was to attend Rowan Junior High under one of the desegregation plans being considered, and immediately my parents put me in the car and took me somewhere off Mill Street to a newish-looking building that was so out of place in the surrounding neighborhood that it might as well have been a spaceship. It was Rowan, and it was built at a time when our leaders were trying to demonstrate that blacks were being provided with separate *but equal* educational facilities. We were taken on a tour by the principal or his assistant. In the hallway we passed a black student with facial hair carrying a knife in his right hand. My mother: "Do you allow the students to carry knives on campus?" Our guide, who had not seen the knife, simply turned his head and said over his shoulder, "Well, we always try to take them away when we find them." My parents were strong, progressive people of good will and true believers in integration, but Rowan shook us up. There was an atmosphere of menace there unlike any other school I was to see. It exceeded the limit of what was acceptable to white students and their parents. Just the threat of being sent there caused white people to get an apartment or a fake address in north Jackson, or to chuck it all and join the Citizens' Council or throw in with the segregation academies. My criticism of the white families and students who abandoned the public schools should be understood in view of this Rowan caveat. We all have hypocrisies to admit when dealing honestly with racial issues in Mississippi.

Ultimately we were sent back to Bailey for the spring semester of our ninth-grade year, 1970. When we arrived we found that a lot of the student body of our rival, Chastain, had been transferred to Bailey. I remember being quite pleased with the influx of pretty Chastain girls, for they were many and exotic, though I know now our Bailey girls were every bit as attractive and perhaps more elusive. Never ignore or minimize the importance of having pretty girls in the vicinity; in fact, that happy confluence of females in the same place influenced many school-choice decisions in the very early days of integration. Those of us who knew we were staying supported our parents' decisions by deluding ourselves that we already knew black people given our experience with "them" at Bailey. It was our version of the most common and reprehensible self-deception white people still use when talking about African Americans in any context: "Don't tell me. I know blacks!" We really didn't have a clue. But even that deluded bit of hubris paled in comparison to our misjudgment on the depths of feelings among a huge majority of white parents and their children about black people. They responded to integration viscerally, rejecting it out of hand in reliance on the oldest and meanest political slogans like George Wallace's and Ross Barnett's "NEVER!" or, worse, Theodore G. Bilbo's warning that "mixing" with black people inevitably lead to "mongrelization" and "miscegenation" of the proud white race. This was January 1970, and whether they would admit it or not, vicious racism of such caliber still controlled the actions of the majority of white parents and students.

About 30 minutes into that first morning at newly and truly integrated Bailey, three buses pulled up to the Riverside entrance and unloaded about 100 black students, followed by about five more buses in short order unloading 200 more, mostly from Rowan. White students reacted like a nuclear device had been detonated. Pandemonium. Everybody ran around pointlessly, I guess trying to find somebody to make it all go away. Absolutely no one stepped up to assert leadership or even disciplinary authority, which is probably the only reason that our first confrontation didn't turn violent. The Rowan students took advantage of the generalized panic and stayed outside and hooted and hollered at the white students for hours until they were loaded back on the buses and taken away. A few teachers tried to wave them down and force them into the auditorium or classrooms, but they hooted and cursed the white teachers worse than we got it. Not a single black student minded any white person. The older teachers who stayed at Bailey swarmed around the principal's office looking for . . . what? The ones with better control of their emotions just stood at the windows of their rooms and stared out on the anarchy, powerless, more sad than scared.

If you think my description exaggerated in any way, I submit that you were not there that day. In retrospect, I'm surprised that we had no violence. We discovered quickly that we were *not* dealing with the blacks we'd known during the days of token integration. The Rowan students that came over to Bailey, and others who came from other black schools, wanted us to understand one thing about the new integration experiment: they hated us. They showed it in everything they said and everything they did. They were strongly influenced by various cultural manifestations of racial identity and pride: Black Power, Eldridge Cleaver, Stokely Carmichael and others who had jettisoned Dr. King's teachings on "nonviolent resistance" in favor of more aggressive positions advocating black nationalism and identity, including violence toward their oppressors, the beginning of gangs in the most impoverished areas, and, a bit later, John Shaft and SuperFly. The old ideas on how to deal with whites—turning the other cheek, suffering racial injustice with dignity, Booker T. Washington's model of the "good Negro" earning respect through excellence of character, anything that fell within what they called "Uncle Tom" behavior—was far behind our black classmates by the time we encountered them at Bailey. Confrontation seemed inevitable, though none of us, black or white, was prepared to deal with it. The first time we saw what was coming was that morning at Bailey.

And the new white students? Exactly one pay phone was provided for students near the library in the middle of the school, and a line of those same pretty Chastain girls, joined by more than a few Bailey girls, snaked from the phone all the way down two flights of stairs and out the massive southern corridor of the old building. I have always heard that Jackson Prep got started that very night in the basement of the First Presbyterian Church in Jackson. That may be apocryphal, but it is not far from right. The Citizens' Council schools—an ignoble creation of old-line racists called by historians the "white collar Ku Klux Klan"—filled up overnight. On the second day of real integration about one-third of the white student body was gone. Much, much worse for my friends and me, about half the white girls were absent ... permanently. Thus, North Jackson beat a full retreat at the mere sight of so many black students. They never met a single class, never spoke to a black student, and obviously had no basis for making such a harsh judgment to abandon the entire school system. But they did it anyway. They just dropped everything where they stood that day, then took off straight backwards as fast as they could go. It's been 40 years now, and they have never turned back.

Despite that wild start and the early confusion, my experience at Bailey was peaceable, fun and highly educational. For us (I cannot describe the feelings of my black classmates and won't try), the races were at first like two feisty dogs discovering each other in the same place: snarling and bristling, sniffing and probing, angling for exposed parts, both barking at the slightest provocation, then losing interest as their energy waned. Neither race knew the slightest thing about the flesh-and-blood realities of the other. We only knew what we saw and what we'd been told, which rarely matched. Many white students were concerned about the black students in a paternalistic, oh-let-me-help-you way that I'm sure set their teeth on edge. I and others approached the black students with a sort of self-conscious compassion, like a church project, and found out quickly that they had no use for our compassion and hated our pity. The presumption, really just the ridiculousness in how we acted toward them at first, made them laugh and loosen up, and that helped. Then we took jabs and laughed at each other until we reached a stasis that took us through the spring. Ultimately we stumbled into treating each other as individuals because nothing else worked, and that was the key. We were, I think, able to push past the stereotyping so fast because nothing we encountered in one-on-one relationships bore the slightest relation to what we had been told. The clichés proved not only false but the opposite of the truth. When we realized that, we all took a giant step forward.

Unfortunately, the grown-ups were in charge, and the strategy (if that's what it was) of the white decision-makers was retreat and retrenchment: a rearguard action. The frank racism, misjudgments and group-think crap indulged in by school principals and JPS administrators (not all, but by far the majority) were far worse than anything the students would have considered if left alone. For example, all extracurricular activities—sports, clubs, newspaper, cheerleaders, band, student body elections, Class Day, most assemblies—ceased to exist. We were told to hand in our basketball uniforms immediately upon our return because the season had been declared over at Christmas. No Bailey uniform was used for anything during spring 1970. We were thus robbed of the chief unifying activities of any collection of students: our team and a common enemy in the opposition. We had nothing to identify us apart from anybody else; we didn't even have a homeroom. The grown-ups apparently thought the situation too volatile to risk placing us in extracurricular activities or any setting where the students could deal with each other directly rather than through a teacher or other monitor. Like all decisions made in fear and expectation of the worst possible response, these judgment calls were not only wrong but wrong-headed. The people at the JPS central office and many white principals and teachers approached integration like it was a proven failure before we met the first black student. Their self-fulfilling prophecy of failure answered every problem or difficulty they faced, and "I told you so; this will never work" took the place of an effective response. If there were leaders back then who took a different approach, I never heard from them.

Lenda Taylor Brown:

Overnight we had churches forming private schools; that really disappointed me and drove me away from organized religion, for a church to turn their backs and open all white schools—that I will never understand or tolerate.

Steven Jenkins:

I was there [in Mississippi] to see the succession of buffoons and demagogues who served as governors of Mississippi from 1960 to 1972: Ross Barnett, Paul B. Johnson, Jr., and John Bell Williams. They were unabashed racists, segregationists and obstructionists, and they always appeared to me to be dumbass rednecks. I wanted nothing to do with them.

The people I admired most at the time were NASA flight controllers. Space flight relies on principles; violate those principles and missions fail and people die. So, for example, when Apollo 13 experienced the famous "Houston, we have a problem" failure, they didn't roll some ponderous Southern Baptist preacher out to pray, "Lord, we ask you to watch over our Oxygen tank no. 2 and restore its integrity." They got to work on principles: What's working? What isn't? How can we contain the damage? How can we use the remaining systems to get the crew home safely? No histrionics, no recriminations, not even a raised voice. Next to them, the Mississippi governors, and Allen Thompson, Douglas Hudgins, Byron de la Beckwith, William Simmons, Sam Bowers, were all repulsive troglodytes.

Against that background came the 1969 Supreme Court decision in *Alexander v. Holmes* that put an end to Jackson Public Schools' so-called "freedom of choice" policy and forced the city, at long last, to actually integrate its schools. I don't remember how I got the news that I'd be transferred to Bailey at mid-year, but I remember sitting in my eighth-grade classroom at Chastain and thinking how wrong it was that I had to move from one predominantly white school to another in order to achieve some sort of racial balance. We as a nation have struggled with just this problem ever since: Is it enough to ensure equality of opportunity, or do outcomes matter too? What if the opportunity is equal only in word but not in fact?

In January 1970 I arrived for classes at the dreaded Bailey Junior High, but it wasn't so bad. Of course it was no longer predominantly white, and so for many of us our first experience as a minority. It was revealing to see what black students were like on their turf, so to speak. I remember being surprised at the energetic, rambunctious flow of kids between classes, the loud cheering (or booing) at assemblies, the graffiti that covered every hallway poster in short order. (Remember, I was an Episcopalian.) But we got along. One good thing that I noticed immediately is a lot of the trivial crap that the Chastain faculty and adminis-tration obsessed over, like hair length and socks, and many of the people that obsessed over them, were no longer around. I didn't miss them. (I remember one Chastain coach accosting me in the hallway because I was wearing a peace sign. It ain't the end of the world if an impressionable junior high kid wears a fashion accessory, and acting like it is just made him look stupid.)

Roslyn Allen Clopton:

I was a member of Murrah's Class of 1973, that class whose unenviable fate it was to have to move to another junior high school, in the middle of the year, due to forced integration by the state of Mississippi.

At the time the law was enacted, I was a freshman at Rowan Junior High School. Keep in mind that I loved Rowan, since it was all I had heard about since entering elementary school. It was, as junior high was for any student, the rite of passage into teenhood and all other sorts of coming of age activities and experiences. I had finally made it to ninth grade and was so looking forward to moving from there on to Brinkley High School, where my siblings had gone before me (although one brother had gone to Lanier). All of my fondest imaginings were dashed against a rock with the untimely enactment of this law. I was forced to relocate to Bailey Junior High. I had never really paid much attention to Bailey, as I considered it did not really concern me. Upon having to go to school there, I realized just how much it looked like a prison—an observation shared by all of my friends who had to go there too.

Not only did I find out it looked like a prison, I soon learned that the "prison" had numerous prison wardens! We—me and my friends and classmates—soon learned that "they" did not want us there anymore than we wanted to be there! What a mess this was. Even now, in the twenty-first century, given a choice, people tend to socialize with those with whom they share the most in common. So just imagine a whole school full of postadolescent teens (if that wasn't enough all by itself!) being forced to go to school together and learn something at that!

I distinctly remember that my algebra teacher (a coach of some kind; at least, that's what they called him) would give us an in-class assignment and then proceed to go to every white child's desk to see how they were doing—quite noticeably skipping over the black children. Just one of the unspoken gestures that told us how unwelcome we were. Needless to say, I did not do well in algebra.

How I missed my former instructors, who were all black and who, for the most part, took an avid interest in our learning. Mr. Douglas Anderson, who taught us math/algebra and went on to serve several terms in the Mississippi House of Representatives. Mr. Basil Twyner, who so ably and colorfully taught us biology. Mr. Twyner made all of his own suits! This list could go on.

I remember this being the first time in my entire school history that I *hated going to school*! I had always loved school. I also remember this being the first time in my life skipping school. I remember I had gotten within yards of the school that day. It was looking like rain and I had secretly told myself that if one drop of rain fell on me, I was going to turn around and go back home. Well, as fate would have it, that drop fell and it hit me! So as not to disappoint myself, I turned around and started the long trek back home. We walked to school in those days. As I made my way back home, I encountered many others who wanted to know where I was going (I had never considered myself any leader of sorts), but, I think the idea of *not* going to school was too enticing to pass up for many of the children I encountered. We ended up at someone's house—easily thirty or more of us and proceeded to pass away the time until it was time to go home. Well, the next day, we were all in serious trouble. Somebody told somebody else and soon, the school officials found out and some way, by hook or crook, I was named the ringleader! I remember they put a big "H" on my slip that I had to carry to all my classes to be signed by my teachers. You can imagine the disdainful looks that got me. This humiliating event put a serious end to any further thoughts of playing hookey. Although I did continue to be a leader—in a good way, of course.

By the way, I was able to attend Brinkley, after all. After all the initial mess, Brinkley was made into an all-tenth-grade school. Different, but I was glad to have had the opportunity to go there.

Betsy Grimes Triggs:

Cassandra and I became fast friends soon after integration while we were still at Bailey Junior High. The first time I remember her, she and Karen Bell were cutting up in history class. They were both so funny and *so* good at never getting caught. Our friendship grew over the next four years and we were frequently at each other's houses.

Willie Miller:

At a Murrah reunion gathering at Sal and Mookie's restaurant in Jackson, I asked Willie Miller: "When they first changed it up in the ninth grade, what did you think about that? What did your mama think about that?"

"My mother and father were working stiffs. They wanted me to be open minded. You see my mother and father, they worked fast. If you messed up at school you got a whipping when you got home during those days. And whatever the teacher said, regardless of race, the teacher was right. So Mom . . . if you do right, everything will turn out good for you, so you can throw that race card out of the equation . . .

"I went to Bailey with the goal of achievement . . . it worked out. I can remember my first day at Bailey; there were police officers at the entrance. They were looking for some type of big commotion, I guess. I mean we had scrimmages, there were different scrimmages that came up in the bathroom, and there were some people, for whatever reason they just had to show the ugly side of themselves . . . But as a whole, I think my Bailey days, even though it was just a half a year, Bailey was good. We got melted at Bailey, we were poured into the mold at Brinkley and when we got to Murrah we came out as a masterpiece."

Mary Al Cobb Alford:

When integration began in 1969 there was never a discussion of pulling out of the public schools within the Cobb household. Upon reflection, I realize that my parents and many others took a bold and significant step by staying the course with public education at such a turbulent time. The only talk of attending private school came much earlier in my life when Mom was strongly encouraged by the St. Richard's priest to enroll her children in parochial schools. Dad wouldn't hear of such and years later Monsignor Chatham apologized to my parents for this effort explaining that he was a "company man" at the time of the attempted recruitment.

Doug Levanway wrote:

The desegregation that was going on in Jackson, Mississippi, at the time wasn't really on the minds of the 8,000 or so inhabitants of Spencer, Massachusetts. There was one African American family in the town, to my knowledge. Boston would later struggle with its own racial issues, but I doubt that had much of an impact on Spencer either. What I knew of desegregation I learned through letters from home, which some of my friends were kind enough to write. I didn't know what to make of it. I remember watching the Ole Miss-Alabama game (it was the first college football game to be shown on national television at night) on a little black-and-white TV in the lake house, and being giddy watching Bo Bowen from Murrah High School burst through the line on national TV. While my year in Spencer had turned out fine, I was ready to go home and start high school over at Murrah with my friends.

Freddie Funches:

"That year was a trying year for everybody. Everybody was tossed in a situation where they didn't have control over it, and everybody was just trying to survive. You know, trying to figure out what's going on. It was just pretty chaotic at that time." *Freddie said someone had asked him who was the first white person that he met after the integration of Powell Junior High:* "I vaguely remember it was Jimmy Fields. Looked like Opie on 'Andy Griffith'—little red-headed guy. He was silly too, and I think that's what made it so good. He didn't have any fear . . . most people, they . . . didn't know what to expect. They didn't know what to do. They was kind of like, man, what is this here. He was just a bubbly little guy. But he hung out there, and I think people started liking him because they didn't know what to expect from Jimmy. I don't know what his family history was or what was he told before he come over there, but he pretty much fit right in."

Freddie said he didn't have any problems during integration because he likes people, "and I was just ecstatic about the moment. It was chaotic to some people but to some people it was just an experiment . . . But being young teenagers, we didn't know about what to expect . . ."

Debra Lindley Ruyle:

I remember the seventh and eighth grades at Chastain as uneventful. The ninth grade, after Christmas holiday, are when the changes occurred and the integration of the school began. Interesting enough my parents did not have any problems with my returning to Chastain after Christmas until I was threatened with a knife over my coat. My parents were called to the school and the principal recommended that my parents take me out of Chastain. I was upset at the time and felt I was being punished for something I didn't do. Anyway, by the next day I was off to Council Manhattan where a lot of my former classmates were already enrolled. School was OK but something seemed to be missing. I attended Manhattan for the remainder of the ninth grade and continued throughout the eleventh grade.

Lele Winter Gillespie:

In the fall of 1969 I was a ninth grader at my neighborhood middle school, Chastain, enjoying an innocent and carefree adolescence . . . Toward the end of 1969 the US Supreme Court called for complete integration of the Jackson schools and the school district followed this directive. To my dismay I learned that I was going to have to leave Chastain, my bastion of familiarity, and finish out my ninth-grade year at Bailey Junior High School, across town and a little foreboding. Bailey had always reminded me of a large prison and I was very sure that I didn't want to go to school there. One of my first realities, when it was announced that some of the student body living in certain neighborhoods would be sent to Bailey, was that of leaving friends behind. Even worse, though, was the stark realization that some of my really good friends weren't going to be staying in the public schools. I had never given much thought to the fact that this was where we would go our separate ways, take different paths. Private secular schools, in my opinion, mainly served as havens for troubled or struggling youth. Now, though, with some of my best friends seeking refuge in those same private schools, like the Citizens' Council schools started in the early fifties for the sole purpose of segregation, this was a reality that I would soon get used to. It was an unwelcome reality not to be going on this journey with childhood friends.

Thankfully my few months at Bailey turned out to be a fairly uneventful experience and it allowed us to meet new friends from other parts of Jackson. This move proved to be incremental but there was a bigger challenge awaiting many of us the next school year.

Laurel Propst Ware:

I had gone to Chastain for two years when I was sent to Bailey, which was so far from my house. My street was the dividing line between Chastain and Bailey, so all of my friends stayed at Chastain. Although I knew people at Bailey, it was not familiar and I was not happy. I would not say that I was miserable, but I did miss the familiar surroundings and people at Chastain. My parents used a friend's address, said we moved, and I went back to Chastain. More than anything, it was more convenient because Chastain was so much closer; the racial makeup of one school over the other did not influence their decision. I don't remember if the racial makeup was different or not. As a parent, it is very hard for me to believe that my parents lied to allow me to change schools. And, it was no secret that we did not move.

Amelia Reagan Wright:

My parents could not afford to send children to private school, and they were staunch advocates of public education. Sticking with the public school system was more than an education for me. It was a learning-experience that was/is invaluable. Thank goodness my parents did not shield me from the real world.

I loved Bailey Junior High School and realized just how much I hated Chastain Junior High School when I got to Bailey. Being transferred to Bailey was one of the highlights of my public school years. The people there were real, and no one cared about the color of one's skin. Just as important, no one cared about what label of clothing one wore or where a person lived. The popular people at Chastain would have faded into the woodwork at Bailey. They would have been fish out of water, because they wouldn't have been able to cope with not being center stage. The Chastain world was so superficial, sickening, and small . . . sad but true.

Fred Sheriff:

Even though the number of court cases was mounting regarding the integration of public schools, I was unaware of the impact they might have on me. Not until I heard in the fall of 1969 that the Jackson Public Schools were to be integrated in January 1970 (just after the holiday break), right in the middle of my ninth-grade year, did I feel the effect of what had been going on for years, that is the fight for equal education between blacks and whites. At the time I was attending Powell Junior High School.

Once it was clear public school integration would take place, my parents and I began, like others, to make necessary arrangements to attend a new school. Of course there were discussions among family members and friends; no one really knew what to expect. I don't remember the substance of any of those conversations now (I guess they weren't that important after all).

There was some apprehension, on my part, as in any new school situation. To some degree, I've always pretty much rolled with the punches in my life. I guess that's why a close friend of mine called me "Roller"; I never asked him if that was the reason. This was one of those situations. I do remember one regret however— I was so looking forward to attending Brinkley High School the following year.

When I started at the newly integrated Bailey Junior High School in January 1970, it was comforting to know that some of my friends from Powell were with me, probably my best friends. For the rest of the year, I did basically the same thing I would have done at Powell; that is, hang with my friends and try to do well in school.

My story:

I have never had a problem with school integration itself, but I do believe that it could have been planned in a much better way in Jackson, Mississippi. As a fourteen-year-old child, I was forced to switch schools during the middle of my ninth-grade year. My own experience was not good. I hated that year, and actually became sick in the process of trying to adjust. My parents had just separated, and our once very happy, stable, and carefree family was in economic and emotional turmoil. "When it rains it pours." I write this from the viewpoint of the child I once was: Massive integration here was, frankly, like enduring an invasion from a foreign entity (our government). Everything in public education changed and kept changing year by year. Organized educational systems became chaotic. The landscape had to be rebuilt into a new community of thought, which was difficult to assimilate into the very structured and social-minded lifestyle of some northeast Jacksonians.

There was an unexpected announcement over the loudspeaker at Bailey Junior High. It stated that we were to all go home and check the newspaper for citywide zoning maps that would designate new schools of attendance. This was a bizarre occurrence lending absolutely no time for parents and students to prepare. We did not understand why it had occurred or what was going to happen with our education and our lives. The federal government sneaked up on us during Christmas break. I can't call it anything but sneaky. Frankly, the way in which it was done was extremely disrespectful to individual freedom. It was unprecedented—disrupting children midyear during an educational process. Angrily, we thought, "It must be the Yankees causing all of this havoc."

During this time of radical transition, I had an awakening from a sheltered life. Suddenly, I became aware of protests about the Vietnam War, seeing hippies wearing beads, and giving the two-fingered peace symbol. The winds of change were upon us with no clue of what tomorrow would bring. The news reported that, even if we lived across from our school, we could not go there. How silly was that! They got rid of the neighborhood schools around which homes and lives were built. I was zoned to Rowan, a junior high school across town in an all-black neighborhood. I did not even know where Rowan was, so my mother and I drove to look at it. Mama was nervous while navigating her car through the streets leading to the school location. She had a job in another part of town; this school was completely inconvenient to accommodating her work schedule. What was said to be a "dangerous area" (for white people) in 1969 was out of our comfort zone. I was scared to death every day that I was forced to attend this school.

It was not that we were prejudiced; our feelings had nothing to do with race. I had walked to school under safe conditions. Now, abandoned by everyone, panic ensued. I pleaded with my mother to take me out of school. I had obeyed the rules and attended the designation to which I was assigned, but where were all of my friends from Belhaven? They had deserted me by using fake addresses, or renting apartments in order to return to the formerly white schools. I have blocked out most of my memory of going to Rowan because, for me, that was a traumatic experience. My mother informed me that I had to catch a bus to get to school; I cannot remember that. As one of the few white girls (I do not remember any others in my classrooms), I remember shaking in fear and frequenting to the restroom to throw up and cry. No one talked to me, and I could not concentrate on any reading assignments, so I just looked down or out the window. School was supposed to be about education, not about equal racial numbers—which was a civil rights fantasy that year. The numbers were not equal. There were not many white students at Rowan the spring semester of 1970. Boys would stare at me and call me "honky." I was pushed against the walls of the hall sometimes, which taught me to create a personal space and stay away from people. I held on by my faith in God with many prayers. I wore the mustard seed necklace, given to me by my Sunday School teacher, Miss Mary Weems, as a protective symbol.

Why was I sent to Rowan? These thoughts flowed through my mind as a child who was without a deep understanding of the history of racial segregation and tension that existed in our state. We were innocent children who went to school to learn and play with friends. I had always thought that the government—America—was supposed to protect me, but it had not. My country advertised freedom yet, I was like a prisoner to the times. That year in the Jackson public schools, only the collective was important not the individual. My ninth grade was wasted. I do not remember anything I learned that year except avoidance techniques.

Mother always picked me up from school, but one day she was late. I stood outside of the school, alone with no idea of how to get back home. Two boys walked by me and flipped out a switchblade. They said, "Do you want some of this?" I said nothing and just looked at the knife. I had never seen one that opened so fast, and I wondered why they would take one to school. They just laughed at me and walked on. I guess they thought it was funny to scare a little girl, but I had not experienced any sort of violence before my time at Rowan. (The closest threat that I had seen up until that point was when I visited a Baptist church and the minister slammed his fist on the pulpit and yelled, "Repent of your sins now, or burn in the fires of hell for eternity!") When mother finally arrived, I cried as we rode home, "Get me out of here!" There was no choice . . . I had to go back.

The way I coped with this oppressive situation was by shutting down and becoming stoic. I stopped brushing my hair and caring about my appearance; hopelessness began to influence my body. I broke out in hives of unknown origin, my nose bled spontaneously in class; I was sick. It was at this low point in my life that I began to feel sympathy for the young boys in town who were receiving military draft notices to Vietnam. To graduate from high school and be sent unwillingly (by the draft) to war, with no way out, just because they needed your body . . . was not soul inspiring. They needed my body at Rowan, just because I was white. The government demanded to fill the numbers to prove some point. That year it was indeed all about the numbers and color of your skin. When I thought of America, I envisioned: freedom, free will, and volunteerism—not forceful control!

My mother realized that she had to take action; therefore, she removed me from Rowan and placed me in the Council Manhattan school, as an opening had become available. "Council," which we viewed as a private prep school, was closer to our home and my mother's workplace. She took a second job to pay for my private school education. Finally, I began to learn and care again. I only stayed there for a month or two to complete the ninth grade. Prejudice later appeared at Council and at my church. I withdrew from that, like the water fountain experience—it did not feel right. My desire was to be where I could walk to school again, to Murrah, where my brother was attending the eleventh

*grade and basically unaffected by events. I learned one thing that year: "No
choice" is not good.*

Carole Sanders Bailey:

Gosh, all I had ever heard was about Murrah, Murrah, Murrah, and how great
of a school it was on a national level. Having had three siblings who went there,
it's the only thing I ever wanted to do. My expectations were as high as they could
get. I wasn't really aware of all the upheaval of desegregation because I was so
young—seventh grade. I remember having some friends who stayed in the public
schools during the junior high years and they were bused across town. Seemed so
stupid to me at the time, when before we used to walk to school or ride our bikes,
all the kids in the neighborhood, to the neighborhood school. We all went to the
same school (Spann). I didn't understand why when I went to Chastain, all of a
sudden I couldn't go back there after Christmas break. No one could, for weeks
and weeks. Everything seemed so out of sorts during that time. Then I went to
a private school that I had never heard of, where I knew NO ONE. Maybe five
people. Meeting new people was fun, but I remember I missed what I had had at
Spann and Chastain. I didn't understand why all the changes. It was so unfamiliar
to me, and I missed the familiar.

Alan Huffman: *essay*

Integration, which came midway through the 1969–1970 school year, was the
inevitable court-ordered follow-up to the sham of desegregation, and it changed
everything. Over the Christmas holidays, formerly white Chastain Junior High
became predominately black. A few students took advantage of the minor turmoil
that resulted to stage walkouts that didn't otherwise seem related to integration. It
was just because they could. There was upheaval in the air. I don't remember any
significant racial incidents at Chastain but I do remember the latent prejudice the
school's transformation brought out in me. I was indignant over being subjected
to the substandard education that, as was now painfully evident, had long been
the lot of some of the city's black students. In particular, I didn't like being taught
English by a teacher who butchered the language.

Bill Patterson:

Coming into this world with older parents, and with my father serving as
Mississippi's attorney general when I was born in 1955, was not just about my

beginning life, but the beginning of radical change to the social fabric of this state, as predicted by my father. According to my mother, when the United States Supreme Court handed down its landmark decision in *Brown v. Board of Topeka*, which declared that separate was not equal, my father commented that public education in the deep South was destined to change, and there was nothing that could keep it from happening.

My father died spring of 1969. I, along with my Chastain Junior High School classmates, were sent home for a week spring of 1970, returning to a fully desegregated school system one week later. Again, according to my mother, my father's plan was for me to continue in the Jackson Municipal Separate School System post-desegregation. My mother followed his wishes, with a backup plan for me to attend St. Joseph, the city's Catholic High School if "things didn't work out." They did, and that has made the major difference in my life.

Susan McBroom was my best friend in high school. Her mother, Mrs. Susan Culbertson, opened her home to our classmates.

Mrs. Susan McBroom Culbertson (Parent):

"Well, we had to move. Unless you wanted to go to Rowan, you had to find a private school to put your child in. I asked somebody, and they said with Susie's stature, as small as she was and everything, that going to Rowan would *not* be a good thing for her. I was a single mom, so I had a real hard time finding a school to send her to until it all got ironed out . . . she went to Council school."

Myra Stevens Myrick:

The memories of desegregation in the seventh grade ('69–'70) were interesting. I know the teachers were as freaked out as we were. My homeroom teacher (Williford) talked to the class, she separated the blacks and whites and tried to reassure us and calm us down. I think she was scared of fighting and the black boys bothering the white girls, which never happened. The first day of eighth grade at Chastain ('70–'71), as I was walking to my first class, a huge afro wig came sailing over the lockers. Two black girls were fighting and one of them pulled off the other one's wig . . . As long as I had my friends there, I was OK. It was the first year we lost a lot of classmates to private academies . . . I am thankful to the principals, teachers, and coaches who looked out for us. It was all a big experiment and I think it was more interesting and educational than anybody realizes.

Mark Flanagan:

The black students assigned to Chastain were bused. They were not happy being bused. It was utter chaos. Many of the white parents removed their children and put them in Jackson Preparatory School and Council Manhattan. The discipline and pride of Chastain Junior High School was never the same. The tension was intense. There were numerous incidents in the hallways. Disorderly conduct became the norm.

David Flanagan:

I felt sorry for those black students being bused to Chastain because they didn't want to be there any more than we wanted them there. The classroom suffered. It was a period of feeling each other out, trying to understand the differences, and just plain trying to get along.

Robert Hand:

I came to Bailey in the ninth grade from Whitten and Lester Elementary after my family upgraded by moving from south to north Jackson.

I wasn't bused to Murrah, but remember when busing started my parents did not know what to do with me, so my brother and mother pooled their money and sent me to school in the tenth grade in Sweetwater, Tennessee. My only memory of Bailey is attending football games and hearing the song, "Wendy" and thinking, boy, if I were playing and that song came on, I would surely run back a touchdown.

Laura King Ashley:

There are many stories like these: Kids ending up in private schools who would never have considered it, kids in private schools being taken over, kids from all over Jackson being bused to places they never heard of far, far away; parents being forced by pudgy yes-men in making their thirteen-to-seventeen-year-olds fight the hard fights, going to schools they did not want to go to, all in the name of a better education for all? Do you really think it worked? . . . Stupid, insensitive, unreasonable, middle-aged, pudgy yes men . . .

My mom had just settled into the routine of managing four different carpools for four different kids at four different schools (yes, school districts existed pre-December 1969, but the logic and rationale for the school a child was assigned to attend was based on location between home and school—it made sense) and then Boom! Right in the middle of a school year and without the luxury of a summer break to work on it, four new carpools had to be formed and managed within a few short weeks. Though we may have been assigned to attend the same school for the remaining of the school year, school-age neighbors did not necessarily go to those schools—many families opted to rebel and not to deal with the madness and drove their kids to St. Joseph, Council Manhattan, St. Andrews, St. Richards, so even when families chose to remain in public schools, it was so much harder for many, many families.

Not to mention the students who were high school seniors and had only a few months until graduation; even if they were allowed to remain, the entire dynamic of their senior year was forever changed—some students may have been forced to go elsewhere, whether public or private—the WORST time for change in the life of a young person is in the middle of a school year. This was crap. For black and white students, black and white families, for all who were forced to make such a drastic change at such a sensitive time—it was thoughtless of the middle-aged men.

Based on the disruption and chaos of where students were assigned to attend, many parents' thinking in December 1969 was to send their kids to private schools in January 1970 for one semester until things settled down and then figure out what to do in September 1970 because by then, surely, children would be assigned a little more reasonably based on location. Ha!

… For me, I stayed at Chastain (in a different carpool) and finished the rest of the year with a really good science teacher (Mrs. Sweet, black) who was transferred from another school and kept my good English and algebra teachers. Chastain, for those last five months, worked out fine; lots of new black students, a lot fewer white students, but we all seemed to get on quite well. Maybe a little tension just because of the new logistics and meeting new people, but overall, no problems. OK, that was the ninth grade for me.

Laura's essay brought to me the reflection of a simple truth: that the adults in the government made the children fight the hard battles which mature elected officials, in our state of Mississippi, were unable to resolve. The method and the maelstrom in which we were expected to create a social miracle was an unreasonable burden to put on young teens. Yet, we did just that.

William Winter Interview:

In an interview, Johnny Jones and I found some answers to what was going on at the state capital.

I asked Governor Winter: "When they integrated the schools in 1969 what was going on in the background with the legislature and the state politics. Was there any attempt to change things? Also when they changed the schools every year, it was like they would not know from one year to the next what school we would be going to. What were ya'll talking about?"

William Winter: "Well, John Bell Williams was governor at that time. To his credit he did not get out and agitate people as Barnett had. But I think John Bell was a true believer. He was ideologically committed to maintaining segregation. But he was also a political realist, that from an economic standpoint he had to maintain order in the state. He came with an educational program; they stayed in session in the legislature, the regular session in 1968, his first session until August, primarily about education. Then [Hurricaine] Camille came along about that time and prolonged the session. But anyway, he made a bonafide effort to pass pretty sweeping education bills, but I think the climate limped home without much in it. He was very conservative in his attitudes, and by conservative you mean maintaining the status quo. He was not a dynamic governor."

Johnny Jones: "There weren't any voices back then that were calling for either massive resistance to continue or any kind of accommodation of the federal courts' orders. I mean Mississippi politicians at '69, '70 basically kind of closed down. We didn't get much leadership one way or the other that I recall. Was there?"

William Winter: "It was not strong; there was no strong leadership on the basis of trying to adapt to accommodate a new relationship between the races."

At another sitting Johnny inquired of Governor Winter: "Do you think the way they went about it in '69 when they shut us down, gave us two extra weeks at Christmas, and then we came back to a whole new world, do you think that was the right way to do?"

The governor replied, "No, I did not. I thought it was a terrible way to try to accomplish the mission. I think it almost ensured that it meant we would have a re-segregation. I hoped it wouldn't happen. But at the same time, let's also say this: If the Jackson school board had started out on a softer course and we had had an opportunity to work our own plans, I think it would have worked."

Adrienne Day:

Desegregation took place when I was in the ninth grade. At the time the experience was exciting and scary with new people, new environments and new teachers. Many new people were now attending Bailey and I did not miss most of the people who left public schools and went to the all-white private schools that were quickly established. Some of these people's choices were made by their parents, who feared change, cultural differences and felt that racial integration was unsafe. My British-born mother related stories of parent meetings in which some individuals were tearful and clearly upset at this federal mandate intruding on their lives. The melodrama she described at these meetings struck me as amusing. I was glad these people were disappearing from my life. Too many were mean-spirited, impressed with their own status and wealth and their departure was welcomed by me. At Bailey, Brinkley and Murrah we were involved in some of the significant transformations of the sixties and early seventies. My white middle-class life was being transformed. It felt radical and I loved it . . .

Unfortunately, this was not the case for my sister, five years my junior. She attended Casey Elementary, Powell fifth and sixth grades, Bailey Junior High, and Murrah High. Her school experience was painful, alienating and dangerous. She was harassed constantly, physically attacked and injured several times. A girl tried to strangle her twice at Bailey and Powell. While at Murrah she was attacked by three male students who cornered her in a room during lunch, and she was successful at fighting them off. While most of her tormentors were African American, she thinks this could have happened no matter what race. One of her best friends was African American and visited our house many times.

Katie Barwick-Snell:

I remember when desegregation started for me in 1969 at Chastain Junior High School. Barbara Miller and about seven others were the first black students to attend Chastain. Barbara was very nice but I felt sorry for her because she did not have many white friends in junior high school. We were in many classes together and we talked but we did not socialize outside of school. Now I realize she was blazing trails. My love of home economics started at Chastain with a new teacher who was black, Ms. Thomas; integration was a new adventure for her also. I believe she had been in the Jackson Public Schools and was moved to Chastain so she could keep her job. I know the changes were hard on the faculty as well as the students . . .

I felt that desegregation was a thrilling challenge and painful for the people that could not let go of the past. I remember my parents going to meetings to discuss the changes and after major discussions with me and examining their fears and finances, my parents decided to keep me in the public schools. I vividly remember my mother coming home from a meeting of neighborhood mothers, crying, feeling like maybe we should go to the Council school down the street because all of the horrors of integration. Many people were saying that fights, knifings and raping would happen in the classrooms and the quality of education would suffer. My daddy put his foot down and said we had already decided to stick with the public schools because it would be character-building for me and we shouldn't let others' prejudice influence us. We should support public education because all children deserved to be educated equally and we needed to stay in the public schools and not leave. He was right—I formed friendships that I would not have otherwise had and became so much more culturally aware of how other people live.

Lindy Stevens Clement:

"There was a black girl named Barbara Smith, when they had freedom of choice and she was very well loved . . . very well loved. And when the courts hit, she had to leave, and she cried and cried. She didn't want to leave Chastain . . . but she'd put on that little red skirt and white shirt on game days."

Margie Cooper Pearson:

During an interview Margie said that when she attended Powell Junior High (before the schools were integrated) she walked to school with her friend and neighbor Cassandra Fowlkes. Midway through the 1969–1970 school year, she was sent to Bailey Junior High for the remainder of the ninth grade.

Margie said, "Well, I really didn't, you know, again, buried memory here, but I didn't think one thing or another about it because I really didn't know what was happening . . . See, you guys probably talked about it a whole lot more than we did because it was probably a bigger deal for you than it was for us . . . Because we really didn't think, I didn't think one thing about it. It was not a discussion in my household . . . That's my memory now. Of course, maybe the adults were talking about it a whole lot more than I was aware of . . . All I knew was we broke for Christmas, and after Christmas I was going to a different school. And we did take the bus."

She allowed that after walking to neighborhood schools for all those years, "It felt a little weird to me, to walk there [to the bus stop], and then all these folks—classmates—are gathered there to catch the bus. That was new to me."

1969 Memories from Those at Murrah

In 1969, Murrah High School educated the tenth through twelfth grades. Changes to this institution are revealed by some of the Murrah students who were sophomores at the time.

Charles Miller:

I attended Murrah from 1969 to 1972, being all three grades 10–12. Certainly, desegregation was introduced as abruptly as possible and with maximum disruption when we were "changed" under court order during the Christmas holidays in tenth grade. Midyear introduction of desegregation was foolish and did nothing other than make a great, social change even more disruptive and get off to a bad start.

Michael Bounds:

"Desegregation started in the tenth grade, so the first half I went to Murrah, the second half I went to Callaway. Then whatever strings my parents pulled, I wound up at Murrah again for the eleventh and twelfth grades."

Chryl Covington Grubbs:

We were rolling through football season way too fast when rumors started flying around about our school being shaken up. Students would be required to go to a different school no matter whether they were seniors or not. When my parents were legally informed in January 1970 that I would have to attend and graduate from Callaway High School I was devastated. How could the administration and the government make me graduate from my school's main rival. I had a very good friend who attended Callaway that was going to have to attend Murrah and graduate there after attending Callaway for two and a half years. She, like me, was totally devastated.

No matter how much we prayed, talked and cried, change came. In January my parents had to rent a house in the Murrah district so that I could graduate from my beloved Murrah. My friend's parents did the same for her so she could graduate from her beloved Callaway.

Change came quickly to Murrah. The old Murrah was no more. The new era brought good and bad changes to our school. People always say they want the truth, but sometimes the truth hurts. I began the second semester of my senior year with four different teachers. How is that for a senior year? On the flip side the students at the school from where those teachers came had the same thing.

Before forced integration we had black students at Murrah. I knew each one by name and had several classes with Sheila Evers. She is the daughter of Charles Evers and the niece of slain civil rights leader Medgar Evers. I used to wonder how Sheila felt being in school with us. She was always friendly and she did well in class. I knew her on a first-name basis but I never had the nerve to really ask how she felt being in the minority at Murrah. I do however remember one incident in which a fellow black student attended one of our victory dances. He even asked one of our Murrah Misses to dance. Well, of course she said yes and danced. A fast dance at that! Well, it was common knowledge that someone leaked this to the people in charge. The word was that the Murrah Miss was warned with being kicked off of the squad if it happened again. I think that was the only time I was embarrassed and disappointed by my school.

If I could sum up my last semester at Murrah it would be controversial. It was not pleasant for the black students or the white students that had been forced from their neighborhood schools. I think the desire for equal schools was justified. I think the method and timetable were horrific. I am not so naive that I think any time would have been perfect for desegregation. I do however feel the adults in charge neglected the one fact that binds students together—school spirit. Giving people time to try out for sporting teams, cheerleading squads, or dance teams would have eased the transition. It also might have lessened the "white flight" to private schools.

Cy Rosenblatt:

When I entered the tenth grade, my high school had less than ten black students. If you were to ask me whether Murrah was integrated, I would have said yes. The Jackson Municipal Separate School District operated under the freedom of choice guidelines that allowed students, regardless of race, to choose the school they wanted to attend. The reality of the day was that black parents wanted their kids in neighborhood schools, and Jackson's neighborhoods were segregated. Therefore, the geographic distribution of the population worked against large numbers of minority students attending schools in white neighborhoods.

The federal court saw the situation a bit differently in 1969 and concluded that Jackson Public Schools, in fact, were very segregated. Relying on the *Brown v. Board of Education of Topeka, Kansas* ruling, the federal judge determined that Jackson's school district was operating under the separate but equal framework that clearly was unconstitutional. Having "separate" in the school district's official name was probably a good hint to the judge that he should take a close look at the racial makeup of the city's schools. A handful of black students in an overwhelmingly white school did not constitute an integrated school.

Court-ordered desegregation was in full throttle during the first half of 1970. A sizable contingent of black students was forced to move from their neighborhood school to Murrah, and likewise, a number of white students were sent to a black high school. The decision as to who would go where was determined by zones created by the school district. Where one lived dictated where one was schooled. Distance from your home to the school was irrelevant.

Zones were paired with schools with the sole intent of overcoming de facto segregation that existed in neighborhoods. The consequence of this decision was that, literally, white and black students probably passed each other on Northside Drive as they drove a considerable distance to attend the others' school. When deciding where students should be educated, counting student miles traveled was of less importance than counting how many black and white students would be placed in a particular school.

My parents sold their home shortly after the court decided to mandate real integration. Mama and Daddy gave me a choice regarding my education. Private academies were popping up, marketing themselves to white parents who were concerned or afraid to have their children in a classroom with black children. Some families were exploring out-of-state prep schools, and I was given the choice of attending McCallie School in Chattanooga, Tennessee, or enrolling in St. Joseph's Catholic School in Jackson. The bishop, a friend of my family, nixed the latter idea given that my family was not Catholic. I had great friends choosing all of these options. I decided to stay at Murrah, so my parents moved to an apartment on the edge of the Murrah zone.

The first year of integration was rather uneventful with the one exception that Murrah's new students really did not want to be Murrah Mustangs. I did not blame them. Their high school identity was just as important to them as being a Mustang was to me. Their identity had been jerked from them, but I still had mine.

Joe Reiff:

Ridiculous rumors of daily knife fights at the black high schools (Brinkley and Lanier) were common at Murrah and in northeast Jackson as January 1970 approached. This reflected a reality pointed out by various cultural critics, most notably the early twentieth-century black intellectual W. E. B. Du Bois: we whites knew very little, really, about the black community, while blacks understood us better. Since the white perspective was the dominant worldview, blacks could scarcely avoid knowing something about it, while they also knew their community's worldview intimately. But to white families, even those who resisted the Closed Society/white supremacist perspective, the black community and worldview were mostly foreign and mysterious.

This was illustrated for me most clearly in that spring semester of 1970 in my sophomore English class, taught by the legendary Meda Bonne Crawford. There were probably ten blacks in the class of thirty students, and they all sat on one side of the room because the teacher had seated them that way. One day in reviewing the distinctions among simple, compound, and complex sentences, Miss Crawford invited us to propose a sentence and challenge others to say which type it exemplified. This turned into a back and forth between a black student named Charles Yarn and me. We had three or four exchanges, neither one succeeding in catching the other in a mistake. After class, Charles approached and tipped his hat to me as a worthy opponent. I did not know how to respond and said virtually nothing back to him. That night, I wanted to call him on the phone to reciprocate and searched the phone book in a futile attempt to find his number. But I gave up, realizing that I knew nothing about him as a person or about the community in which he lived. Obviously, I could have pursued that at school, but I did not, I am sorry to say. I think most of us, white and black alike, were unsure of how to cross the color line in that spring of 1970.

When the additional black students arrived at Murrah in January 1970, a dozen or so were assigned to another of my classes, and again the teacher sat them all on one side of the room. She usually began class with a few minutes of recitation, going up and down the rows asking us specific questions from course material. A correct answer earned a recitation point; if we answered incorrectly or were too slow to respond, she would ask the same question of the next student. On the black side of the room, she would noticeably speed up, giving them less time to answer. One day a black student frustrated with this treatment jumped in with an answer to her question right as she called his name. His answer was incorrect, and she paused briefly, looking at him with disdain, before continuing. Many viewed this woman as an excellent teacher, but I was disappointed at the way she treated her new students that semester.

In another group interview Johnny asked Michael Bounds and Kip Ezelle about any violence that they evidenced during this year.

Michael Bounds said that he was sent to Callaway for his sophomore year, where he saw his first bad episode: "Yeah, because it was all happening in the tenth grade. People were just angry. I remember one time they just sent us home. At Callaway, the second half, they just said, 'Go home. Leave.' People were coming out of classes, and there were little bitty fights in the hallway. I remember Don Butler just jumped in his car and went home. I couldn't wait to get back to Murrah."

Kip Ezelle said Janice, his wife, left Bailey "because of black guys touching, going down the hall, and just being blatant about it. Of course, her daddy was not going to put up with that."

Johnny: "I wouldn't put up with that, either."

Kip: "So she went back to [Council] Manhattan for the tenth grade and then came back to Murrah of her own accord."

1969 Memories from Brinkley

Robert Gibbs was a sophomore at the all-black school, Brinkley, when the changes took effect. Brinkley was a powerhouse in sports, with its own proud traditions. Johnny Jones and I asked Robert to describe this year in his life.

Robert Gibbs:

"We had a couple of white students at our school. It was the first time . . . I stayed at Brinkley. That year they didn't do anything but move students around. At the end of that year they changed the schools. Brinkley became a tenth-grade center and all of the students that would have been there and graduated were sent to Callaway, Murrah, or Lanier, based on where the lines were drawn. And where the lines were drawn at my house I ended up at Murrah."

I asked Robert, "How did you feel about that? About Brinkley being changed?"

Robert responded: "Well, I was disappointed, it seemed like I could never get to Brinkley. Let me explain that. Brinkley was initially where Walton was located on Bailey Avenue and when I became a first-year student they moved the school. They renamed the school. They renamed Brinkley to become Walton, and Brinkley was a new school that they built on Albermarle Road. When I finished my six years in elementary school and was getting ready to go to Brinkley they had built another school on Albermarle Road, and Brinkley was on Livingston Road, that became Powell Junior High School. So I didn't make it to Brinkley then either. [laughs] . . . so three years later when I finally made it to Brinkley, I was only there for one year before I ended up having to go to another school. So Brinkley was like this thing that I could never reach to . . . You know, it was a great school, had a great basketball team, bands, football team, and my sister was two years older than me so it was following in my sister's footsteps. I really thought that Brinkley was this ultimate school to be at and so I looked forward to graduating from it, except for we were sent to Murrah."

Johnny reminded Robert that Coach Orsmond Jordan had won the state basketball title at Brinkley during his tenth-grade year.

Robert said: "That's right. They had some of the best basketball players around, and I would go to those games. Again, my sister was a senior so I was able to go to almost all those games hanging around her and her boyfriend. So it was really great to see all those basketball players."

1969 Teacher Memories

Coach Orsmond Jordan: *Johnny, Kip Ezelle, and I interviewed Coach Jordan.*

Coach Jordan told us he was born in Carthage, Mississippi, and graduated from Alcorn State University. He began teaching at Flora High school and later came to Lanier in 1962. He won a national basketball championship at Lanier in 1964. Then in 1967, he went to Brinkley. Coach remembered saying, "I am going to work at Brinkley. They had better talent than we had at Lanier, height wise, everything, but never could win . . . 1969, won the only state championship I had ever won. In 1970, I came to Murrah."

At Brinkley Coach Jordan taught driver's ed. "You didn't have to get everybody through there, [just] the ones that want to take driver's education. Most of the white students had a driver's license, or had permits . . . most of them had their family car or their car. So I didn't have any problems there. It was a good transition for me."

"I stayed at Brinkley until the year was out. They made me transfer . . . after basketball season was over. Really and truly, I didn't know where I was going," said Coach.

Johnny and I went to the home of Mr. and Mrs. James Merritt for an interview. Mr. Merritt was our high-school principal; his wife had been a teacher. Their son, Greg, was a year behind us at Murrah. The Merritts answer many questions about the integration process that I had never understood, as to who was in charge of zoning and placement of teachers and students. I remember an English teacher, Mrs. Ainsworth, who said she drew the paper-name of her next school assignment out of a hat, in a lottery style of selection. Mr. Merritt explains the situation as it affected him as an educator and administrator.

Mr. James Merritt (Murrah principal): "In 1970 after they had gone through massive court cases and everything that you can imagine, the court came down with a strong ruling. School was dismissed in December, and in two weeks' time we had a group of new teachers, a large number of new students, and we had to reschedule by hand everyone between Christmas and, well, two weeks' time. It was not related to education; it was related to other reasons, because in no way could you justify that as an educational deal. It was a trying time for everyone because we had new staff, a lot of new students both ways. You didn't know who was going to stay there and who was going to leave. You had most of the secondary high schools, other than the public high school, were born at that time . . . You had Council school, and Prep opened up in '70. So it was a time of fantastic change for all of us, not knowing what was going to take place, and it was some difficult times for everyone."

Johnny Jones: "Did you know it was coming in that drastic a form?"

Mr. Merritt: "No, well, we didn't know what was going to come. Had no way of knowing. If you had told me one time that it would be possible to go through what we went through without any bloodshed in any way, I would say it wouldn't hardly be possible."

Johnny: "Why do you think there was not any bloodshed or violence?"

Mr. Merritt: "There was a lot of other things, but there was nothing that required things like police being involved and all that deal. But we were prepared for it because we didn't know what was going to happen."

Johnny: "Why do you think Murrah was different than the other schools that did have that kind of violence?"

Mr. Merritt: "Well, I don't know. If we had had only the students, we wouldn't have had any problems at all, but when you get parents involved and so forth, because not many students would have left if they had had the opportunity, but the parents were more involved than anything else."

Johnny: "Weren't going to let them go to school with black people and so forth?"

Mr. Merritt: "That's right. Well, athletics was one of the first things that really was a cementing area and something you could deal with."

I asked Mr. Merritt, "Who made those decisions about making a ninth-grade school, or a tenth, and then changing Murrah to tenth, eleventh and twelfth grades?"

Mr. Merritt: "That was the courts. That was all court ordered."

Johnny: "They didn't involve y'all in that?"

Mr. Merritt: "No, no. We didn't have anything to do with that. At one time, we didn't have any tenth graders at all, but we didn't have anything to do with it. It was court ordered. Actually, the school administration had nothing to do with it. They were doing what they were ordered to do. It was a trying time."

Johnny: "You think it was a social experiment?"

Mr. Merritt: "It wasn't an experiment; it was a matter of just doing something, and Jackson schools were used as pretty much an example in that deal. But we have a lot of schools in the state that didn't go through anything like the situation that Jackson public school went through. Really, from an educational standpoint, it has damaged the school system in Jackson, as such, for years. Down through the years, things have been done to kind of remedy some of that in some ways, but it was a mess at that time. It impacted the school system in a fantastic way."

Johnny: "What do you think, if you would have had the best of all worlds, you knew integration was coming, you knew there was going to have to be a change and more black people were going to be at Murrah, but what would have been a better way to do that than what they did, in your opinion?"

Mr. Merritt: "Well, I don't know. The thing that bothered most educators at that time was they felt it was forced on them. We felt like it was going to come and was going to come in a natural sequence in some way, but the courts didn't think it was moving fast enough. And it wasn't moving too fast. They were trying to put the brakes on it all the time, but it just finally was an overriding thing, and really that final decision came in '70 when the major deal occurred where there was no other way to do it, it is going to be this way. I forgot the title they gave them, but the outside people would come in. They were the ones who arranged all the school deals and where the schools would be and what schools would be this and that or something else. I have often felt, like I said, I went to school at the University of North Carolina at Chapel Hill. The Charlotte, North Carolina, schools went through some of the same deal we did, but they had an outcome that they have lived with it. What they did, which the courts would not allow in the Jackson school situation, was to merge the county and city school system. The county and city schools were one school district. They put elementary schools, junior high schools, and senior high schools in districts. For instance, if I moved into Charlotte, North Carolina, at that time and I wanted my kids to go to a certain high school, they started in this elementary school, go to that junior high school, and then to that high school. Well, that wasn't true in Jackson. You never knew from one year to the next where you were going to be. Just like Greg. One year he was in one place; one year he was in another. What that did, it achieved what they had to do, but it was done in a manner that did not affect education and parents could live with it."

Johnny: "It retained the neighborhood school concept."

Mr. Merritt: "That's right, and you knew if you went to these elementary schools that you were going to this junior high and this senior high school. Well, you had a community support deal and so forth built in. Athletics and so forth just thrived under that kind of deal because you knew if changes were taking place, parents would know what to do and what the situation was and were able to achieve things in a much smoother way. But Jackson was just chopped."

Johnny: "As far as I know, we were the first school district in America that had to go through that radical change."

Mr. Merritt: "I don't know. I don't know. I was too busy trying to find out what was going on at that time. But I know the court rulings that occurred just vastly impacted the educational system in Jackson . . . It was [all] court ordered. And the one thing that has just disturbed me more than anything else is at one time (now it's a little bit different) I did not know what teachers I was going to have. I always said if they would let me hire the teachers that I wanted, I'd take my chances. I remember one year, don't remember what year, guess it was the year they had the tenth grade over at Brinkley, I had twenty-six, I believe it was, teachers. Not all of them were black, but most of them were black. I had twenty-six teachers, at least a third of my staff that, I had never recommended, had never seen, and I was to take them and integrate them in to staff and have a good staff. That's not educationally sound."

Johnny: "No. That was in our time. The court also ordered that the teachers moved from black schools to white schools and white teachers to black schools."

Mr. Merritt: "That's right. Yes, my wife was teaching at Duling, up the hill here, when the lottery took place, and that's what it was. Some of the teachers didn't think it was a lottery. They thought it was staged. Anyway, my wife was one of those that ended up going to one of the largest inner-city all-black schools. I think they had one white student at that time, and there was probably over a thousand students. They had six groups of every grade . . . N C Jones. The one in the same area that Lanier is located . . . Now it is a community center of some kind, not a school. But she was lottery chosen to go to that school, and she went."

Johnny: "Before then, you selected your own teachers and had your own staff?"

Mr. James Merritt: "I would recommend. I never had one recommended that was not approved. But during that court-ordered time and the early stages of that deal, I didn't have any say; I didn't know who were going to be teachers and who weren't going to be. It was awful."

Mrs. Bee Donley describes her experience as a teacher during the first year of upheaval and change. She was transferred from Murrah to Brinkley.

Bee Donley (Teacher):

Brinkley listed two white students among the all-black student body. Perhaps they were there; I never saw them. I did see young white teachers who brought their husbands to sit in their classes and after a week the teachers were gone. (Some returned to white schools to answer telephones.) I saw an auditorium filled each period with students who had no teachers for their classes. The superintendent came to faculty meeting to tell us he was sorry there were not enough teachers to go around. And all of us, black and white, knew that was not true.

I complained to two friends. Ann Allin, wife of Episcopal bishop Jack Allin, said she could teach home economics. Al Brady, just graduated from Law School, volunteered to teach history. Thus two classes were filled.

I inherited the senior and junior English classes Mrs. Merelyn Graves had taught; she began teaching my classes at Murrah. I also taught a speech class. Changing teachers in midyear was not easy, but my Brinkley students accepted the changes with good grace. They were respectful and interesting and fun. The girls in my after-lunch class took turns calling the roll. They could imitate me perfectly. It gave us a daily laugh. In that spirit of fun, one wrote in my yearbook that they tried to teach me how to talk.

When it was time for one of my classes to have an assembly program I let the class choose our format. We had studied Paul Laurence Dunbar's poetry and they voted to use several of his poems. The students cast the performance; they set the poetry to music; they did the choreography. The finished product was completely professional. The music, the dancing, the acting showed amazing talent. I've never seen a better high school student production. I wish I had videotaped it; I wish I had taken it to Murrah to show those students. My students and I were very proud; the student audience loved it; the black teachers did not like it because the poetry was in dialect.

One occasional stress-reducer was a message piped into all classrooms that a fifteen-minute "social" would be held in the gym at a certain time; teachers could take their students or not. I always took my class and for fifteen minutes the group had a great time dancing. Afterward we went back to class and easily took up where we left off.

One truly stressful time was after the May 15 tragedy at Jackson State where two students were killed: Phillip Gibbs, a junior at Jackson State, and James Earl Green, a senior at Jim Hill High School. [Note: The shootings took place during a protest at Jackson State University, when police opened fire on the protesters; the incident received little national publicity because it roughly coincided with the killings of four white students, also by police, during an antiwar protest at Kent State University in Ohio.] The black high schools planned marches to protest. Early morning when students walked in Brinkley's front door each student was given a slip of paper. This had the time of a walkout. Some of my students asked if they could stay in my classroom because they were frightened of students from other schools and the possibility of fights . . .

In my few months at Brinkley I spent no time with the black teachers except in faculty meetings and occasionally at lunch, but one teacher, Vivian Calloway, was a constant source of support and friendliness. Actually I saw little of my white friends; we were busy in our classrooms.

We survived the first semester of the 1970 year. In our minds, things would level out and go back to the way it had been—attending schools close to our homes. Perhaps we would move on to our planned high-school situations. Life would be good again. I prayed and hoped to attend Murrah in the tenth grade. But more changes were to come.

The Holding Pens: Holding on to Segregation at Private Schools

Alan Huffman

■

In the spring of 1971, my father sat down in the office of a man named Bill Simmons, head of the segregationist organization known as the Citizens' Council. He'd come at Simmons's request to discuss a series of letters I'd written in response to articles in *The Citizen*, the organization's blatantly racist periodical.

I was a tenth-grade student at one of the Citizens' Council's academies and had attracted Mr. Simmons's attention by writing rabid rebuttals to *The Citizen*'s claims that, among other things, black people had been scientifically proven mentally inferior to whites and that the Bible had ordained their subjugation.

My letters were fueled by a fifteen-year-old male's natural eagerness to challenge authority. I was not particularly liberal, though my experiences at the Citizens' Council academy, which was known as Council Manhattan, proved illuminating, in a perverse way.

A few years before, I had left a matinee of *Gone with the Wind* at Jackson's Capri movie theater feeling rather amenable to the idea of owning slaves, and until Chastain Junior High was integrated, midway through the 1969–1970 school year, I had known comparatively little about the lives of the black people around me. But attending a school that was founded on racist principles made me look at things differently. For one thing, *The Citizen* offended my sensibilities because its pronouncements demeaned two people I had great affection for—my family's and my grandmother's maids, Johnnie and Helen, who were both generous, fair-minded, and smart. My true education about race was beginning at, of all places, a segregationist academy, largely as the result of my exposure to propaganda.

Council Manhattan had some good teachers but it was not a complete school. Because there was no gymnasium, I spent the hour that should have been devoted to P.E. class in study hall, in the library, which was about what you'd expect at a hastily organized segregationist academy in 1970s Mississippi. Likewise, aside from driving for about a week, my driver's ed class was spent in the same library, and because the classes ran back to back, I spent two and a half consecutive hours there every day. After perusing everything I found interesting to read, then spending countless hours drawing caricatures of my teachers, I discovered the library's stockpile of *The Citizen* magazines—cheaply printed, staple-bound periodicals with covers of various colors, inside of which were articles committing every imaginable printed offense against black people. For some reason this fascinated me.

I was a bit of a young Turk, prone to skipping school with my friends and defiantly speeding past the security guard at the gate, who for some reason never turned us in, though we occasionally veered so close as he stepped from the curb, motioning for us to stop, that he had to take a step back. One of our favorite destinations when we skipped school was Brinkley, the integrated public school that we would have attended had we not transferred to Council Manhattan. I spent a lot of time looking for fun and the rest of it looking for trouble. Hours spent reading every vile word of *The Citizen* had the unintended effect of opening my rather volatile young mind.

In addition to writing zealous letters to Mr. Simmons, I took it upon myself to steal the library's entire *Citizen* collection, one edition at a time. I'm not sure why I did it. Maybe I wanted to take them out of circulation; maybe I just wanted to possess some serious racist porn. After I completed the heist, which took a couple of weeks, I hid my collection in a box at the back of my closet. There it remained for several years, until I decided I no longer wanted it in my possession and threw the issues away, which I now regret.

My father kept a copy of one of my letters to Mr. Simmons, which he afterward enjoyed reading aloud at family gatherings, but in the years since it has gone missing. All of which means that I don't have any of the original documentation, and because my father and Mr. Simmons are both dead, I can only approximate their exchange, based on my memory of what my father told me.

It must have seemed odd to Mr. Simmons that a Council school student openly felt the way I did. The Citizens' Council had made it its business to monitor everyone's viewpoint and behavior on the issue of race for the better part of two decades, and did not tolerate dissent. After court-ordered integration, the organization had hastily opened several campuses of prefab buildings for white students fleeing the Jackson public schools, and the presumption was undoubtedly that everyone there felt the same way about integration.

As a result of integration, my previous public school, Chastain, had gone from having a couple of black students during the first half of the 1969–1970 school year to being 60 percent black and 40 percent white after the Christmas break. A great many white students had not returned after Christmas, but I had. I found the change less than satisfying—from my perspective, integration was basically a nuisance, though it caused no real problems other than preventing us from having class day (a rite of passage for ninth graders until that point). And there was one rather glaring affront: Black teachers now wielded unexpected authority over me—more, even, than Johnnie and Helen did. I remember feeling rather indignant to be subject to teachers who were a product of a substandard education system, particularly the woman charged with teaching me how to use the English language, who so badly butchered it. And yet: There was Mrs. Sweet, a tall, intelligent, very dark woman with shoulder-length, heavily pomaded hair who didn't shave her legs, so that her long, thick leg hair was grotesquely plastered flat beneath her stockings. I found Mrs. Sweet's appearance unfamiliar and creepy, and she was meanwhile not at all subservient, which was an important component of my interactions with unfamiliar black people. She clearly would not have fallen to the floor each time I playfully fired my toy pistol at her, as Helen had, over and over, when I was a child. Where, I wondered, had Mrs. Sweet come from?

For her part, Mrs. Sweet recognized where I was coming from immediately. She was straightforward—and utterly accurate—in her indictment of my attitude toward her, as that of an insolent white boy. In the end I learned more about biology from her than in any science class I took in the years afterward, but more importantly, she showed me that there were roles for black people other than yardmen, field hands, and maids.

I don't remember feeling strongly either way about the idea of attending the tenth-grade center at formerly all-black Brinkley High School the following year, but in any event I convinced my parents to let me transfer to all-white Council Manhattan, which was a few blocks from our house, because my best friend Roe Looney was going there. I also liked the idea that the classrooms were air conditioned and students were allowed to drink soft drinks, neither of which was true of public schools. Like most fifteen-year-olds, my worldview was fairly narrowly framed.

My parents were average white Mississippians of the era, which is to say they didn't exactly look down on black people but didn't want to eat in the same restaurants with them, either. Their approach was that we were in charge, and that we should treat everyone as individuals and just try to get along. They taught my sisters and me to be polite with everyone, to never talk down to anyone nor to allow anyone to talk down to us, and to never use the word "nigger," except, for some reason, when referring to "Niggertown" (and even then, not if a black person was in the room, when, in a form of deference, we called their part of town "the Quarters"—a throwback to "slave quarters"). The bottom line was: We were to treat everyone with what *we* construed to be respect. I cannot explain the leaps of logic that an average white Mississippian of the era was compelled to make, but I do know that when we deliberated whether I should go to Council Manhattan, race wasn't part of the debate. The big issue was whether I should be in a carpool with my friends when we lived only two blocks away. To me the carpool was absolutely essential.

Until that time there'd been no mention at our supper table of Martin Luther King, Medgar Evers, or Byron de la Beckwith. My sisters, my friends, and I had had no real concept of what was happening around us in the socio-political sense, or, for that matter, in the sense of what black people we knew truly thought. I do remember thinking it unusual that Johnnie's daughter, a pretty young woman named Juanita, had been arrested and held with a large group of "agitators" in the cattle pens of the state fairgrounds following a civil rights protest, but that had only made Juanita more exotic, and made me curious about her world.

Frequent civil rights demonstrations during my early childhood had been mysterious yet welcome in that "trouble downtown" precluded my mother and sisters from dragging me down to Capitol Street on Saturdays so they could window-shop all day. In that sense I had rather liked civil rights, early on. Then again, I had rather liked the idea of owning a personal slave. It was all about me.

I was fascinated by Johnnie's and Helen's neighborhoods, by the serpentine alleys wending their way through rows of shotgun houses, where I observed women talking from porch to porch as our car rolled past on our way to pick up or drop them off. It looked like a fun place to live to me, though I was perplexed as to why there were so few men around. When I asked my mother about it, she said, "I don't know, maybe they robbed somebody and had to leave town."

Like most white children of the era, I was also intrigued by the presence of racially segregated facilities on "our" side of town. Once, like countless of my peers, I had surreptitiously drunk from the "colored" fountain (at the Sears department store, where my father worked) when no one was looking, to see what the difference was. I was disappointed that I could not detect any difference at all. I also remember being a little jealous when my friend Owen Patterson's mother took her down to the Blue & White Shopette to watch a civil rights march pass on State Street. In her mother's view, it was a part of history. My parents had instructed me to not leave our yard that day.

Despite these variations in the norm, I assumed it was routine for families the world over to pass the ruins of bombed rabbis' houses and burned churches on their way to their grandparents' home. And even when I began to realize something was amiss, it seemed a foregone conclusion that we would be the ones to decide how it should be fixed. Interestingly, considering her liberal views, Owen's mother agreed to send her to Council Manhattan, too, for the tenth grade, though she also transferred to Murrah the next year, and graduated early.

As my own worldview began to broaden, I went from seeing civil rights in terms of how it affected me to seeing it in terms of how it affected us—"us" being white people. I held a decidedly egocentric vantage point, which is, I suppose, the way it typically works for those who enjoy comparative privilege. Even as we began working on this book, it was apparent that many of my fellow white Murrah alumni still saw integration as something that happened to *us*. When I told a black friend that the nexus of this book was an argument between two white people, his response was: "Isn't that just . . . the world?"

Not surprisingly, my understanding of people who did not share my unearned privilege was at the time wholly lacking in nuance and detail. I have no idea, for example, what Johnnie's or Helen's last names were, though they were a part of my entire childhood and were much beloved by my family. I'm sure my parents knew their surnames but I never heard them use them. As white people, we didn't have to be overly concerned with such things, and for whatever reason did not choose to know many of the basic details about their lives that we would have known had they been white like us. As a result I don't have a clue what happened to Juanita, though I wondered about it, years later, after the Jackson public schools were racially integrated in large part because of the movement she had participated in. For the first time, after school integration, I had an inkling of what Juanita had been about when she disturbed her family's status quo by getting involved in civil rights, and for the first time it mattered that black people actually had last names.

I don't recall my parents talking about any of this back then, and by the time we started having conversations about such topics, they had become more open in their views. More than a decade later, I remember my mother saying she was voting for Jackson's first serious black mayoral candidate because the city was by then becoming predominately black, and crime was increasing dramatically, and so, she reasoned, "maybe a black man would have a better idea what to do." It was not a position she would have taken way back when, though in her defense, she had few opportunities to defer to black people which didn't involve cooking or pruning roses. As a result, I don't know what it was like to be in their shoes, either, back then.

In one of the interviews Teena and Johnny undertook for this book, Governor Winter observed that it was far easier for a white Mississippian to be a racist back then than not. He said that when he was giving political speeches back in the 1950s, he was always careful not to identify himself as "an integrationist," which, he said, "would have been not only the end of my political life but I would be totally ostracized." The day after the *Brown* decision came down, he recalled, Walter Sillers, the Speaker of the Mississippi House of Representatives, issued a statement about forced integration that basically said, "Well, it's not going to happen in Mississippi!" Sillers, Winter said, boasted, "We don't have to maintain public schools. We will create private schools, but we are not required to educate everybody as a public obligation. We will just convert the public schools into private schools, and so be it."

Governor Winter remembered that there had been borderline hysteria in Grenada, where he lived, over the prospect of integration—a feeling that, "You let this happen, and the white folks will just have to move out of Mississippi." He said that when he was invited to a group meeting in Greenwood to discuss the future of the state's public schools, "We heard the most ominous stories about what was going on, that there were secret meetings of black people, they were going to take over the government, they were going to take over the schools. All this burst of activity was going on, and white people had to organize themselves. That was really the beginning of the organized Citizens' Council. And they were saying, championing, 'What can we do? We'll just go to private schools.'"

To me, Council schools had seemed an outgrowth of temporary disarray in the Jackson public schools, when in fact they had sprung from a long legacy of organized hatred and mistrust. Winter recalled that he had stood up at the Citizens' Council meeting in Greenwood and said, "Now, I want you to know I'm a segregationist. I agree with the concern expressed," but that he had added, "I don't know that it's going to be as simple as just converting our schools to private schools, because the court is not going to let us. All the decisions are to the effect that you cannot do indirectly what we have precluded and prohibited directly." The response, he said, was that, "Folks looked at me like, 'Who is this guy?'" Winter was later invited to join the Citizens' Council in Grenada; he declined, but was careful not to alienate the group. Then, in the fall of 1954, a state constitutional amendment was filed to repeal the mandatory public school system. "I had voted against it before the [*Brown*] decision," Winter said, "but then the tide began to run so strong." This time he voted for it, and it passed.

In the end, there was no effort to shut down public schools. Desegregation was held off until a few minor changes were made in the late sixties, which redistricted schools in such a way that most received two or three black students. Once the federal courts decided to bring the hammer down—to force full racial integration of the schools, white flight rapidly escalated, beginning with the creation of white-only academies, including, in Jackson, the Council schools, Jackson Preparatory School, and Woodland Hills Baptist Academy. The student bodies of previously existing private and parochial schools—St. Andrews Episcopal Day School, St. Joseph Catholic High School, and Jackson Academy—simultaneously swelled.

Teena also attended Council Manhattan for a time. "In Jackson," she recalled, "private schools could not be built fast enough. Trailers," she said—prefab units used for classrooms—"were being shipped from everywhere, and people were demanding an immediate solution to the madness. Council Manhattan school had a waiting list, so my mother made the decision to enroll me as soon as possible."

Teena said she actually had a lot of fun during her two months in private school, but was uncomfortable with the evidence of racism she encountered at Manhattan. "During one of my classes at Council school," she recalled, "a student became a little loud, and the teacher slammed down a gavel, saying, 'You have no reason to be disrespectful. We saved you from those niggers. If it had not been for us, you would have been in a lot of trouble, boy.'" Even more surprising, she said, was encountering racial prejudice in her church. "At our youth meeting, one of the children began criticizing the 'niggers,'" she said. "I told them they should not be saying those things in church. The teacher verbally attacked me. Red-faced and flashing teeth like a growling dog, she said that I did not know what I was talking about. I left there and stopped going to the Methodist youth fellowship, thinking, 'This craziness has infected the church!'"

Her few months at Council during the ninth-grade experience was, in the end, a happy time, Teena recalled. "What I enjoyed the most about Council school was looking at Jerry Cruise every day," she said. "Jerry was a blond-headed, blue-eyed athlete who had a beautiful smile and a cheerful disposition that showcased his perfect teeth. He exuded happiness and confidence." Jerry, who was also a friend of Johnny's and mine, died young, at twenty-three; Teena said that when she thinks of Council Manhattan now she is less likely to think of racism than of Jerry, smiling in his football letter jacket, on his way to class. So it goes with high-school memories.

Despite the racially charged environment of Mississippi at the time, Governor Winter said he never considered sending his daughters to private school, and that he eventually did penance for having voted for the amendment to repeal mandatory public schools by pushing through a sweeping education reform act, to try to correct the cumulative failings of the state's public schools. As for keeping his daughters in public school, "We thought it was important," he said, "as much as we disagreed with the process of the massive dislocation of so many kids." He and his wife, Elise, wanted their daughters to experience going to school with black students, he said.

Such sentiments were not widely shared. At one point, as whites were fleeing the public schools, Governor Winter said he phoned a member of the school board and asked him to go on TV with a statement urging parents to keep their children in public schools. He said he was told: "That's not our business."

Students like me, who temporarily abandoned the public schools, may have provided a sort of relief valve, by removing from the equation those who were most hostile to integration, but the students who remained felt some resentment over their departure. The hope was that the students who fled would eventually return, and the situation would stabilize, and a few did return, including Teena and I. My own views on race were evolving, partly because of my exposure to *The Citizen* and partly due to the ministrations of my liberal friends, including Owen. At that age, new ideas can be very seductive, and it was obvious there was nothing new about what was behind the Council schools.

The summer after our tenth-grade year, Owen managed to get the two of us volunteer jobs at a black clinic, the Jackson-Hinds Comprehensive Health Center, which disastrously assigned us to operate a daycare center—by ourselves, at sixteen—in a church in a predominately black community known as Pocahontas Heights, just north of town. I remember children throwing rocks at us after we got out of Owen's flashy Camaro SS and walked house to house, handing out flyers about our new daycare center. We did an abysmal job of operating the daycare. The children ran roughshod over us. Glitter no doubt filled the cracks of the church's worn wooden floors for many years after.

I remember thinking we were pretty cool, riding in Owen's Camaro with a political activist who worked at the Jackson-Hinds Comprehensive Health Center, who sported a huge afro that made her look a bit like Angela Davis. Her hair grazed the ceiling of Owen's car as Sly and the Family Stone played on the 8-track, and in my mind, Council Manhattan was already ancient history.

Obviously, 1971 wasn't exactly a showcase for racial harmony. That year a black militant organization known as the Republic of New Africa, which maintained its headquarters in Jackson, was involved in a shootout with Jackson police. But the civil rights movement was no longer as volatile as it had been in the 1960s, and the Citizens' Council was starting to lose its clout, partly because it was no longer fashionable to be overtly racist, and partly because the Council schools never got as good as other private schools, which soon began accepting small numbers of minorities, if only to maintain their tax-exempt status. With enrollment declining, Council school representatives actually tried to recruit Ken Allen, who graduated from Murrah four years after us, in 1977. When his family moved to Jackson from Meridian, Allen was in the Murrah school district, and, "Recruiters from private schools came to our home telling my parents I would be hurt and I would get a poor education—all that stuff," he recalled. "Well, my parents did not have a lot of money and I knew that they could not afford to send me to a private school, but when they offered anyway . . . I declined, and went to Murrah."

As is often the case with people who have aligned themselves with dying causes, Mr. Simmons was, by the time my father was called to meet with him, reactionary and intolerant. When Mr. Simmons suggested that I was dangerous and needed psychiatric help, my father asked to see one of the letters. Mr. Simmons responded by pulling out one that he no doubt saw as extremely offensive, and passed it across his desk. My father, perhaps bristling a bit over Mr. Simmons's having insulted me, but also drawing from his own well of basic fairness, read the letter, then looked up and said, "I pretty much agree with everything he said." Mr. Simmons was shocked. My father had seemed like a normal white Mississippian. How could he agree with this dangerously deluded fifteen-year-old?

That night, the decision was made that it was time for Alan to go back to public school.

I had made a lot of new friends at Council Manhattan, and several of them also made the subsequent transition to Murrah. One was Debra Lindley Ruyle, whose parents sent her to Council after she was threatened by a girl with a knife at Chastain in 1970. In an essay she wrote for this project, Debra recalled, "I don't remember being fearful over the incident, just pissed that I was going to have to leave and go to private school." Her parents had pulled her out of Chastain immediately and sent her to Manhattan, which, Debra said, "was OK, but something seemed to be missing." She attended school there for the remainder of the ninth grade, as well as the tenth and eleventh grades. "I wanted to go to Murrah so bad, but my parents wanted no part of it after the incident in the ninth grade," she wrote. "I begged and pleaded the entire eleventh grade year. Finally, my senior year, my parents caved and let me return to public school. I remember being ecstatic and couldn't wait for the first day of school."

Kathy Wilson Phillips had a similar debate with her parents over public versus private school. She was also at Chastain when integration took place, after which her parents enrolled her at Council Manhattan. For the eleventh grade, she recalled, "I begged to go to Murrah and told them they were being racist; they finally consented."

Laurie Propst Ware said her parents never considered allowing her to be bused across town to Brinkley for the tenth grade, and so sent her to Council Manhattan. "The thing that stood out the most to me about that year was that it was a lot of fun, but I don't think I learned much!" she wrote in her account.

Susan McBroom, a fellow Council Manhattan alum and later, a Murrah cheerleader, recalled that her mother pulled her out of public school during the 1969–1970 school year out of concern that she would be bullied because she was physically small. Her mother had expressed those concerns to the principal of Rowan Junior High, a formerly all-black school where Susan was to have been transferred, and he agreed that she might have problems, she said. So she went to Council Manhattan for the remainder of the ninth grade, then returned to public school.

Brothers Mark and David Flanagan went back and forth as well. Their father had died of cancer when they were children, and Mark became "the little man of the house," he said. In the summer of 1970 he worked as an orderly in the emergency room at University of Mississippi Medical Center, and with his salary bought a Volkswagen Beetle for $500 and used it to carpool with his younger brother and sister to Council Manhattan. The family could not afford the tuition there, so Mark and David paid their way by working as after-school janitors at the school.

"The educational process was disorganized at Council Manhattan," Mark recalled. "The school was extremely overcrowded and the ability to learn was weak due to the confusion. It was like a mass exodus of white kids from public school to a confined space with limited facilities. In the summer of 1971, I visited with Dr. Alton Cobb and we decided to return to public school."

His brother David said he also found Manhattan to be "unorganized" and "chaotic," and remembered that his science class had no lab. His teachers, he said, were "nice but not great, and the students were pleasant and friendly," but in the end he told his mother he wanted to go back to public school to get the best education he could.

Another Manhattan-Murrah alumnus, Arthur Minton, said he had little understanding of what Council schools represented at the time. "Much later," he said, "I learned the organization that founded the school had as its sole purpose the preservation of the status quo of racial separation. To this day that fact embarrasses me."

I remember feeling a little embarrassed myself, for a time. As a student at Murrah, I did not play up the fact that I had spent the tenth grade in private school. It was only later that I began to realize that it had been a useful experience, and I ceased to feel embarrassed about it. Those of us who attended both public and private schools got a unique education. Brinkley was no doubt a memorable experience, but confronting racism at close range actually helped galvanize—and liberalize—my own views about race and about how to interact with anyone whose background was different from my own.

At Murrah, we found a place where everything seemed new and untested, which I liked. We seemed to be on the cutting edge of something, whereas at Council school we had been part of a relic mentality. There was a feeling among my friends at Murrah that we were far cooler than the students who attended private schools, that we were learning about a new world even if the process was at times challenging and uneven. Despite the occasional confrontations, the random car thefts in the parking lot, and a few unfortunate incidents in which white girls were harassed or even molested by black guys, we realized that there was something worse, and it was ensconced in the downtown offices of the Citizens' Council and in its substandard schools. We tried to see the unfortunate episodes as setbacks during a period of transition. We assumed that once the transition was complete and it became obvious that there was no need for white students to seek refuge in private schools, they would all come back and we would achieve true integration.

Mr. Merritt, our principal at Murrah, observed of the exodus to private schools, "It happened for a lot of reasons, and . . . a lot of it is choices the parents made." He said he continues to be amazed that parents pay high tuition to send their children to private schools, "and pay for public schools at the same time, but that's what they are doing, but they will do anything. Hock their house, borrow, do anything in the world they can to send their children to school. A lot of it is more peer pressure and so forth, and now it has reached the point where the percentage of whites and blacks in a school is a certain deal, that just turns a bunch of people off in a hurry."

Sadly, our small demographic—private school students who returned to public schools—did not sustain itself. Though the Council schools eventually folded, the student bodies of other private schools grew larger with each passing year, and new academies sprang up in suburban areas. As Governor Winter pointed out, the white students who stayed in public schools—or returned to them—demonstrated to others of their race that integration could work, that the schools were generally safe, and that the quality of education had not seriously suffered. That, he said, encouraged "those children whose parents had sent them to these newly constituted private schools that they really could come back to public schools." Governor Winter said he does not believe his children suffered academically by attending public schools, "and I know they benefited immensely from a social standpoint, bringing themselves into a world that prepared them for different kinds of folks."

The initial years of coming and going between public and private schools seems like a strange exercise now. My old all-white neighborhood is now almost all black, as is the student body of Murrah. The white exodus from the public schools was not temporary. Those of us who left and returned were just an interesting aberration, going against the grain.

Governor Winter said he had hoped the private schools would be a temporary adjustment, "although I also understood that if the schools tipped too far in terms of desegregation that they might not be able to come back. That has been a pattern in some other places." He added, "You know what an economic hardship it was on folks that really couldn't afford the tuition in the private schools. I thought if you want a reasonable option, staying together was the way. I thought it was going to work."

Teena Freeman Horn's Murrah "M". The blue slash indicates that this is her second.

Teena, a dentist and mother in Houston, Mississippi, in her senior portrait. This book would not exist without her personal vision, dedication, commitment, and extremely hard work.

Alan Huffman's senior portrait. Alan was feature editor of the *Hoofbeat*, and went on to become a professional journalist and author of nonfiction books.

Johnny Jones's senior portrait. A practicing trial lawyer, his e-mail to the class of 1973 started the discussion concerning desegregation methods used in 1969–1970, white flight from the Jackson Public Schools, and the effect of both on the Jackson Public Schools then and now. His "small argument" with Teena in 2009 framed the issues.

James Merritt loomed large in Murrah's history, both before and after the Jackson Public School system's court-ordered desegregation. Mr. Merritt was the school's head football coach when Murrah first opened and was principal for many years thereafter. He was one of the few constants through those tumultuous years.

From the 1972 *Résumé*, too, Mrs. Carol Clanton. She carried the sobriquet "the lady in the cage" for occupying the secure area of the school's front office. Together with her husband, Doug, the Clantons devoted innumerable hours to Murrah and its students.

A stalwart of both the old and new Murrah, Pauline Carter. Miss Carter worked closely with students on completing their college applications, as well as serving as the longtime sponsor of the Student Council. After retirement she became a fixture at local voting precincts as a volunteer on election days. This picture appeared in the 1972 *Résumé*.

Pictured, from the September 1972 *Hoofbeat*, are seventeen of the approximately twenty-seven new teachers from the 1972–1973 academic year. The addition of a sophomore class that year led to the marked increase in Murrah's faculty.

"Something old and something new was [*sic*] tried in the English department this year,'" according to the 1972 *Résumé*. Claiborne Barksdale—a graduate of the "old" Murrah—and Mattie Weathers—a popular "new" teacher—rearranged their classrooms to enhance a less stringent learning environment. Seated on a sofa or easy chairs students were immersed in a crosscurrent of southern literature, studying such works as Willie Morris's *North Toward Home* and Margaret Walker Alexander's *Jubilee*. An inspiration to Alan Huffman, Claiborne would later become president of the Barksdale Reading Institute.

The fall of 1971's Speech Class, depicting a mix of juniors and seniors, blacks and whites.

MUSTANGS '70
MURRAH FOOTBALL FACTS

Head Coach Bob Stevens: improviser, offensive genius, winner.

Passing Tradition: The cover of the 1970 *Murrah Mustangs Facts Book*. *Left to right*: Team captains S. T. Ray, Richard "Stump" Russell, Pete Markow, and Coach Jack Carlisle. After the last game of the '70 season, Coach Carlisle and all but two juniors on that team left Murrah and moved operations to the new Jackson Preparatory School.

Coach Freddie Lee: backfield coach, coordinator of swarming defense that improved with every game, later head coach and legend in Mississippi high-school athletics.

The Surprising 1971 Mustangs: With only two players who had ever seen Big 8 action before the season, this cobbled-together team went 7-3-1, winning the Mississippi Bowl 30–0 over Mendenhall.

Coach Doug Clanton: line coach, head baseball coach, inspired maximum performance from 160-pound linemen, rejected all offers to become head coach in academy leagues.

The Immovable Defense, 1972 Model. Junior Craig Cole (67), supervising.

New and Improved Mustangs, in new uniform, 1971. *Left to right*: senior Willie Ray Purvis, sophomore Tommy Bodker, senior Dan Henley.

Stars 1971: junior Willie Miller (51) leading quarterback Wyatt Washington (19) on sweep.

Stars 1972: sophomore quarterback Billy Denny (10) pitches to junior Kenny Burns (32).

Five Horsemen of City Championship Team: starting seniors 1972–1973.

Orsmond Jordan: Murrah head basketball coach 1971–1993. With a 722-232 record over a thirty-five-year coaching career, most successful basketball coach in the history of the JPS, matched and extended Coach Jack Carlisle's 78-18 record as head football coach at Murrah 1960–1970 and "tradition of excellence" in Murrah sports after integration.

Big Tummie: senior catcher George Coleman after walk-off homer, 1973.

Invincible: senior Mike Brown hands baton to senior Willie Taylor in relay, 1973.

The 1971–1972 Murrah cheerleaders. Gail Wellford in the center and, *clockwise from the upper left*, Teena Freeman, Susan Daily, Terry Tiller, Lee Porter, Pam Mayer, Susan McBroom, Gloria Donelson, and Nancy Powell.

Selected in the spring of 1972, the 1972-1973 cheerleaders were, *back row, left to right*, Susan McBroom, Cassandra Fowlkes, Nancy Powell, Teena Freeman, and Marilyn Jamison. *Front row, left to right*, Ann Ritter, Myra Stevens, and Jeanette Darby. As did the Marching Band and the Misses, the cheerleaders toiled through months of practices and performances.

A new homecoming for everybody.

Mr. Roger Dollarhide, Murrah's band director for decades and mentor to many hundreds of young musicians. In a 1964 tribute to him, the *Northside Reporter* described him as "A modest, unassuming man with a rare ability to inspire respect, confidence, and devotion from his students."

The band's drum major John Weeks, perhaps leading his troops in "The Horse." In the background Murrah students are occupying the visitors' bleachers at Newell Field, indicating that the game is against Callaway and the Chargers are the home team that year.

The 1971–1972 Murrah band, comprised of thirty-seven seniors and twenty-two juniors. The band practiced for incalculable hours, beginning in August before the school year began and continuing into January. The band possibly reflected the demographics of the student body more than any other organization.

Diane Jamison, class of '72, delivers a presentation on black literary achievements during the fledgling Black History Week at Murrah.

The 1971 Homecoming Court. Pictured, *left to right*, are Mary Al Cobb, Gloria Donelson, Vicki Willis, Lee Porter, Karen Bell, and Joyce Johnson. Debbie Horn was also in the court but was not pictured.

From the 1973 *Résumé*, the class of '73's Mr. and Miss Murrah High School, Fred Sheriff and Nancy Powell.

The Fall 1972 theater production was "The Odd Couple." 1973 classmates Robert Kelly and Jim Matheny played the eponymous pair.

A football pep rally from the fall of 1971. Ubiquitous at the pep rallies and football games, the Murrah Misses are in full dress, including their iconic hats.

The 1973 seniors erupt in a cloud of confetti at a football pep rally.

The spring of 1973 Junior/Senior Prom was held in downtown Jackson's Hotel Heidelberg. Evocative of another era, the Heidelberg was razed in the late 1970s to make room for a new South Central Bell building. Excepting graduation, this was the last time the class of 1973 would celebrate together as a class. Here a well-turned-out A. C. Williams dances to the music of the Independents.

Pictured are the *Résumé* staffers for the 1972–1973 school year. Along with the editors Cassandra Fowlkes and Mary Al Cobb, this crew is braving a particularly cold winter day in the school's courtyard.

The Murrah Debate Team for the 1972–1973 school year, Curtis Hall, sponsor. Coach Hall was a popular government teacher, debate team sponsor, and defacto cheerleader at the football pep rallies.

The junior class officers during the 1971–1972 school year. *Left to right*, Fred Sheriff, Annette Johnson, Robert Kelly, and Mike "Ike" Adams. The next year Fred would be the president of the entire student body.

The Student Council circa fall of 1972 from the 1973 *Résumé*. Meeting in the Choral Music room, the council tried to address some of the vexing problems affecting the student body. This must have been a tranquil year, however, as according to the *Résumé*, "Rarely were there disagreements or discord, if any."

The Junior Classical League during a February 1973 trip to Nashville. Latin teacher and JCL sponsor Jim Barksdale was known fondly as Magister to many years of Latin students. Who but a classicist could teach unfailingly and unflinchingly through so many years of tumult?

From the March 1973 edition, the 1973–1974 *Hoofbeat* staff. Cindy Wilson was its editor, Anne Gibson, its sponsor.

The Class of 1973's Tenth Year Reunion.

An ad from the *Jackson Northside Sun*, encouraging Murrah graduates of the early 1970s to participate in the project that would become this book. Identical ads ran in the *Northeast Mississippi Daily Journal* and the *Clarion Ledger*. Not many graduates replied.

The response was much better to the second ad to run, picturing Teena Freeman in her cheerleader's uniform.

The Experiment: The 1970–1971 Academic Year and Other Pre-Murrah Experiences

Narrated by Teena Freeman Horn

■

After Jackson schoolchildren and their families survived the initial shock and meltdown of half a year of chaos in the public school system, we dared to dream that things would improve. Those of us who were about to be sophomores hoped our educational experience would return to normal. More school district lines were drawn from a federal, not local level. The new lines disregarded the traditional neighborhood school system and the immediate needs of local Jacksonians. Who was to blame for the unprecedented sacrifice and the inconvenience that we children endured in 1970? Was it the Mississippi state government, who was slow to implement national standards? Alternately, was it federal employees who forced immediate movement without regard to the effect on current individuals—just focusing on statistical black/white ratios and projected long-term hypothetical results? Short notices given before each school year ensured that no one could plan ahead! As resilient young people, we reacted in different ways: some enjoyed the new experiences of seeing new people and places, while others had difficulty with adjustment. There were a good deal of lawsuits and appeals going on that eventually worked into the establishment of the 1970 school year that is now history.

The *Clarion-Ledger* on Tuesday, June 16, 1970 (pages 1, 2, 4) displays discussion and maps of "New High School Zones—Four zones are provided in the new integration plan ordered in U.S. District Court for the Jackson City Schools [from the HEW Plan A]. The school district opposed all three secondary school plans submitted by HEW." There were five zones for the junior high schools with the most contention involving the elementary schools and busing considerations.

Billy Skelton wrote, "The schools had suffered an 8 per cent loss in enrollment, presumably to white private schools, when the integration plan was put into effect last Feb. 1." He continued, "The Judge, under orders by the U.S. Fifth Circuit Court of Appeals to select one of three integration plans for the junior and senior high schools proposed in January by the U.S. Department of Health, Education and Welfare, ordered Plan A, which combines zoning and pairing, put into effect.

"The appeals court May 5 ordered the adoption of a new plan because the present plan did not produce sufficient mixing . . . One section of the order sustaining the function of a Biracial Committee might be interpreted as a potential counter to any resegregation that might develop as a result of the implementation of the plan." Their job was to suggest to "school boards ways to attain and maintain a unitary system." The HEW plan was said to be too costly in the transportation-busing implementation.

In this new plan, I was zoned to distant Central High School, an old established school in downtown Jackson. It was designated the tenth-, eleventh-, and twelfth-grade school for those of us from the Belhaven area, and those from other areas of central and south Jackson. Central turned out to be a good place, though it was inconvenient and costly to my family unit. It was "the school" of an earlier Jackson, which was centered on downtown. My Jackson had moved north. Central High did not have the amenities of Murrah High, but my time there allowed me to blossom a bit. I had an outstanding teacher named Mrs. Ainsworth, whom I really liked. She awakened in me the love for reading and helped me learn to think, analyze, and be critical of published works. Mrs. Ainsworth was a bright, positive, cheerful black woman who appeared untouched by prejudice. She was excited about teaching, and treated all of us the same; in that I found comfort. For some reason, Mrs. Ainsworth picked me out of the class as having leadership potential. Reflecting back, my assertiveness as to becoming engaged in activities began from her placement of confidence in me. Of all my teachers, I believe that Mrs. Ainsworth was the most influential, as I found a voice.

Education was good at Central and I enjoyed the faculty, friends, and safe environment, yet it was not my desired destination. My family bought a house in the Murrah district and took control of my destiny.

The north Jackson residents were sent to Brinkley for the tenth grade, and those in classes behind us muddled through Powell, Bailey, and Chastain Junior High schools. Like all shocking events that happen to people in the course of a lifetime, things got better with time. I talked to one white student who went to Rowan the year after I left and she said that school was a lot of fun. The old adage, "this too shall pass" comes to mind. My classmates continue their accounts of the 1970 to 1971 school year.

The Brinkley Experience of Johnny Jones:

The first day at Brinkley was memorable. At assembly that morning we heard from the black principal (a holdover and kind man), followed by the white co-principal (a military type looking for trouble). They both told us that the eyes of the nation were on us, that if we could make integration work at Brinkley, it could work everywhere. Before the white co-principal got a minute into his speech he was shouted down by the assembly, which made him furious. This was unprecedented for us, and we sank into the seats and tried to disappear. Right as the confrontation built toward critical mass, a bump from the rear of the auditorium followed by an eruption of screaming drew our attention. We saw a 300-pound white history teacher named Crowson tumbling over backwards and a black male (he looked ten years older than us but was apparently a student for that day) finishing his haymaker punch. He'd clocked Mr. Crowson. He stepped over the poor man and rapidly descended the stairs two at a time, flinging away the hands of teachers trying to grab him, and ran out of the auditorium holding his fist in the air in a black-power salute of pure defiance. The whole place went nuts. Within the first hour at Brinkley we saw our first and last assembly where both principals spoke, followed by general chaos that drew police officers, fireman in their ladder trucks, and two ambulances (which were completely disconcerting). We had no teachers, no class had even met, and we just sat there for a couple of hours waiting on order to be restored, scared to talk and draw the attention of the crowd or, worse, an angry individual looking for a white to pick on. I don't remember how the assembly ended, but I do recall thinking that the whole integration thing was over.

That same day my friend Tinker Miller and I walked into shop class for fifth period. A very dark African American classmate named "Wolf" (if one had any doubt, he wore on the day after Labor Day a black leather motorcycle jacket cut to shreds from, we inferred, knife fights, with a crudely drawn green and yellow wolf's head on the back, over which was written his moniker in old-English script) walked up behind me and put a straight razor to my throat. "We don't like white people around here," he hissed. "I don't either," I got out, and two of his pack mates and then Wolf laughed. He withdrew the razor (it was dull) but kept his wolf-type aggression for as long as he could see we were still scared, and that was a while. But we didn't report him, even to our parents because the response would have been inevitable; somehow it didn't seem that threatening. By my senior year Wolf was the centerfielder for the Murrah baseball team, looking the same—downright menacing, even when his cap sat on his Afro without contacting his head till he cut it to play ball, which showed me a lot—but now I considered him a friend. We swore we would defend our friendship (I really don't know if Wolf thought we had a "friendship" back then, but I did), but of course I haven't seen him since ... I don't know about Wolf, but I learned a lot from our relationship.

There was very little educating going on at Brinkley. Every Friday for at least the first month of school the black students held a "walkout." I asked Wolf one time what they were protesting. He thought a minute, then looked annoyed and said, "Discrimination, fool!" I nodded, said, "I know exactly what you mean." Most of the black students walked out the front doors, gathered on Albemarle in front of the school, and protested against ... Brinkley, I guess, or, like Wolf, discrimination as a general concept. I never knew. The cops came and stood around too, everybody laughing and joking, happy to be outside (they did not call a walkout when it rained). After the first two even the local news reporters quit showing up. Those Fridays were lost, and we usually went home early.

The teachers had it worse than the students. Some couldn't take it. In the wholesale transfer of teachers all over the district Brinkley somehow ended up with a majority white faculty, including older ladies like my English teacher for whom the changes were just too rapid. She was from Provine, still attractive in her mid-fifties, petite, friendly, staunchly Baptist, well mannered and perfectly spoken, a lady of the old ways of the white South, and absolutely terrified. The black students treated her ... with a sort of aggressive indifference, utterly unmoved by anything she said. She tried for about a month, and then she quit, the fight drained out of her. We ended up reading her children's books (she was a published author, albeit of the "Tommy and Tammy Visit Grandma's Farm" school) aloud in class while she stared out the window and drifted farther away each day. Our final exam was a ten-question multiple-choice puff piece which was meaningless because everybody got a "B". Then there was our geometry teacher: a mildly attractive young white lady, unmarried and unhappy about it, probably on her first teaching assignment, determined to keep good order. She called down a black female for some infraction, told her the next time the student would be sent to the principal's office. She was shocked, as were all the white people there, when the student shouted back at her in full voice, calling her everything she could think of that was nasty, then stood and started toward the teacher amid the catcalls and "ummm-hmmmmmmm" of her many friends. Horrified, the teacher ran out the only door, held the doorknob until help came, then collapsed in the arms of the white co-principal. I remember her expression: A face completely blank except for mouth slightly agape, like someone who had just received awful news but didn't want to react or cry. She never tried to discipline another student. One Friday the geometry teacher gave us our assignments and wished us a good weekend, and we never saw her again.

Other white teachers brought their boyfriends or husbands to class on most days but especially Friday. Some sort of confrontation occurred every Friday I can remember, at least until late in the year. Older white female teachers were occasionally protected by black males, usually gang members, and were walked to and from the parking lot daily. Among the true believers in integration, and there were some among both races on the faculty, the problem was not racism but power or influence at faculty meetings. As with most of the civil rights organizations, there came a point at which the influence of white "do-gooders" became suspect if not resented thoroughly, and their effectiveness in improving things, and then their desire to do anything but get through the day safely, fizzled out. In my view, integration failed primarily because of white racism and intolerance, but, like everything we learn about life as we get older, nothing was all one thing or all the other.

What did we learn that year? Honestly, I don't recall a thing I learned in a Brinkley classroom, except typing, but it was the most intense education I ever had. We simply had to find a brand-new way to communicate with people, to bend our will to fit ever-changing circumstances, forget our pride and find something else to pin our hopes to. Like children of fighting parents, we desired peace above all, and we learned how to achieve it through our own actions. I was still learning when I returned to Brinkley in June 1971 to get my final report card from the office. I walked out of the office, happy I'd passed (not a given for me in high school), and being immediately confronted by a throng of black gang members roaming the halls looking for white kids. The teachers and administration had given up confronting these throngs. They locked themselves in the only air-conditioned part of the building and left every student, teacher or civilian to himself, not even looking up when I tried to open the office door that locked behind me. I took off as fast as I could go, and Tinker had the truck moving when I reached it and jumped in. We didn't look back; didn't even talk about it. By then we were no longer scared, just practical and ready to move on. Adieu, Brinkley.

Dealing with each other, somehow we were able to maintain a sense of proportion through it all. A case could have easily been made that the races were warring at Murrah or Brinkley or Bailey that gang beatings, use of brass knuckles and straight razors were commonplace in bathrooms and other places where teachers would not be found, and therefore massive intervention was demanded. We all knew of something that happened to us or in front of us that could have, if stripped of context, been made to look sinister if not deadly. The solution would have been to install the 101st Airborne, or at least local cops, and we would have lost all semblance of control over our own destinies. The few white parents who were committed enough to send us to Brinkley would have jerked us out that minute and the whole experiment would have been declared an immediate and irredeemable failure. People can respond to so much change hysterically, but for reasons that still escape me it didn't happen in the early days of massive integration to those of us who were there and saw what was really happening on the ground. I think it was just that nobody actually subject to it wanted to make the case that violence was out of hand, primarily because the fix would have been worse than the problem. Looking back on it now, informed by a lifetime of over-estimating the capacity of people to simply do the right thing, particularly under pressure, I am amazed that nobody lit the fuse.

In truth, the situation improved day by day until it was at least clear that violence would not take place between classmates. We knew each other. Most of the violence I experienced or knew about was the work of students from rival schools. One morning by the Murrah tennis courts Tinker and I brawled with three Lanier students who kicked at us with razor blades in their shoes, knock-ing my books out of my hand but missing skin. It ended when Tinker tackled one and I hit another with a grazing and painless punch to the face and ear, after which they scattered amid vile curses and threats. That was pretty typical of the extent of the actual physical confrontations. Among our black classmates whose names we knew, if threats came they were usually mere posturing, more about intimidation than hurting anyone, designed to further a self-image based on one being "bad," as in the John Shaft/SuperFly/(later) Michael Jackson sense of "bad" with a snarl and a quick kick. Nobody wanted to back down—not so much with the opposition but in the presence of his fellows. Nothing new about that; it is simply the high school experience, and it didn't have anything to do with race. The students intuitively understood what it meant, kept the context, and just moved on.

Governor William Winter: Interview

"I think not a lot of civil rights workers would agree with me then or now, but I think we would have had a more satisfactory result, permanent result, if we had had more gradualism in the process of desegregating the schools. We would not have had the problem that you and Lele had in 1970, when kids were bused all over Jackson and I think that is what doaked the process down."

Governor Winter allowed that one of his daughters had a difficult time at Brinkley, that her year there was "absolutely miserable. She would come home really almost shell shocked. She was harassed. She was one of maybe a half a dozen white girls in the whole school. I don't know if she had any close white friends that went there, maybe one. But it got so bad that by mid Octo-ber, Elise [his wife] and I called the principal and talked to him. We said our daughter is having a real hard time. The kids were running up and down the halls, obviously no discipline. Eleanor wouldn't even go to the bathroom. She would go all day without going to the bathroom. We said, 'We want to talk to you about our daughter.' He got up and closed the door—an old, white professor. He said, 'I knew this integration wasn't going to work. I tried to tell them it wasn't going to.' He was almost ensuring that it didn't work by his attitude." *The Winters afterward withdrew their daughter from public schools and sent her to St. Andrews Episcopal School.* "I never apologized for them going to St. Andrews because St. Andrews, I guess, was desegregated before public school," said Winter.

Lele Winter Gillespie:

In the summer of 1970 it was announced that for our tenth-grade year many of us would be attending Sam Brinkley High School, an all-black school located in what is now known as the Medgar Evers Historic Neighborhood District of Jackson. Brinkley had been established in 1966 and named for an outstanding black educator in the city. I remember feeling like we were "invading" this school and this newfound neighborhood in a part of Jackson I had never been to and I wasn't sure exactly how the neighbors would like us. Although admittedly a little scared in the halls at times, my academic experience there was a good one—I had an exceptional art class, learned to type with Ms. Ainsworth, studied classics like *Lord of the Flies* under the tutelage of Eudora Welty's niece, Mary Alice, and learned the ins and outs of driving as we cruised the neighborhood in Ms. Roulette's driver's ed class. It was a very positive experience and ultimately a fun one.

Velma Robinson Chisholm:

The busing disrupted my plans. I had always dreamed of going to Brinkley High School, ten minutes away from my house, being with a class I grew up with and had attended school with most of my life. Instead I got half of the class and new classmates.

Doug Levanway:

Brinkley had its own proud past as an all-black high school, but it was clearly out of the comfort zone of many white northeast Jackson parents (and their children, if we're being honest). I don't know whether it was by design or the result of our city leadership's stubborn refusal to follow the law and desegregate without a court order, but the court-ordered desegregation plan we ended up with all but assured that we would have a strong private school system in Jackson. I'm certain many parents would have pulled their children out of the public schools no matter the school or where it was, rather than let them attend a racially integrated school. But I'm convinced a lot more would have given the public schools a try if the plan had not seemed so harsh and punitive. It's true that some of those who went to private schools for the tenth grade came back to Murrah for their junior and senior years, but the private schools would not have gained the same traction, in my view, if kids weren't being sent across town to an all-black enclave of Jackson into which most of them had never set foot.

Brinkley lived up to its moniker: It was merely an "attendance center" in every sense of that phrase. No teams, no cheerleaders, no class leaders, no student council, no school singers, nothing that seemed like high school. We were marking time until we could go to a real high school ... Brinkley turned out to be OK.

I found out a few weeks before school started that my mother had arranged for me to carpool with four girls. I knew one of the girls, I think, before we started carpooling. Some had cars they could take to school and some didn't, so mothers would be driving us on some days. Let's just say this wasn't exactly how I envisioned starting the tenth grade. My worries didn't last. The girls were all pretty, smart and fun. One of them became my girlfriend for the school year. I was envied for my carpool, or at least that was what I thought.

I was held up for my lunch money in the bathroom my first week at Brinkley. I refused to give up the money when asked, so my arm was grabbed and held behind me and twisted in opposite directions, like we used to do when we gave someone a "rope burn." I had two older brothers; we used to do this for fun in my neighborhood. The situation became less scary. The other two guys just looked at me and my "assailant" standing there awkwardly while he put the old rope burn on me. Finally, someone else came in the bathroom, a large guy who I believe was Willie Miller, but I'm not sure. He laughed and shook his head "no," the guy let go of my arm, and we all went off to class. That was it.

I made some new and lasting friends at Brinkley. The alphabet ensured that I would be sitting behind or near Steve Laney throughout high school. Steve had a natural mind for math and he was a security blanket for me in the advanced math courses we were in through high school (college calculus put this premed major on the path to Law School). But it was at Brinkley that we started our debate about music that would last for years. Our discussions were always before or during class, when we should have been paying attention, and we disagreed about everything musical. I would throw out Derek and the Dominoes and Delaney and Bonnie, and he would counter with Grand Funk Railroad and Black Sabbath. If I wanted to talk about the Allman Brothers Band, he would bring up Iron Butterfly ("Laney, seriously, Iron Butterfly?"). It was fun.

We had several bomb scares at Brinkley. Guy Gillespie and I used them as excuses to leave and skip school, though what we were skipping was debatable. The kids who went to Council school often showed up at Brinkley to hang out when we had a bomb scare. How did they know? Did they ever go to class?

I started a paper route in the tenth grade and would have one through high school. Friends started getting paper routes too, and there were times on the weekends that other friends would join us just to be out and unaccounted for in the middle of the night. Sometimes we would meet up after we threw our routes. I remember all of us sitting in the Krystal on State Street, the sun just coming up, eating eggs, grits, and bacon, and drinking chocolate milk. Good, good times.

Betsy Grimes Triggs:

I remember Roosevelt, a black boy I met at Brinkley, who was in the Wolf gang. We talked about gangs at school way back then. He dropped out of school and became a paratrooper. Came to visit me at my home in his paratrooper uniform and scared the shit out of my parents!

Kip Ezelle:

At Brinkley Kip remembered being part of "a bunch of lily-white kids that went over into that area of town, which was an experience, from locking the rooms down when we had a motorcycle going through the school, or some gang running through the school. But as far as the education went, because we were all put in the same classes, we got a good education. You had people like Awad, who was a great biology teacher."

Lindy Stevens Clement:

"I met Freddie Funches and he kinda was my buddy, and Ms. Olsen, she was my tenth-grade English teacher, and she basically had to send me to the library because I was the only white kid, but I was so far ahead, that she couldn't—she told my momma and daddy, 'I will just have to send her to the library and give her stuff to do 'cause I'm trying to catch everybody else up.' I mean, we would have walkouts. I don't know why, everybody would walk out. It wasn't just black or whites, we would just all walk out."

Steven Jenkins:

The next year brought me to Powell Junior High. Going from being a minority at a formerly all-white school to being an even smaller minority at a formerly all-black school was another big change. We carpooled to school and carpooled home. No extracurricular activities, no socializing. I remember almost nothing of it.

Faced with the prospect of another similar year at Brinkley High School, I took two summer school classes in 1971 and another half-credit by correspondence (typing!) to qualify as a junior, and showed up at Murrah, no doubt to the puzzlement of the rest of the Class of 1973. Having looked forward to attending

Murrah for years, I finally felt like I was where I belonged, even though the circumstances were a little different.

Robert Kelly:

"The integration process didn't work too well, because we were not able to pull a lot of the white kids into Brinkley. I think that is when a lot of the white folks in Jackson got together and built Jackson Prep . . . I remember hearing about 'the white folks are building their own schools.' I think there were just a few white people at Brinkley. I can't even recall . . . I really enjoyed going to Brinkley, because I was able to walk to school. It was right in the neighborhood. That year flew by. You know when you are fifteen years old, and a teenager, times are tough already, because you think you know everything."

Freddie Funches:

By the time Freddie got to Brinkley, "things started to round out a little bit. I think kids started giving each other a chance, because I remember a time over there, I met Charles Irby, and Charles and I became good friends . . . We played football in front of the school before we entered, and things started getting a little better."

"They had a walkout one time. I don't know, pretty much right now, what it was all about, but it started around in the office . . . it was brief . . . I was in Ms. Odom's room. Ms. Odom was a big lady. And you didn't do too much messing around up in her room. I couldn't go home and walk out of that schoolhouse and think I'm going home and telling my momma I walked out. Naw, she didn't play that! Just some people had a lot of respect."

Freddie sometimes visited Charles Irby at his family's house in Eastover, the city's most affluent neighborhood. "We started sharing with each other. I would go to Charles's house. Charles's mom was a great lady. She wasn't outspoken. She didn't come out that much . . . she was just a mother at home, and she done a great job . . . He told me one time, the thing to realize in life, regardless of what you do or how you do it, you still had to deal with certain people at a particular time. And by prolonging it was gonna make it even longer to have to deal with, so get tossed over in that salad. Toss it up and make it happen . . . That's why their business was so successful, because they knew how to deal with people, not isolating themselves from different things."

Margie Cooper Pearson was interviewed by myself, Johnny Jones, and Claiborne Barksdale:

Margie: "Powell was the junior high, Brinkley, senior high, and that's what we were all aspiring to because some of the kids had older siblings who were already at Brinkley, and so they were already looking forward to that. I'm the oldest, so I didn't have that necessarily, but still, I was looking forward to going, because it wasn't just the education, it was also the sports. You know, you looked forward to being whatever Brinkley was at the time . . .

"We were just doing what the law required us to do, OK? That's how I remember it. But you guys, typically, had other choices. You could have gone to some private school or some prep school, but you came, and I wondered how did you come to that decision and how did your parents get to be OK with that? I have questioned that, because, to me, that was a big deal for you, because you were coming into a neighborhood that, you know, it wasn't an unsafe neighborhood back then, but still, it was all black and that had to be really big."

Johnny: "I didn't even know where Brinkley was until the first day of school. We had to find it. And it took us a long time to realize what a fine place Brinkley really was . . . But that experiment at Brinkley was so strange because I don't think that anybody was prepared, the teachers or anybody else. I didn't get much education at Brinkley. Did you?"

Margie: "I think I did. I had this great teacher. I can't remember his name. He was white . . . It may have been civics. I'm not real sure. But he made an impression on me."

She said she remembered one white student, Charles Irby, who came from an affluent family and chose to attend Brinkley and later Murrah, which surprised her.

"Now, that was a shocker because I just remember how much money these people had and I'm, like, he could go anywhere he wanted to in the world, and so that was really something to me. That was like 'wow.' That said a lot to me. That said that there were people who—and it had to be coming from their parents—were open to letting their children have this experience for whatever it brought, good or bad, and that was big to me."

Johnny: "There were people of good will, but there were only eighty-three white people at Brinkley with six hundred black people."

Margie: "I didn't remember that."

Amelia Reagan Wright:

After the incredible experience of attending Bailey, going to Brinkley High School was icing on the cake! I thought Bailey would be an impossible act to follow, but Brinkley surpassed all my grandest expectations. The burden was on our parents, as they had to arrange (carpools, as no buses were provided) for us to attend a school so far away from home (at least ten miles) just to satisfy the federal government in maintaining a supposed racial balance. We were not allowed to attend the school within our designated district. Brinkley was a black high school. It did not belong to us. We were interlopers/outsiders, though we were accepted. For that, I will always be grateful . . . I loved Brinkley and my classmates. We had the best of everything, with everything being that we were in it together. Sure, there were rough spots . . . Remember the riots? Do you remember the guns at school during the Black History month riots? It was scary, but it was, again, reality. If I could go back, I would.

Fred Sheriff:

At Brinkley High School it was more of the same—hanging with friends, doing schoolwork. I was actively involved in the marching band, which provided a good outlet. Other than the classroom, the band became another place of interaction with white people. Those "white guys" in the band seemed "cool" to me.

Mary Al Cobb Alford:

My carpool friends included Betsy Grimes, Rebecca Smith, and Lele Winter. We rode to Brinkley, the historically black high school converted to a tenth-grade center, with anxiety well beyond the typical adolescent drama. Brinkley was a fifteen-minute drive across the railroad tracks into "foreign" territory in Jackson. We had never strayed further than a mile or so to school. Lele's dad would often break the tension by singing along to "Bad, Bad Leroy Brown" as though he were a chauffeuring Jim Croce!

The quality of education at Brinkley was diminished from that at Chastain. I can recall sitting in biology class the entire year with no significant instruction. It seems our teacher was frequently sick—did we even *HAVE* a substitute teacher? Madame Prater was a delightful French teacher and we enjoyed receiving extra credit by bringing French food on Fridays! My grades were not particularly exemplary and my mother attended several teacher conferences to defend my academic efforts. The Brinkley atmosphere was chaotic and a sense of confusion prevailed. There were frequent fights in the halls as we struggled to know and understand one another. It was at Brinkley, however, that I formed my first close friendships with African American students including Cassandra Wilson and Fred Sheriff. I was captivated by Cassandra's many talents . . . Fred Sheriff's mother worked with my dad at the Health Department and Dad had great respect for her. Fred and Cassandra were strong leaders and role models in our class and gave hope to the beginning of this experiment.

Bill Patterson:

I was a good (not great), but indifferent student at Chastain. I was no athlete at all. Stereotypically, I was defined by that school, its administrators and teachers, and fellow students to be such, and never more. Tragically, in retrospect, I accepted those judgments. Then, I went to Brinkley, and everything and nearly everyone was different. I thought, why not be different. Why not study more? Why not run every afternoon on your own for the satisfaction that comes with simply doing something that takes some effort and discipline? Why not, it turned out, begin again?

So, I did. Those decisions, prompted by the changes in our school system and reinforced by a fateful trip to a scholarship camp in upstate New York following my tenth-grade year, which convinced me that I controlled my life and future, made me the person that I am today, both intellectually and physically. But it was another beginning that complemented my personal rebirth and that rounded out my soul and my life. That other beginning was the company of folks, both African American and white, with whom I studied, interacted and ran track while at Brinkley, then Murrah.

Foster Dickard:

[It was] personally and generally perceived as a major inconvenience and unpleasant experience to be forced to travel out of my community into an unsettled and tense atmosphere as an outsider (Brinkley). The educational and social experience I feel sure was significantly less valuable than if the students (black and white) were allowed to go to school in their own communities. While there are always lessons learned by facing adversity, it undermines academic or social development. My impression was that the black students that lived in the community did not consider Brinkley to provide the same (less than their expectations) experience than before it was deseg'ed. It had "lost its identity" of the community school. I had several black friends in the band talk about "how good Brinkley used to be." There seemed to be an attitude by most students and staff of "nobody wants this but we have to deal with it."

I was not one of the socially elite or the type of person that looked forward to school or structured environment, and so whatever social climbing experiences missed from the upheaval of desegregation do not compute for me, at least not negatively. I did however expect that there would be a safe and a sense of community support and pride in the school programs. The sense of community and school tradition was lost or degraded because of the forced busing out of communities into a situation of forced cohabitation with others that would rather be at their own community school. Many of our friends escaped the situation with "white flight" to at least three or four different private schools. Hmmm, it would be interesting to know their perspective . . . I am not aware of any scenario where forced integration improved the academic and social success of the school system. I think the teachers (black and white) at Brinkley and Murrah did an admirable job with a general lack of discipline and respect from some (too many) students.

Doug Minor:

Those of us from Chastain who would have gone to Murrah, took a dramatic detour in 1970–71. Brinkley . . . is where real integration began. Remarkably, on their turf, in their neighborhood, in their school, most black students welcomed us. We were invading their world, and in their eyes, boy, were we different. We came in our own cars, new clothes, white skin and white ways. The contrast was stark . . . 90 percent black, 10 percent white, as I recall. We were strangers from another world; they knew nothing about us, and we knew absolutely nothing about them. But that changed.

There were some great teachers at Brinkley, among them: Mr. Rollo (math), and Mr. Awad (biology). English class is where I first experienced one of the designed benefits of desegregation, as I became friends with three very special people (who happened to be black): Cassandra Fowlkes, Karen Bell and Fred Sheriff; all are friends today. Also, the black guys I befriended in P.E., mainly members of the basketball team, became my biggest supporters, and protected me, even though I didn't know it at the time. I don't remember their names, but I can see their faces, and fondly recall the competitive games of three-on-three with them in the gym.

We had a great carpool. Layne Turner, Bill Patterson and the lovely Lenda Taylor (beautiful legs, long blonde hair, and the shortest mini-skirts in the school) . . . what a treat it was to see her get in and out of Layne's green Rambler! Each day we drove past Grove Park golf course, (near Powell Junior High) the only public course available to blacks back then. Layne and I played that course in the spring, and I would venture to say we may have been the first whites ever to play the "Grove" . . . and probably the last. We were treated with dignity and respect.

Lenda Taylor Brown:

Tenth grade I went to Brinkley (it was an all tenth-grade center—no sports, no bands, just tenth graders; whoever planned that planned for it to fail). I had a blast, not much in the way of learning facts but I did learn life skills. I remember driving to school in my 1960-something blue-green Comet; I did not even have a driver's license, only a permit. I had the best, all-boy carpool: Layne Turner, Billy Patterson, Barry Dent and Doug Minor; my mama did not worry about me being with boys. I remember a kick in my butt the first day of school by [a female]; we interrupted their school, we had no football, etc., and it was a hardship all way around. Many Fridays no one showed up for school. I remember protest in the halls, especially one day when lots of older guys (early twenties) were running up and down our hallways handing out flyers demanding we celebrate black history—nice to know we were in the preplanning stages of the initial Black History month. Debbie House was a good friend of mine and we had planned to leave school early one Friday to go to the local rock show (real rocks, gems, etc.) and Debbie's mother was going to pick us up but she got busy at work and had her co-workers pick us up. She worked for the local police department and sent a paddy wagon for us; you should have seen the looks we got that day—was a lot of fun.

I remember a lot of kids in Jackson dropped out of the public school system to go the Council school (white Citizen Council school; when I think of that today it scares me; good I was young in the seventies and not paying attention to the meaning of things). To think they were going to a school supported by the local KKK shows you the hot bed in Jackson and may explain the white flight? Just a thought.

Susan McBroom:

I lived three blocks off of Riverside Drive and had to go to Central HS in downtown Jackson. My mother worked at UMC and we were a one-car family. So, my mother decided to use a friend's address for us and then we went to Murrah my last two years of high school. Unfortunately, my older brother, William, had to go to Central his senior year after being at Murrah his sophomore and junior year. We still have his senior class ring from Murrah, which he had to purchase during his junior year!

I felt like everyone was just blowing in the wind. We just landed wherever we landed, and had to make the best of it. I was upset about being separated from the people I had become friends with at Bailey when I moved back to Jackson in the middle of the eighth grade. I was not too concerned about my poor mother's situation at the time. Looking back, I think it brought those of us who are still friends closer than we would have been otherwise. How did it make you feel then and now? Back then I was upset about having to go to a school where I did not know anyone other than my brother, Teena Freeman, and Nancy Powell. We made lots of friends there but most of the folks at Central looked at us as "those north

Jackson girls." You do remember the north Jackson/south Jackson thing, don't you? Now, I don't think about it too much. I was glad I got to work in the coaches' office at Central and get to be friends with Coach Stevens and Coach Clanton. I now laugh about how upset the Central folks were that "we" were taking two of their best coaches and half of their football team with us to Murrah. Oh, I left out the part about Teena, Nancy, and me skipping school (with parent's permission of course) to go to Murrah and try out for cheerleader! And we all were elected! Needless to say, the Central folks did not take too kindly to us after that. Do you blame them?

David Flanagan:

In 1972, I was bused to Powell Junior High from north Jackson. Powell had a ratio of 70/30 black to white. I learned to get along, stay clear of certain situations, and watch my back at all times. There were fights, boy against boy, black against white and even girl against girl. Powell was in a terrible area, as was Brinkley Junior High . . . I met some good friends at Powell. We, whites, learned to stick together. I felt totally out of control to change the situation, as this is where we were told to attend if we opted for public school. We won the citywide football championship. We went undefeated and that was sweet. Some good news arrived. They decided to make Murrah a tenth-, eleventh-, and twelfth-grade high school once more. No going to Brinkley the following year in a worse section of town than Powell. Yeah! I was excited to be going to Murrah. My brother and I would be able to attend the same high school, ride together, etc. The sad part was that half of the Powell students would be going to Callaway and half would be going to Murrah. Football players included. The good news was that I had friends at both schools. The thing I most remember at Powell was when the last bell rang, get to the bus. If you missed the bus it was scary to wait on a ride to come get you.

Katie Barwick-Snell:

I was "bused" to Brinkley even though I don't remember ever seeing any buses. (But really I had a great carpool.) I attended Murrah High School during the 1972 and 1973 years. Many of my friends from Brinkley went on to Callaway and we missed them. I was blessed with a great group of friends that gave me social support that met at Brinkley and traveled on to Murrah . . .

Many rumors circulated that year about school violence in all the schools. I think some of the private schools fueled the fires by rumor-mongering. I think most of the students enjoyed the "walkouts" that happened at Brinkley because it meant we did not have classes and not much really happened. I know many people felt that the government stepped in and made people go to different schools without much thought but in graduate school my education classes discussed how many states chose to integrate their schools. Our discussions were quite interesting and after hearing and reading how other places integrated, I think Jackson did a great job of having "same grade centers" in the tenth grade and eleventh/twelfth grades—this helped cut down on age harassment (seniors picking on freshmen, etc.) and it also mixed up the school loyalties for both white and black students. Brinkley and Lanier had been the most beloved black high schools in north Jackson and Murrah and Callaway the beloved white high schools.

Some classmates said that they took buses to designated schools, others did not.

Johnny Jones explained the busing situation in an e-mail he sent me:

The facts: as can be seen from the Clarion-Ledger maps [1970] we have, the redistricting of the JPS created school zones for certain neighborhoods that ended up constituting a swap of the white students and the black students along gerrymandered lines developed first by the federal courts and then by the US Dept. of Health, Education and Welfare (a defunct federal agency that contracted with "experts" to "draw the lines"). For instance, the black neighborhoods surrounding Brinkley were gerrymandered and the students formerly sent to Brinkley were told they had to go to Murrah or Callaway. For the white neighborhoods like Amelia's and mine, we were gerrymandered into Brinkley's former school district for the tenth grade, and in that process Tinker and I (we drove to Brinkley every day in Tinker's old yellow truck and my father's 1956 Plymouth station wagon, stopping at Campbell's Bakery every morning because Tinker always had money for some reason). We were just much closer to Murrah, Callaway, even Central, and had we chosen to drive that way (e.g., down Woodrow Wilson to Brinkley by the Jackson Mall), we would drive past Murrah another four miles to achieve "desegregation." Blacks had it worse: they had to drive out of the neighborhoods adjacent to Brinkley, Powell Junior High, even Lanier, to get to Murrah, and that was a hell of an inconvenience that Margie Cooper told us led to their just walking four miles until JPS bought enough school busses in the summer of 1971 (from my father, ironically, driven from the Kosciusko plant to Jackson every day that summer by Tinker, Kip, Jerry, Spencer, others and me) and offered bus rides. Very few blacks had carpools.

The real problem was elementary schools. They were the traditional "neighborhood" schools, and when desegregation hit white kids had to drive by three and four closer schools to the black school to which they were assigned. Blacks had worse problems because they had less transportation, or fewer housewives to do the driving.

It wasn't the JPS administration's "intransigence" that caused the bussing. It was the federal courts, later (there was no written plan until the summer of '70) the HEW, that came up with these plans in accordance with the US Supreme Ct's mandate in 1968 that *Brown v. Board of Education* did not mean merely ensuring that the black kids who wanted could go to Murrah but required school districts to do whatever was necessary to achieve a "unitary" school system that in each school reflected the racial make-up of the community—in Jackson's case in 1970, every school had to have a student body at least 40% black. That's the "radical" desegregation methods of which we have written, and also the methods that drove whites out of JPS to attend academies opening up closer to home. For instance, Alan had to go two blocks to get to Manhattan Council school rather than the eight miles across uncharted (for white kids like us) territory to get to Brinkley."

So, yes. It *was* what created much of the white flight. Not so much that whites didn't want to put kids on school buses; it was that no one (not even a good liberal like me) could defend a plan that required kids to drive past perfectly adequate schools in and around their neighborhoods into areas of town we'd never even seen to attend schools we knew nothing about, all for the purpose of achieving radical desegregation . . . It was the core of the problem that led to white flight. I think it was more of a cause of it than raw racism or refusal to attend schools with black kids.

Murrah High Students Remember 1970 to 1971

Cy Rosenblatt:

When school opened in September, there were noticeably fewer white students in the halls. The student body was approximately half black, and there seemed to be increasing tension at Murrah. Sporadic fights broke out in the halls between a very small minority of black and white students. I always thought that dividing anything in half would guarantee that everyone would be happy with their allotment of whatever was being divided. Being equally divided along racial lines did little to forward understanding between the races.

Robert Gibbs: *Interview with Johnny and me*

Robert: "Well, the good thing was a good number of us went together. A large number of my friends went there. One of my friends was Wyatt

Washington; Wyatt was a great football player and Wyatt encouraged me to go over with him to try out for football. Of course I wasn't a football player, but I went over with him because he didn't want to go by himself and he wasn't getting a lot of cooperation from other folks and I remember I went over and met Coach Carlisle and got assigned a jersey, number and . . ."

Johnny: "Really?"

Robert: "I did. Still remember my number was 43, but I knew I had no intentions. I played in the band . . ."

Johnny asked if Robert was angry about having to accommodate white culture after integration and whether he was political back then.

Robert responded: "I can't say that we were militant about it. If you had asked me would I rather have graduated from Brinkley than Murrah, the answer would have been yes. I would have much rather been at Brinkley because I liked its tradition and I would have liked to have been a part of it, but having been integrated into that system and meeting people that became friends, it was OK. The thing that I think caught us and caused us to rebel some, was some of the [white] teachers. Some of the teachers were just not used to having black kids in their classrooms. I think they had the mentality that we could not learn or at least that we could not learn as well as the white students and their way of showing us that, you could tell it had a racial bent."

He mentioned the teacher, Mrs. Ruff. "It seemed like nothing we could say in class was right," Robert said. "And you know we would raise a hand, and her whole demeanor would just change when she would look at us. It was a difficult time to deal with her and yet, I remember I think I made a B in her class which she probably didn't expect and it probably should have been an A. But I don't think she felt she could give an A to a black student. And there were others, but hers just resonated, because so many of us just felt that type of racism in her class."

I asked: "Were there any other times that you felt that from anybody?"

Robert: "Well, you know, again, in band, with Mr. Dollarhide. It took a while to get him to change. He was this way, this is the way we're going to do it and we're not going to do it any other way. And so we followed him right and left to give in and let us try another way . . . he evolved. It took him a while, but he did it."

Coach Orsmond Jordan:

Coach Jordan told us in an interview, "My father was a high-school principal, and you have to learn to deal with people. You let them have their way, and you have your way. So, that's the way it ought to be. My first year [at Murrah] I taught general science. The next year I taught general math, from then on I taught driver's education, which I was teaching at Brinkley." *He said when he got to Murrah,* "Coach Carlisle tried to make me feel okay. They didn't quite know me, so Coach Carlisle told me, 'We heard about you. We know all about your record and everything. They say you a good football coach. I said, 'They also say I'm a good basketball coach.' And really, I didn't have any problems."

We asked Coach Jordan if he saw any racism on the part of the coaches, and he said it was just competition between coaches trying to encourage players to go for one sport over another. Coach said that Merritt would repeat, "We need to work together."

"I didn't have any problems. Mr. Merritt was our principal, and I got along with him real well . . . he worked along with me. Every principal I had at Murrah I enjoyed, but one. I won't call his name. He didn't like me and I didn't like him. But otherwise, the problem was we could hardly get any white boys to go out for basketball after a couple of years. Couldn't get them to go out . . . I really think it was the black boys were better athletes. That's the way I tried to figure it out. But, most of the black boys went out for football . . . You know if you look at professionals now, you see football and you see basketball almost predominately black . . . But I think what happened is, I guess a lot of parents, they came and looked and said they didn't want their kids going with these blacks. So sooner or later they started going to Jackson Prep, then Manhattan." *He added that sometimes people just want to go to school with those they go to church with or have some familiarity.*

Joe Reiff:

In the fall of 1970 as my junior year began, more change took place. Murrah became an eleventh- and twelfth-grade school, paired with Brinkley (formerly all-black), which was the place for tenth graders in that district. This included the junior highs—in our district Bailey housed seventh and eighth graders, while ninth graders went to Rowan, a formerly black school. That arrangement persisted for a few years; my brother, two years behind me, attended four schools during his secondary education. Many white families responded to this arrangement by sending their kids to private school.

The 1971 Murrah yearbook has about 523 individual student pictures from the junior and senior classes who attended that year; 144 of them (over one-fourth) are black. The senior class includes 60 blacks among 264, while my class includes 84 blacks among 259. Although my class was not affected by the pairing with formerly black schools, almost 200 whites (just over half the class, based on yearbook picture numbers in sophomore and junior years) had departed Murrah for private schools by the fall of 1970 (a few went to Callaway or Central, both public schools, because of redistricting).

I had the most interaction with black students in gym class, and my most vivid memory is something the black guys did on occasion as we were dressing. One would call out "Well!" in a loud voice, and several others would respond with a "Well!" Now I understand this as a variation on the "call and response" phenomenon from the black church, but it was new to me then. It went something like this:

"Well!"	"Well!"
"Yes!!"	"Yes!!"
"Well!"	"Well!"
"Uh huh!"	"Uh huh!"
"Mm hmm!"	"Mm hmm!"
"Yes!"	"Yes!"
"Well!"	"Well!" (repeated a time or two)

It is amusing to recall how bewildered we white boys were by that bit of black culture.

Charles Miller:

My class (unlike the class behind us with you guys, Bob Lampton, Doug Minor, etc.) did not have the unifying experience of going to Brinkley. We had tasted the "old Murrah" of prancing Murrah Misses and Jack Carlisle football glamour; desegregation threatened that Camelot. My classmates ran for the hills to Council Manhattan, Jackson Academy and the beginning of Jackson Prep. A double standard quickly emerged—parents sent their daughters to private schools and their sons to public school, presumably to protect them from the threat of black teenage boys. By the time I graduated, my class's white population was two-thirds male.

I never really had any close black friends at Murrah. My black classmates were virtually unknown as individuals to me. Some certainly stood above the rest and were very likable, a few seemed like thugs, and most were in the anonymous middle (obviously, in hindsight, an exact reflection of my white peers). One of my most memorable experiences at Murrah was being a student assistant in a math class in my junior year, with all the kids being black and mostly seniors. I graded their papers and never will forget how many people added 1/3 and 1/4 and got 2/7, simply by adding the numerators and denominators across to get an incorrect total. It dawned on me—above anything else, many of my black classmates were academic cripples and nothing "magical" happened, or would ever happen, in an integrated Murrah to change that. It was too late for them.

In an interview, John Mixon, Kip Ezelle, Michael Bounds, Johnny Jones, and I discussed bomb threats and variations between the grading scales.

John Mixon: "Well, you know, we had a lot of bomb threats. I don't know if you had them at Brinkley like we did at Murrah."

Johnny: "Yeah. We would get to go home."

Mixon: "We didn't ever get to go home. We just had so many we would parade out in the streets for thirty minutes and then they'd call us back in."

Kip Ezelle: "I do know this. When we went to Brinkley, school was so easy. I remember having, I don't remember his name, but it was tenth-grade history."

Johnny: "Wasn't Krauss, was it?"

Kip: "And I had a 106 average in the class. So the black teacher that I had by the spring part of the year, sixth period, I'd say 'you mind if I go over to the Quick Chick,' which was the convenience store across the street from the school. We'd go over there and get stuff, bring it back to class. Then in the twelfth grade I had Mr. Harris. Y'all remember him? He about killed me. We were doing an experiment, and it was to make . . . I don't remember how it happened, but you never heat a closed system, and of course he didn't particularly tell us that, and we ended up making chlorine gas in the closed system. It blew the top off and I took a full hit of straight chlorine gas. I ended up at the emergency room."

Johnny: "Wow! Damn!"

Kip: "We had to have an epinephrine shot and other stuff like that."

Michael: "Oh my gosh!"

Kip: "I couldn't breathe. But the funniest thing about Mr. Harris, he always did this. His grading scale was 0 to 20 was F, 20 to 40 was a D, 40 to 60 a C, 60 to 80 a B, and 80 to 100 an A. That was from the black schools."

Mixon: "You know what, when the blacks were merged with the whites, they brought their grades from ninth and tenth and the next half a year, two and a half years' worth, and merged them for the next one and a half years. All of a sudden, but I was not a good student, I went from maybe the top half of the class to near the bottom of my graduating class because of their GPA."

Johnny said that he was not aware of this and wondered how he achieved his class rank. "I don't remember learning a thing at Brinkley, except how to type. Ms. Hatton taught me how to type."

Mixon: "I remember shutting down, as far as study wise. I never studied a lot, but it was cruise control the rest of the way on out."

Johnny: "Me too. I didn't open a book the whole time. Did you?"

Mixon: "Naw. My mother couldn't figure out why I never brought any home."

I said, "Then you didn't take Awad's class."

Kip: "No, they didn't take Awad or didn't have Ms. Tramel."

Mixon: "I had Ms. Tramel when I was in the tenth grade."

I said: "She was a good teacher."

Kip: "She was an excellent teacher. She taught all the math courses, all the advanced."

Johnny: "See, I didn't take that."

Kip: "We did have some really good teachers that stuck it out. Whether they were doing it for retirement, I don't know."

Johnny: "There were some really good teachers."

(I cannot verify or remember the grading system comments included here, but I think I received an A in Mr. Harris's chemistry class. It may have—only— been because there was a twenty-point spread. I liked Mr. Harris.)

James Merritt (Parent of Greg Merritt ['74] and Murrah Principal):

"One year he [Greg, his son] was at Rowan. He had a good experience at Rowan. It was kind of a little side deal. I don't know what it was, but Greg and some of his cohorts, a group of about forty or so that went over to Rowan. They were a close-knit group and a lot of good students in it. Some of them doctors and so forth now, a lot of them. They went over to Rowan. I don't know what happened, but there was a German wrestler in Jackson at that time. He used to wrestle down at the coliseum. His name was Waldo Bonair . . . I don't know what happened, but word got out over at Rowan that Greg was Waldo's son. Greg was blond, had a crew cut, and that's exactly what that Waldo looked like. So a lot of the students over there thought Greg was Waldo's son. It got him, the fact that he played football along with his other buddies, was a good student, he did well . . . Well, he did something that was absolutely unreal in that school, where there was a population of forty-some odd or fifty whites to maybe four hundred blacks, Greg was elected Mr. Rowan. At that time, that was unheard of, but a lot of it came because he played football and they thought he was Waldo's son. But he didn't tell anybody differently because that was an end for him. Some of his best buddies still call him Waldo."

Home Life and Mixing of the Races

Narrated by Teena Freeman Horn

■

The seventies were special times. It was an era of great bands and a plethora of music genres, which my children love to listen to today. Like a renaissance, 1970s music was awakening, emotional, and vibrant. We danced often: the monkey, the twist, the swim, the go-go, the pony, and of course the occasional slow dance where shy teens held hands, as adult chaperones monitored the scene. Riverside Park (in Belhaven) was the Saturday hangout, where we picnicked on a blanket and listened to local rock bands. Young boys were drafted and shipped to 'Nam. Perhaps the uncertainty of the seventies is what created the unique and sometimes "wild" expressions of music, style, and social gatherings.

My time at Murrah was from 1971 to 1973. John Bell Williams was the governor of Mississippi, followed by Bill Waller. I met Governor Bill Waller once at a small gathering he hosted in honor of his niece, a classmate.

In 1971, integration of the public schools in Jackson, Mississippi, was an established fact. It was at this period of our high-school experience that we began to socialize outside of our school environment in our homes and community; we had our driver's licenses! I mean, that was the point of forced integration, wasn't it, to mix the races and change the structure of our local society?

This chapter reveals the home life and encounters of both races in a quest to understand each other and just simply be friends. The stereotypes that we previously held toward each other are explored and remembered by my classmates.

Owen Patterson Phillips wrote:

> All my friends had a crush on W. T. He was the football star and the fact that he was black didn't keep us from swooning when he walked by. It *would* probably have kept us from going out with him (if he had even been interested enough to ask).
>
> It was all new: White kids and black kids now together in the halls of a once all-white high school, jostling open lockers between classes, sitting next to each other in class, shoulder to shoulder in the stands at the pep rallies and at the games. We had desegregated. But had we integrated?

134

W. R. was also a football player. I'm not sure I had ever spoken to him, except to say hello in the hall. As I left school one afternoon, he stood on the sidewalk near the student parking lot. I walked past and then stopped, turned around and went back. "Do you need a ride home?" And, he said yes.

His mother had forgotten that there was no football practice that day, he said. He climbed into my Camaro and off we drove. I don't remember if a single word was exchanged. Willie gave me directions as I drove, up Northside Drive, off Watkins Boulevard, down alley-like streets to his home. I pulled up into his drive-way that led behind his home. I was uneasy and I was hoping it didn't show. He thanked me as he got out of the car. But halfway to his door, he called back for me to wait. I assumed he may have left something in the car. He came to my window, I rolled it down; he leaned in and kissed me square on the mouth. And it was a good kiss.

Before I got home, I began to worry. Worry that he might call my house. Worry that he would ask me out. Worry that if he called to ask me out, I would have to say no. And then, it would have been obvious: I was a fraud. I was all talk: About the better days, about the new beginning, about my parents' generation not understanding, about our collective vision. I was all talk and no action.

Only now do I consider how W. R. must have felt. Worry about who I might tell. Worry that his phone may ring late one night or that there would be a knock at his door. But nothing happened. Nothing but the usual hellos in the hall.

I think we were hoping for big changes, very fast. We had desegregated two years earlier. And because there was little chaos and no violence, we thought it had happened; the worst was over. All we had to do was hold ourselves out as the example and the world would see. And I wanted to be brave.

Robert Gibbs: *Interview with Claiborne Barksdale and Johnny Jones:*

Claiborne Barksdale: "What about the dances? Were the dances well attended, completely integrated and the social life outside of school, Robert, when you were a junior or senior?"

Robert: "You know we had a prom at the school my senior year. The prom was at Murrah, in the gym and it was well attended. I had a good time. I don't remember who the band was. We had dances after school and I do not remember any problems with any of those."

Johnny: "No violence at all during your time?"

Robert: "No. I remember, 'cause I was in the band, when the games were over with, we would walk back to the school, put up our instruments, and hang around the school until they told us it was time to go home. It would be everybody, blacks and whites, we all had a good time just hanging out.

Eventually, I guess when they ran us away, there was a McDonalds on Livingston Road and most of the blacks would end up at that McDonalds. I am not sure where the whites ended up. Things kind of segregated as the night went on because we congregated over there as it was closer to where we lived."

Johnny: "Over by the Jackson Mall?"

Robert Gibbs: "Yeah, but we had good times at those events. I know of dancing with white girls at those functions. Nobody thought anything about it. I am sure if Mrs. Ruff had been out there [laughs] then it probably wouldn't have happened. We are not going to have that!" [laughs]

I drove to Birmingham, Alabama, to interview Robert Kelly at his place of business, Kelly Construction. We had not seen each other since high school, yet we shared a mutual respect knowing what we had survived together in the 1970s, and that we were both concerned about our old hometown of Jackson. It was a fun day. I met his staff and brother (also a Murrah graduate) and saw photos of Robert's family. He told me some wonderful stories. Basically, I gave Robert the tape recorder and asked him to recount what he remembered about integration in Jackson, Mississippi.

Robert Kelly:

"One of the great things I got a chance to witness as well in high school, and I think all the other black kids would say the same thing is the fact that we found out that there were basically two worlds. There was our world where we always thought that we were doing pretty good. I wouldn't say that we were poor, but a lot of times we were broke, as a family. But then to be integrated into a school system where you were going to school with some of the richest white folks in the state of Mississippi and get a chance to—I remember going over to Charles's [Irby] house, in Eastover, and I walked in there and I thought I was walking into a movie. I am like damn! [laughs] This place has got to have at least thirty rooms in it. Now I grew up in a three-bedroom house with one bath and I thought we were on top of the world, 'cause the bath was on the inside. But to walk in there and see the help that Charles had—people working there and everything. I remember going outside to the pool and they had a big pool house and big tennis court behind there. It was like one part of the world has no idea how the other part of the world is living. So that was an amazing experience. You would see something like that on TV, but you didn't think that people actually lived like that. For Charles to be as privileged as he was, he was a real cool cat. You never would have known it by just having a conversation with him. I remember that is when I went over and said, 'Man what the hell does your daddy do?' . . . and we never would have experienced that.

"I will never forget going to Jack Ritter's home for a little party or whatever ... It was a two-story house. I'm like my God, this has to be one of the biggest houses I've ever been in before in my life. Now of course I went there before I went to Charles's house, OK. [laughs] This is unbelievable! We were sitting around and things just [were] in place and looked like you had enough room to do something of anything in there. My God I wished ... I would go home and tell my mama, 'You would not believe this house I was in.' I thought that was some fine living, but when we got to Charles's house, I mean come on. His dad had to be one of the richest people in Jackson during that time ...

"We added on to my mama's house and now we got two bathrooms and four bedrooms. It is real nice and I always like going back, but driving into Eastover, I could not believe how big those homes were. I am like, man, this is just unbelievable. From Shady Oaks and Brinkley, you know where just about everybody's home in Jackson, in that part of town is three bedrooms, one bath. Three bedrooms, one bath and like I said on the inside you were doing good. The socioeconomics were just totally different and there were different backgrounds. You know it makes me think of what a guy said about standardized tests years ago. If you asked a kid that lived in Eastover, what was a canopy and they would say, 'that's a cover over a bed.' You ask someone in my neighborhood, they would have said, 'it's a can of pee that's on the bed.' [laughs] That's a big difference. You understand? My grandmother, when I would go to my grandmother's house, who lived in west Jackson, she lived in a shotgun apartment, where you looked through the front door, you could see all the way to the back door and they had outdoor plumbing. That was my grandmother. Now, some of my most memorable days were over there, having a good time, having good meals and just a lot of fun. So as you can imagine, to finally get a chance to walk into Ritter's home and my God, Charles Irby's home—it was mind-boggling."

I said, "It might have set a new standard to strive for."

Robert: "Yeah, jumping in the swimming pool, I remember jumping in the swimming pool over at Charles Irby's house."

Robert and I drove to eat lunch at a Chinese restaurant. He laughed at me, as I tried unsuccessfully to maneuver chopsticks on fried rice. He was much better at the task than I. Interesting were the people that began watching us, as a black man and white woman eating and talking together. Birmingham is a cosmopolitan city, yet some southerners are still curious.

Robert continued as we dined, "You know most of the people in our neighborhood, on Friday and Saturday nights, we were not going out to dinner, eating at restaurants and stuff like that, for a couple of reasons. Number one, really couldn't afford it, number two, we wouldn't have felt too comfortable trying to go into a restaurant for service anyway. You understand what I am saying? It was a thing that black folks just didn't do. You know we weren't going to Primos for Sunday brunch, or going to Primos for dinner. You know Primos . . . I believe it was . . . all those nice little restaurants that you all went to? When we went to a restaurant, when we ordered something, we were ordering off the wall. Do you understand? No menus. We would walk in and stand up and say OK, I'll take that, that, and that, and typically that was the experience. You know the first time I experienced going into the Piccadilly, I think I was like in maybe the tenth grade. I thought that was a wonderful experience, to be able to walk into the Piccadilly, get a tray, get some food, and then sit down and eat and then try to figure out how I was going to pay for it."

"Now I look at my kids today and they just automatically think that it is just normal to go to restaurants and have dinner, and have cocktails and travel and stuff like that, but that wasn't the case when I was in the eighth, ninth, tenth, eleventh, and twelfth grade. I was probably twenty-three years old the first time I got on an airplane. Our families, we didn't do vacations, unless you want to call going to the country to see your kinfolks a vacation and going there and staying a couple of days. We weren't going to Atlanta, or New Orleans or New York to see shows, like you good white folks. Don't talk about going to Europe or places like that! So you know in socioeconomics right now is still one of the things that challenge the school systems in just about every major city to this day. There is a difference, but one of the things I've always tried to say is—embrace those differences. I love the fact that I work and live in a diverse environment. I just love it! I think when people don't embrace it, not only are they gonna find themselves pretty ignorant when it comes to a lot of things, but they miss out on just a very valuable and wonderful experience."

Robert told me about some vacations that he had taken, as an adult, to Europe and other areas. I made known that he was far better traveled than I, having never been to Europe and wishing I could go one day.

Lindy Stevens Clement:

During an interview Johnny Jones and I asked Lindy Clement about her experience with integration.

Lindy: "I felt like our parents deserve a lot of credit—a lot of credit [for supporting public schools]."

Johnny: "I do too. Were your parents, like I described mine, as William Winter Democrats?"

Lindy: "Heck no, Republican . . . my mother's from Smith County!"

Lindy told us that her mother offered to go back to work as a nurse, when the schools changed so that the family could afford Jackson Prep—Lindy declined. "No way, just wasn't for us!" *Lindy also said,* "I didn't want to go to Council schools! They wouldn't let us go to Council schools."

Johnny: "Your parents wouldn't have it?"

Lindy: "No! They [Council schools] were so antiblack . . . It was the Citizens' Council."

I said: "See, I didn't know that back then. And y'all were aware of that?"

Lindy: "Yes, yes. Mom and Daddy were . . . Republicans, I consider them, but any black . . . that ever came into my house, my mother never blinked an eye. And I can remember . . . when they asked them, when I was a junior at Murrah, to chaperone a dance . . . and one of Daddy's tennis buddies or somebody said, 'Well, what are you gonna do when your daughter gets up and she's dancing with a black guy?' And he said, 'Well, knowing Lindy, she already has.'"

Johnny: "Well, you were saying something about you didn't want to go to Prep but you didn't really say why."

Lindy: "I guess the entitlement . . . I feel like for me and my sisters, I wouldn't have the opportunities at Prep because I wasn't moneyed and I didn't have a Jackson name and I'm sorry, back then that mattered."

Johnny: "Sure, it did, and to some extent does now but I hate that, I hate that side of the coin, too, and there was so much of that."

Lindy: "I would have never been captain of the Misses, never, ever, ever! I might . . . would have gotten on!"

We asked Lindy about other interactions she remembered and she said, "I do remember one time . . . we had to go to Bruno's and get our skirts made [for the Murrah Misses] and so Momma and I were picking up a girl to take to Bruno's because she didn't have a ride and when we pulled up in front of a shotgun house. I mean that kinda hit home for me. And Momma said, 'you know, I'm gonna figure out a way to pay for her skirt.'" *She also mentioned:* "I know when we went to the beach, none of the [black] Misses could swim."

Freddie Funches:

Freddie gave a couple of interviews. I am so grateful that he was willing to give us his story.

Freddie: "I left school when I was in the twelfth grade."

I said: "You did? Where did you go?"

Freddie: "I went out a got me a job."

I replied: "I was thinking you stayed the whole time."

Freddie: "No, no. They just projected me to be in the '73 class because that's what I woulda finished in. School was fun and everything . . . but there was a life after school, and I think I was preparing to get to that because my mom was single and was raising us on her own and I saw a lot of things that she had to do for us as a single parent. I didn't like seeing her having to go that hard, doing all that. I just asked her one day. She didn't want me to do it, but at nineteen years old, she didn't say nothing else about it. So, I went out and got me a job, just helping out. You know, getting things for myself, taking a lot of pressure off her. I just got outta there . . . I was trying to prepare myself for the life after school. Like I said, I had a great time with the people that I dealt with at that particular time, and I still deal with them, but school wasn't the one that made me; I made myself—the kind of person that I was. The personality that I had, the people really rallied around who I was."

I asked: "Did you go back and get your GED?"

Freddie: "Yeah, I did."

I asked: "Did you go to college any?"

Freddie: "No, no. You know what? I didn't wanta go to college because I wasn't college material. I didn't want to feel like going to study no more. I had enough of school going through there as it was. But I just didn't have the energy, nor the focus because everybody is not college material."

I said: "Yeah."

Freddie: "And if you're going there for the right reasons, that's one thing, but if you're just going there to let somebody know that you've been to college, you just wasting your time, your momma's time, and all the kind of money. I didn't want to do that."

I asked: "Do you think most of your friends did or did not go to college?"

Freddie: "I think some of them went two years."

I questioned: "Like Hinds [Community College] or something?"

Freddie: "I think Hinds was the preferable school that they went to for a couple of years."

Kathy Phillips recalls,

> I did have black friends and vividly remember asking my parents if one could come over to our house and my parents' response was, "no, what would the neighbors think?" I did have a meeting at my house for one of the plays I was in and didn't tell my parents (oops, I forgot to mention it) that some of the cast was black. My friends and I went to eat, to movies and to other people's houses together.

Kathy said that she had not been in touch with anyone from Murrah since she left high school.

Adrienne Day wrote:

Most of my friends of other races were school buddies. I did not see them outside of school and I think that it had to do more with proximity than anything else. They lived too far away from my neighborhood and I did not have access to a car until my senior year. I had a group of close-knit friends that lived close to me that I saw more often. My responsibilities for my younger brother and sister and my part-time job kept me busy with not much time for social functions and extra-curricular activities. There was always drama in my home life. During this time, my parents had a lengthy separation and divorce and my beloved older brother was serving in Vietnam. His safety and well-being was in my thoughts daily.

Betsy Grimes Triggs:

The first time she [Cassandra] spent the night at our house, it really tested my mother's liberalism. Having a black girl sleep, eat, bathe, and use the bathroom as an equal in her house was almost too much for her. It helped me realize how deep racism can run even if intellectually you realize it is wrong. It seems so strange now, but just riding around with her in her VW bug could be dangerous. We regularly got dirty looks from both white and black people, sometimes worse.

Joe Reiff:

My parents were active members of Jacksonians for Public Education then, and that organization sponsored a campaign to convince white families to stay in the public schools, including a bumper sticker which said, "We're Sticking." One day during the 1969 Christmas holidays, my brother and I and Mike Stevens, my Murrah classmate and fellow Galloway Methodist youth member, stood at the gates of a factory at the shift change time to hand out those bumper stickers to anyone who would accept one. My family displayed the sticker on our cars.

Group Interview

During an interview, Johnny Jones, John Mixon, Michael Bounds, and Kip Ezelle discussed the Murrah social situation before and after integration.

Johnny: "About that Murrah football team, while we're talking about all this, when Kip and I and Jerry and all of us were growing up, we'd go stand out behind the gym at Murrah, and when the team would come out to jog across the campus, go across that curvy road and down across that foot path up to the stadium, we would run alongside the team and look at those hulking, great big football players and then the coaching staff and then dads and sponsors. And boy that team hit the field and you'd hear 'aaaaah.'"

Kip: "Then we'd climb over the fence while the National Anthem was being played." [laughs]

Johnny: "We never paid. It was glorious . . . you know. That was the glory that we knew growing up, was this beautiful, great football team and the most beautiful women you ever saw in your life."

Mixon: "All intimidating."

Johnny: "Yeah, but also that was the only expectation I ever had."

Michael: "That's what we all aspired to do."

Johnny: "I don't remember wanting anything else, you know."

Michael: "Yeah."

Johnny: "And when the time we got there, there was a lot of people that were real angry that the integration thing took away that."

Kip: "That's true."

Mixon: "Yeah, that's right. We got robbed of it."

Johnny: "A lot of people thought that. By the time I got there, I was happy, but earlier I wouldn't have been."

Kip: "Yeah."

Johnny: "But it was funny the way it changed everybody's expectation. It certainly made, I think, all of us better."

Mixon: "But you know, Bailey, before integration, was just like Murrah was. It was the same way. There was a huge hierarchy."

Johnny: "Yeah, all those that lived in Woodland Hills and Eastover were all up here."

Mixon: "Yeah, they were on the A team. You got to the B team, you felt like you had done something because they would talk to you but that was about it."

Johnny: "That's right. It was a funny world, but that world is gone. Maybe they have reinvented it."

Mixon: "That world carried over to Murrah my tenth-grade year, and once you got to Murrah you knew you weren't going to be on the A team, but you'd still be happy that you could make it to that next level."

Johnny: "Yes indeed. That's right."

Mixon: "Then when Murrah integrated, it was gone."

Johnny: "It was."

Mixon: "It was kind of refreshing."

Johnny: "That's what I'm saying. I liked it much better."

Mixon: "Yeah."

Johnny: "But by that time, we all had a little bit more expectation than just wearing clothes from Persons."

Mixon: "Right."

Johnny: "Remember that place?"

Mixon: "Yep. My mother would go get my shirt and bring it home, I never went in there hardly. Good ole mom."

Johnny: "I went in there and bought something one time. In the eighth grade, well, I picked out something with my mother and came home, and I didn't get it for Christmas. I opened up my Christmas present and there was stuff from McRae's there, it wasn't from Person's. I said, 'what is the deal?' She said, 'well, I could get two pair of shoes for what you wanted me to pay for one pair of shoes at Person's.' I said, 'MOM!' She bummed me out for about ten minutes and then I sat there and told her she was right."

Claiborne Barksdale (teacher in '71–'72 and '68 Murrah graduate) wrote:

This, then, was my life in the Jackson that I grew up in: Relative privilege, relative comfort, and awareness of the realities on the black side of town but little sleep loss about it. I suppose I was a bit more sensitized than the norm. I knew about the Freedom Riders, Pettus Bridge bloody Sunday, the four black girls in "Bombingham." During Murrah Singers one day after lunch I argued in favor of integration with a Christian friend who used the old red chickens/white chickens argument (you remember—birds of a feather, etc.), pointing out to him, aptly I thought, that we were not chickens. (I must confess that I had an inkling that this "liberal" stance might appeal to some of the "liberal" girls in the class; it did.) My closest encounter to the movement occurred one Saturday night in the eleventh grade when a friend and I were the first to come upon the Kotichky's house on Poplar Boulevard in Belhaven shortly after it had been bombed, cross still burning, because they had let Yankee trouble-makers stay there. I detested and was embarrassed by Barnett and the white Citizens' Council. But, for me, the smugness, selfishness and self-dealing, the cruelty, discrimination, enforced poverty, hypocrisy—mostly religious—and utter stupidity of white Jackson, Mississippi, didn't trouble me too greatly. And while I was certainly aware of the vast discrepancy between Bailey and Murrah versus Brinkley and Jim Hill, the sparkling football equipment and the new textbooks we had versus the tattered gear and books they had (separate and profoundly unequal) I did nothing about it and went my merry way. Sure, I could get mad about the blatantly racist idiocy that the *Clarion-Ledger* and *Jackson Daily News* spouted, especially Tom Ethridge, that hackneyed, race-baiting columnist, and the simple-minded twit—his name mercifully escapes me—who drew the cartoon every afternoon featuring "Lefty

Wing" with his beret and cigarette holder. But these were essentially mere annoyances that were tangential to the more important questions about whether I had a date, what should I wear, would the Mustangs win the game that week. The normal adolescent concerns. The issue of race and our collective inhumanity did not appear directly to affect me, and I was too blind to see that of course they affected me, just as they still affect all of us to this day.

When I went to Ole Miss, my eyes were opened a bit, but Ole Miss was so conservative and so racially segregated when I went there that I emerged essentially unscathed three years later. (And, I should point out, about seventy Murrah graduates from 1968 migrated the 167 miles to Ole Miss; think "Murrah-North.") I debated the issues of race and religion and Vietnam and read a lot and studied a little, ran with a liberal crowd, at least by Ole Miss standards. But, still, I remained uninvolved and, unfortunately, largely unevolved.

Some of my favorite places to frequent during the 1970s in Jackson were Brent's Drug Store, in the Fondren area; it was the place to go for a hamburger and milk shake after school. Both races went to Shoney's on Northside Drive after football games, which at that time was located on the very northern edge of Jackson. Dennery's, Primos, LeFleur's and the Mayflower were popular Jackson restaurants.

Gas was cheap during my high-school years. One could drive all over town for a dollar or two. I rode my bike from my house to the reservoir, which was several miles away. Time after school was spent studying, working (I always had some type of job), or attending Bible studies and social functions where we hung out with the white north Jackson kids from Prep, Manhattan, or Callaway. We were in Sub-Debs together and attended these dances and each other's proms.

I remember one evening when I had a date with a boy who attended Jackson Prep. We went to Poet's, a local restaurant and bar. There was a band playing that great '70s music and I happened to pass by a black football player from my school, Freddie Funches. I gave him a hug and danced just a little bit of one song with him. My date and the couple that came along on our double-date were appalled at my behavior and basically wouldn't speak to me the rest of the night. I was a little shocked at this shunning reaction. I don't think I had ever seen that type of rejection—prejudice, with someone I thought I knew, until that moment. Growing up in the same town, with totally different viewpoints – we never went out again.

The Murrah students generally liked one another and had some weekend gatherings at each other's homes. Once, in high school, I attended a Halloween party at the residence of a black football player who lived across the railroad tracks. This was an area deemed "off-limits" by my mother, and she opposed my going. I can remember being a little shaky as I walked alone from my car to the house, thinking, "What am I doing here?" Upon entering the party, everyone was glad to see me, and we enjoyed good southern food and danced to songs like the "Monster Mash." It seemed we were testing our limits in reaching beyond the usual racial mixing boundaries that existed in our minds. But, generally I stayed in my own familiar north Jackson neighborhood.

Jerome Barkum was a football player for the New York Jets, and for some reason he helped us at Murrah High School during his off-season. We used to pester him about getting us a date with Joe Namath, his famous teammate. When I later went to college at Mississippi State University, he came to see me while visiting his brother, who was a State football player. I recall being called down to the lobby of my dorm to see a "visitor" and there he was, Jerome. He was a very handsome black man, and I ran to give him a hug. I remember the crowd of white girls watching us conversing, as if talking to a black man were taboo. We talked for a long time, and then he left, but all the wondering eyes were still on me. I did not say a word, just smiled and went back to my room. It was obvious that I had learned more at Murrah High School about racial interaction and tolerance than most of the girls in my dormitory had ever been exposed to at that time.

During my 1971 to 1973 years at Murrah, all of us mixed together, at school, without the usual socioeconomic barriers that deterred friendship. As John Mixon said about this change, versus the previous social hierarchy that had existed at Murrah, "It was kind of refreshing."

Teachers at Murrah

Alan Huffman

■

We had an odd assemblage of teachers, both black and white, including some of the best and worst products of both former school systems. Some, like Mrs. Jackson and Mr. Barksdale, reinforced the feeling that we were a part of something exciting and new.

Mrs. Jackson was a witty, erudite algebra teacher; Mr. Barksdale (elsewhere referred to as Claiborne) was a smart and inspiring English teacher only a few years older than us, who was also the sponsor of our literary magazine, *Pleiades*. Then there was Mrs. Gibson, the journalism teacher, who took our class to a convention in Chicago on the train, where we mostly got drunk and met Liza Minelli and James Caan at our hotel.

Mrs. Revels and Mrs. Canterbury were history teachers whose innovative methods included letting us learn at our own pace in "learning centers" made out of old refrigerator boxes that we decorated, which did not turn out to be such a great idea. Herr Lowe, the German teacher, took our class to a German film festival in New Orleans that turned out to be mostly soft-porn, which prompted him to strike a deal with us whereby he let us loose, unchaperoned, in the French Quarter, if we would not tell our parents what had happened. Because the statute of limitations has expired, I can say that the film which prompted the late Herr Lowe to stand up and say, "Let's go," featured a farm boy who reached his hand into another farm boy's pants and said, "Laßt uns sehen, was du da unten bekommen!"(which we could understand!), and which translated: "Let's see what you've got down there!" Herr Lowe jumped to his feet and began herding us all out of the theater. We all had a huge time that night in the Quarter, thanks to those German farm boys.

Most of my own teachers were very good, and one of the worst was actually a holdout from the ancien regime. It would be a stretch to say that Murrah was a social or academic model, but it was most assuredly educational, and for the most part, in a good way. The all-white public schools had been strict; Murrah's administration, headed by Mr. Merritt, sought mostly just to maintain order, but somehow we learned a lot about life and its basic disciplines in the process.

Because so many students were chronically late, for whatever reasons, students were allowed up to three unexcused tardies a week, which meant that you could arrive as late as 10 a.m. without being held accountable. As at Council Manhattan, where my friends and I had exploited the chaos by skipping school, my carpool at Murrah abused the tardy policy. Rather than report directly to school in the morning, we would go for long car rides out in the country, or to the IHOP for extended breakfasts, three times a week, arriving at the attendance office just before the 10 a.m. cutoff. Our parents were unaware that we were doing this, of course, and Mrs. Stewart, the attendance officer, was powerless to stop us.

One day we were having so much fun that we decided not to go to school at all, and each member of my carpool found someone—an older brother or older friend—to call in and represent themselves as their mother or father, to report that they were sick and would stay home that day. It was a ridiculous notion, because our carpool was already notoriously untrustworthy, and what were the odds that we would all get sick on the same day? But we were testing the limits. I was the only one who couldn't find anyone to call in for me, so I called Mrs. Stewart myself. She wasn't buying. As soon as we got off the phone she called my house and spoke with my mother. We all got caught.

I remember Mr. Merritt, the principal, telling us afterward that he was going to let it go. We suspected it was because we were remnants of the "old" Murrah, which is to say, white students of generally upstanding families. We were needed. We made good grades. We were on the *Hoofbeat* newspaper staff. We were still more or less privileged. "If I can't depend on students like you," Mr. Merritt said, pausing to emphasize the words, "who can I depend on? I'm going to let you off this time, but if this ever happens again, it's going to be too wet to plow."

Our getting off with only a warning sent a minor ripple through the student body, mostly among other students who had been punished for skipping school, but we now felt a new sense of pride: We were cool because we went to public school, and we were favored by the powers that be for the same reason. We had the best of both worlds. Looking back, I think Mr. Merritt would have reacted the same way if we'd been black students from upstanding families who made good grades and got caught skipping school, just that once, because he seemed like a fair man. But at the time we felt like we were golden.

While my group was enjoying a decidedly self-absorbed senior year, Reginald Rigsby was a sophomore pulling out all the stops academically. By the time some of our less-motivated classmates graduated from high school, he was graduating from medical school. Reginald wrote in his essay that Murrah had a special mystique for him going as far back as the year of court-ordered integration, when he was among forty black students at Bailey Junior High. He was surprised that during his three years at Murrah he had only three black teachers—Mr. Harold Moman, for geometry; Mrs. Gloria Dyson, for biology; and Madame Eva Prater, for French. The three were excellent teachers, he recalled.

"My most negative teacher experience would definitely be a white teacher who assigned the few black students in the classroom to sit in one row and she rarely looked our direction when she taught the classroom," he wrote. "I now understand as an adult that it was a product of the times." It was as if the teacher had refused to even acknowledge that the black students existed. Likely she was just holding on for retirement.

"I know that the education which I received at Murrah was top notch and prepared me for my career," Reginald wrote. "Murrah's diversity at that time allowed me to really understand the Jewish culture and Catholic beliefs; interact with the rich and the poor; but more importantly learn something about me through my relationship with my classmates." He graduated from Murrah at age sixteen and entered an accelerated BS-MD program at Howard University in Washington, DC, which allowed him to graduate from college at age nineteen and graduate from medical school at age twenty-three.

"During all the years of attending integrated public schools, there were only a few times I thought I was subtly being hassled, not threatened physically, but people doing things to me just because I was black," wrote Fred Sheriff, who was our class president in 1973. "I felt one or two teachers may have treated me different because I was black. Again, this is how I felt; whether it was true or not, I don't know. Actually, the most overt acts of intimidation toward me (which basically included tough talk) came from black people, not white ones. From what I understood via (black) friends at other high schools, we at Murrah had it easy as far as the races getting along. Another classmate observed that was due, in part, to the school administration—principal, assistant principals, and others. At the time I didn't appreciate how well they performed under difficult circumstances; now I do."

Teena remembers the teachers at Murrah being "innovative and unprejudiced, in my eyes. I remember that Mrs. Massey taught me everything I ever needed to know about singing harmony and correct pronunciation in my Murrah Singers class. We sang together at some local events and were proud of our group accomplishments. Mrs. Canterbury taught me about playing the stock market. She set up mock scenarios of world events and gave us a set amount of time to invest. Rule of thumb was, 'When things are bad, the sales of booze and cigarettes go up.'"

"Mr. Barfield," known by his students as "Magister"—Latin for "teacher"—was "a kind and mild-mannered man [who] taught me Latin," Teena recalled. "Even though we goofed around in his class, I found years later that Latin was the root of our vocabulary. It helped me in college and specifically in gross anatomy. Mr. Awad was my excellent biology teacher. He made me memorize the Krebs Cycle and Embden-Meyerhof Pathway. I recall my father helping me master these pathways as they were confusing. Mr. Awad said, 'Just learn it, as you have to know it.' He was right. It showed up again in college many times. I later majored in biology because it made sense to me.

"Mrs. Tramel, my advanced math teacher, prepared me well for the basic college math classes . . . I remember Mr. Claiborne Barksdale as being a great English teacher, but I did not learn much in his class because instead of listening to his words, I was watching his every move. A recent graduate from Ole Miss and student from the 'old Murrah,' he had a unique style and sense of class. When he spoke to us, it was as if his mind were in some ethereal world far away from Murrah High School. I noted the clothes he wore, the way he wore his hair, and everything about him, except the subject he was teaching. My friends and I had a teenage crush on Mr. Barksdale. We even had to compile our notes for a test because we were all too distracted to write information down while he was walking around the class. Our 'so fine' teacher made it hard to concentrate. Mr. Barksdale was professional and only wanted to teach us; he did not even notice that all the girls were crazy about him."

Mary Al Cobb had a similar memory, though it had the opposite effect on her studies. In her essay, she wrote, "There were several strong teachers at Murrah and the administration did its best to maintain Murrah's academic standards. I developed a schoolgirl crush on a young English teacher who had recently graduated from Ole Miss. I never studied as hard as I did in Claiborne Barksdale's class! He was enthusiastic and charismatic and continued the strong English tradition at Murrah. Murrah's newspaper, the *Hoofbeat*, afforded many of us an opportunity to experience the challenging world of journalism and I recall an exciting train trip to Chicago to attend a national journalism convention for high-school students. After reviewing several copies of the *Hoofbeat*, I must say the administration afforded us many journalistic liberties not allowed in high-school newspapers today."

When Murrah's student body was forcibly integrated, midway through the 1969–1970 school year, Bee Donley was an English teacher there. The teachers had heard that some of them would be reassigned to formerly all-black schools for the second semester, but, "I was sure I would not be among them,"

Donley wrote in an essay for this book. "I was senior class sponsor, sponsor of the yearbook, sponsor of the literary magazine, and senior English teacher." Then, she wrote, "On Jan. 26, 1970, a letter came telling me to report to Brinkley High School on Jan. 27, 1970, for a faculty meeting. I cried in every room at Murrah, not about going to Brinkley but because I loved Murrah, my students, and the never dull day-to-day pleasure of teaching. On Feb. 6, 1970, I began a challenging and remarkable semester at an all-black school."

As it turned out, Mrs. Donley found her experience at Brinkley rewarding. She took over the junior and senior English classes of a teacher who had been reassigned to Murrah, and a student who was the leader of a Black Angel motorcycle gang walked her to her car each afternoon when she departed for Murrah to meet with the yearbook staff. "I never felt I needed protection but this kindness was typical," Donley wrote. "These students had become very dear to me and their response to me was always positive."

As the school year came to a close, teachers were told Brinkley would be only a tenth-grade center for the 1970–1971 school year. Donley went to the central office to see where she might be teaching, and was told there were no vacancies at Murrah, where she wanted to go. She was referred to a man in the office who was starting "a school for academic excellence," which turned out to be a white-flight private school. She took a job there, but "felt as if I had betrayed my Brinkley students," she wrote. "I did not last long there; however, now that school actively recruits black students." She took a job at St. Andrew's Episcopal School, and taught there until she retired.

"I cherish my small part in integrating a black school," she wrote. "Were there better ways to handle the integration? Of course. But I do think we learned much from each other. I am happy I had that very special time with very special students."

Claiborne Barksdale had graduated from Murrah in 1968 and returned there to teach in 1971, after finishing college early. A decade before, when his older brother graduated, Murrah had had the highest percentage of national merit finalists of any public school in the United States. When Claiborne graduated there were three or four black students in a class of 335, but by the time he returned as a teacher, the student body was about 60 percent black and 40 percent white. He said that because he planned to go to Law School, he took the teaching job to save money for a year.

In an essay he wrote for this project, Claiborne noted that when he returned to Murrah, he was "twenty years old, poorly mustachioed, worse dressed, shorter than many of my students, younger perhaps than some, soon to be married, three years removed as a student stumbling through those hallowed halls."

During his teacher orientation, prior to the beginning of the school year, he found the other teachers, black and white, upbeat about Murrah's potential. "All in all," he wrote, "it turns out that that optimism was completely justified. There were a handful of troubling incidents, but nothing that major." There was, he said, "an amazing lack of tension in the school." He said he developed a rapport with all his students. "The only semi-racial encounter I had with one of my students was when I made Hercules Parker tuck his shirt in," he wrote. "That made him angry and I think he thought about hitting me."

Claiborne was a favorite among students not only because he was young and cool, but because he made learning about English literature interesting. He was inspired, and so, he inspired. In his essay, he does not seem to recognize these things, describing himself as "a very poor teacher."

He wrote: "While some benefited from the discussions of *Look Homeward, Angel* and *The Catcher in the Rye* and *I Know Why the Caged Bird Sings*, much more could have been taught—grammar, writing, American literary history—and learned in my classroom. Looking back, I learned more from my students than they learned from me. I squandered this opportunity and I offer my very belated apologies to the students and to their parents whom I shortchanged. I have carried this with me for well-nigh forty years now and will continue to carry it with me. I am very fortunate, as partial expiation, to be involved with a reading institute that focuses on poor children in Mississippi, trying to give them the fundamental, essential skill of reading. We are making progress, but we have a long, long way to go."

Our principal, Mr. Merritt, had been at Murrah since the school's doors opened, or, as he put it in his interview for this book, "When they laid that first layer of bricks is when I came." He had coached track and football and taught history at Central High School for two years before Murrah opened in 1955—the year most of our class was born. At Murrah he was head football and track coach for six years, after which he became principal, in 1961, a job he held until 1979, when he went to work in JPS administration until retiring in 1989.

Mr. Merritt recalled that Murrah "had a great reputation of being one of the top high schools anywhere. In fact, *Time* and one of the other, *Newsweek* maybe, national publications had an article that listed Murrah as one of the top thirty-eight high schools in the country. Well, people wondered about that, but it came primarily because of the number of national merit finalists and semi-finalists. During that time, we always had a large number of finalists and semi-finalists. Even, I remember being contacted in one of the early years when I was principal, by the Bronx High School in New York City, which was a magnet school for science and math people from all over New York City. I got a telephone call from them wondering how in the world we had so many national merit finalists and semi-finalists and scholarship winners. At that time, we were having normally twenty or thirty. One time we had over thirty. The reason for that is we had great students.

"When you think about it a little bit, at that time we had students of most of the professional people in Jackson. You had people associated with medical school. You had people associated with Millsaps and Belhaven [colleges], the business community, and so forth, and we had a great staff. You put those two together with the community support. And we had great community support. We could get anything done that was practical and good because we had people that knew what to do and could get it done, so we just had one of those unique type of situations where you take good students, good staff, and good community support. You put those three things together and you're gonna have a good school. We were just fortunate, and I have people come up to me all the time now and say how in the world did we have that. I said you were in a privileged situation. And then that changed as we went through the massive desegregation deal."

Linda Hardy also taught at Brinkley, but returned to Murrah in 1972, and taught history there until her retirement. During the first year of court-ordered integration she was a substitute teacher. Her recollection of Brinkley was different from Bee Donley's. Having almost one thousand tenth-graders under one roof posed a lot of problems, she said. "I know there was a white group who had a list of black kids that they were after and a black group who had a list of white kids that they were after," she said. "We had an incident where I remember they told us to get in our classrooms and lock our doors. I don't know what had happened exactly, but I do know they had knocked the water fountains off the wall and water was running down the hall. At the end of that year, they wouldn't let the kids come in the building. They opened windows, and we handed their report cards out the windows."

Hardy, who graduated from Central in 1961, said she remembered that Murrah "was the country club of schools then. Rich children went here." Teena, who interviewed her at the school, noted that when she visited in 2010 the students seemed disciplined and well behaved, to which Hardy, who was still teaching there, said, "Here? Now?" She said that in her view the school's disciplinary problems had grown worse over time.

In her opinion, some of the concerns of parents about Murrah today are justified. There are fights, and there is drug dealing, and in 1991 there was a murder in one of the boys' restrooms, she said. The school is now grades 9–12, and, "The ninth grade is our biggest problem," she said. Then she said, "What did Greg tell you? He teaches AP biology, so he sees a better caliber of kids than I do." Teena said the teacher, Greg Powell, said his students were not aware that Murrah had ever been different. "They think Murrah has always been like this," she said.

"They do!" Hardy said. "And they look in the annual. It's real funny, because when I did the yearbook, I had access to all, well, I still do have some of the other annuals, and like, I would show them the first one. I have it. And they would start looking for black teachers, not realizing, you know, there weren't any here then, in 1955 . . . '56."

Powell, a science teacher at Murrah today in 2011, said the lack of racial diversity at Murrah is a result of the loss of "critical mass" among white students. Once that loss occurred, the white students became entrenched in private or suburban public schools and, "it's hard to get it back from that point." The biggest challenge, he said, is the city's middle schools, which have problems as a result of mixing children with teenagers, and to minimize that, underachieving students tend to be promoted even if their grades are bad to avoid having sixteen-year-olds in classes with eleven-year-olds. So many parents pull their kids out of public schools after elementary school, and they never make it to Murrah, he said.

Those sorts of things were happening when we were at Murrah, too, but perhaps not to the same extent. Everyone remembers the black student who was white-washed by a group of black students, but other incidents seem to be remembered only by those who experienced them firsthand—students such as Barry Dent, who said he had a gun put to his head in the restroom, and Amelia Reagan Wright, who blamed one of her teachers, who she declined to name, for a very traumatic experience at Murrah—when she was sexually molested in biology class while the teacher was at the tennis courts watching matches, having left the class unattended. "I was the only white person in that biology class," Amelia wrote. "Even my lab partner, with whom I thought there was trust (I'll always remember her because I thought she and I connected as friends), did not come to my defense. The classroom doors (front and back) were held shut/barred by classmates while a black male attempted to sit in my lap and grope my body. I ran from the room when the front door was finally unbarred.

"My biology teacher returned to class just before the ending bell. He reported/turned me in for skipping class that afternoon. Of course, that issue had to be cleared up the next morning before being allowed to come back to any of my classes that day. When I told my biology teacher what had happened in his absence and who had intimidated, groped, and bullied me, he was appalled. He should have been. In today's world, that would result in a major lawsuit. Never were my parents told about that incident. I was afraid to do that because I didn't want to be different, and I was also afraid that they would uproot me, making me attend another school with it being so close to my graduation (less than one year away). I didn't want to stand out or cause trouble.

"It was the teacher's fault, and it was the fault of everyone else in the class. Those students were considered to be my classmates and friends—people I could trust, being more than just peers. How could they allow such an incident to occur? However, they thought it was entertaining and funny. The recalling of their laughs and jeers are very hurtful and not understandable, then and now.

"My biology teacher confronted the offending student the day the skipping situation was reported and solved. Later that day, the aggressor told me that I was a 'lying white bitch.' That incident is a very bad memory of Murrah days; however, I do have an abundance of more pleasant memories. There are so many, and I wish there were a way to elaborate on each one, but that would take too much text most would not be willing to read. I could write pages and pages of conversations, occasions, parties, etc., but it would be a laborious task for anyone to read."

Still, she said it galled her to see the alleged molester at class reunions.

Powell, who graduated from Murrah in 1991, and is white, said that just as white parents manipulated the system to get their children into Murrah, black parents of high-achieving students now use the school's APAC program to enroll them there. It's more about socioeconomic than racial integration now, Powell said. Murrah has a mix of black students of different family income levels, and of low and high achievers. "Part of the measure of a good school is being able to take kids that could have turned out nonproductive or not that exceptional and over the course of four years turning them into really well educated people who are going to college," he said. "And Murrah is the best school in the state of Mississippi in that regard—from what we get to what we graduate, the value added, put on it, is enormous."

That was true when we were there, and it was because of the teachers. The difference now is the racial makeup of the student body. In many ways Murrah today is like it was before our time—essentially segregated, with high-quality education. It's just black instead of white.

Common Ground:
Murrah Sports and Traditions

John Griffin Jones

■

The first nonfiction book I can recall reading all the way through was *Murrah Football Facts: Mustangs* (one for each year; e.g., *Mustangs '70*). It was an impressive production, a seven-and-one-half-by-five-and-one-half-inches, professionally bound booklet on glossy paper. Every year's cover featured a color shot of Coach Jack Carlisle and the captains for the upcoming season, unhelmeted in their Beatle bangs except for a few buzz-cut throwbacks, usually linemen, each wearing the royal-blue-and-silver Mustang game uniform drawn on the classic pattern of the Baltimore Colts. Its fifty-odd pages contained in Coach Carlisle's urgent writing style predictions for the coming season, summaries position by position, head shots of each player with a short paragraph of vital statistics and Coach's observations about the player's past performances and areas for improvement, concluding with what the team needed from the player to prevail over the hard season ahead. Because it was as much about the winning tradition of Murrah football as the coming season, the last half of the book contained year-by-year records going back to the first team when the school opened in 1955, detailed statistics from the previous season, "Murrah Individual Records" in every category, then action shots of the storied alumni as Mustangs under the headings "Our Pros," "High-School All-Americans," "All-Star Mustangs," ending with photos of the captains of each team and a listing of "Mustang Lettermen Year by Year." In northeast Jackson where I grew up, it mattered if your name was on that list. Paid for by the "Murrah Booster Club," whose names and contributions were prominently displayed, it conveyed something of Coach Carlisle's "Mustang Creed" of excellence:

> Under Coach Carlisle's leadership, Murrah has become the standard for every
> high school in the State. "Beat Murrah" is the universal cry, and even though each
> adversary has known the futility of this hope, the challenge has become so great

that the effort means almost as much as the actual success. The won-loss record that he has compiled is one of the best in the entire South. However, this tells only part of his success at Murrah. The tradition of excellence that he has developed in his football teams has touched every other activity in the school curriculum. It sets the pattern for excellence in the entire school.

All true. In the 1960s Murrah had the highest percentage of national merit scholars of any school of similar size in the state, winning traditions in the other major sports of the time—basketball, baseball, especially Coach Carlisle's track teams—and more. The yearly stage productions under choral-music director Karen Gilfoy showcased the best amateur theater in the state. In her prime during the 1960s, Karen was Mississippi's premier actress/singer/comedienne before becoming in the 1970s its top criminal appellate lawyer before Governor Winter appointed her to the trial bench in Hinds County in 1982; she was also a very close friend of my mother's and a major influence in my life. We saw every performance of "The Sound of Music" production at Murrah in 1965 or 1966, and, in my memory at least, it was superior to the Hollywood version with Julie Andrews.

In those years Murrah provided opportunities that could not be found anywhere else in the state. It was okay for a popular girl or an athlete to be in the theater production or a member of the "Murrah Thespians" or in the Murrah Singers, or in the Latin Club, playing on stage with your string quartet or garage band, writing for the school paper, the *Hoofbeat*, and poetry or short stories for the yearly publication *The Pleiades*, appropriately named for the seven heavenly sisters of Greek mythology, for true goddesses in their prime walked those halls. If a high-school kid was willing to take the lead, as all were encouraged to do regardless of her or his individual talent, Murrah provided a stage, a place for that kid to thrive, maybe even star. Many did. In our time the extended trophy case in the entrance foyer reflected the accomplishments from what seemed even then a far-off time in dusty trophies, faded-to-colorless ribbons, dingy photos, and newspaper articles about sports primarily but cultural and academic achievements as well. All that talent and beauty came from a relatively small cluster of white neighborhoods extending toward the northeast from the school in the general direction of white migration since World War II. Each year the school was stocked with mid-baby boom kids who lucked into leadership from the faculty and coaches that was superior in every area of endeavor. Without question, however, the public face of Murrah's tradition of excellence was the football team.

Between the first season in 1955 through 1960, under Coach Jim Merritt (who entered administration and was Murrah's principal for twenty-five years, providing badly needed guidance during radical desegregation), Murrah had one winning season. But beginning with his 8-1-2 team in 1961 through his final season in 1970, Coach Carlisle and his great coaching staff made Murrah the class of high-school football in Mississippi. His teams won two "Big 8" championships, the tough city championship five times, and over ten seasons compiled an overall record of 78 wins and 18 losses, with a remarkable 9 ties. If the anomalous 1968 season (for reasons still debated, that team went 5-5) is omitted, Murrah's record under Coach Carlisle was 73 wins against just 13 losses. For a school with a student body averaging around twelve hundred in tenth through twelfth grades, playing against much larger high schools serving entire cities as well as four other white city schools of comparable size drawing the best athletes from their surrounding neighborhoods, consistent achievement like that has no historical parallel of which I'm aware. The only program to come close was boys' basketball at Murrah from 1971 through 1993 under Coach Orsmond Jordan.

Coach Carlisle's last Murrah team in 1970 went 10-1, the only loss coming on a rain-soaked (most who were there recall that the water came from sources other than the heavens, slowing our smash-mouth running game) field in Greenville. At least twelve seniors from that team received major-college football scholarships; of those, six became starting players for Ole Miss and other Southeastern Conference schools. Counting the juniors who signed with Division I schools in 1972, the 1970 team produced eleven players, a full starting team, who went on to major college programs. Those who remember that team consider it the best ever to take the field wearing the blue and silver: the silver helmet with the blue horseshoes over the earholes, wide blue stripe down each gray pant leg, small numbers on the shoulders, long white socks, black Riddell cleats covered to varying degrees with white athletic tape, standard two-bar face masks like Bart Starr's supplemented by a few cages for starting linemen—a *uniform*, without flourish (single numbers were considered hot-doggish and were not allowed) but all class. Yet because of desegregation—more accurately, the white response to it—the '70 team was also Coach Carlisle's last at Murrah.

My brother Jimmy played on '69 and '70 teams. A pulmonologist and critical-care physician in Jackson now, he usually sums up his career the same way: "As a high-school football player, I was a pretty good tackling dummy and future doctor." Coach Carlisle listed him in programs at "5'9", 145 lbs.," but he wasn't. Counting the horn-rimmed glasses he wore under his helmet because he had to, Jimmy weighed about 130 pounds as a senior, and he's never quite reached 5'8". But in surveying his "speedy and small" group of receivers in *Murrah Football Facts: Mustangs '70*, Coach Carlisle predicted: "There is going to be a real struggle here—headed by Seniors Jack Sandidge and Jimmy

Jones." Next to his head shot and exaggerated vital statistics, Coach Carlisle wrote: "Jimmy needs more size and speed but makes up for this in desire and hustle. A very valuable man to have around—Can help us this fall."

I have been proud of my brother all my life, but perhaps never as proud as I was when, as an incoming sophomore two years and four months younger and competitive with him, I realized that Coach Carlisle knew who Jimmy was and actually expected something from him on the field. He didn't much play; like a lot of kids hampered by size and thus speed in equipment, he was a late bloomer, becoming in college and now a splendid athlete. In those two years he played I was there for every home and most away games. Through it all, I never saw number 42 look up in the stands, sit down on the sidelines, remove his helmet, or walk. He performed every warm-up, every pass pattern, even followed the cheerleaders and team captains under the goalposts, at a full-out sprint, maximum hustle. And when he got in, I felt sorry for the opposing defensive back because Jimmy would just maul him, knock him flat, wait for him to rise, and then knock him flat again, usually blocking for a sweep the other way.

My parents didn't get it. They were perplexed when Jimmy chose to attend Coach Carlisle's grueling summer camp—held each year in the blast-furnace heat of August in central Mississippi—rather than fly with us to Acapulco, Mexico, in the summer of 1970. When my mother commented that he wasn't getting enough playing time to justify such commitment, I witnessed a fierce thing I avoided in youth and would never provoke now: Jimmy's anger. But even back then, when, like most brothers, I provoked him as often as he provoked me, I did get it.

Playing football at Murrah in those years wasn't an extracurricular activity; it was a commitment to Coach Carlisle and his "Mustang Creed," which meant eliminating all options except winning, merging and submerging your own abilities and individual qualities into the concept of the team, paying whatever price Coach asked you to pay to help the team win, and, whether your were the star tailback or rode the bench, identifying who you were within that context.

Like my parents, I doubted the wisdom of so limited and limiting a commitment then and for years later, and I didn't play football. But I got it when Jimmy showed me the great 1975 film *The Wind and the Lion*, and made me pay close attention to the movie's final words from Mulai Ahmed er Raisuli (Sean Connery): "Ah, Sherif, is there not one thing in your life that was worth losing everything for?" and then grinned at me. I understood it even better raising my four children, trying to teach each the critical lesson that making hard sacrifices to something larger than one's self is the best path to self-confidence, maybe even happiness, watching them accept that lesson first as a way to understand me, then as part of who they are each still becoming. Such commitment, then acceptance, followed by understanding, comes at different times and in different ways to the fortunate among us, never to the unfortunate and obnoxious, and I'm satisfied to call it what it is: maturity. And I know that, for my brother at least (though he would never say or even admit something so self-serving about himself), Murrah football played a significant part in making Jimmy at once strong yet entirely empathetic, humble but totally reliable, confident but realistic in his self-regard, precisely the kind of "valuable man to have around" Coach Carlisle said he was, especially in a pinch, overall the toughest and very best man I have ever known. Of course it didn't all come from Coach Carlisle and Murrah football, not even most of it; but I believe that the rigors he survived for something he felt worthy of his total commitment helped him find those qualities in himself, then and for all his life. I know of no better instruction.

And Coach Carlisle knew enough to make a prediction about Jimmy that came true. "Size and speed" are wonderful attributes for an athlete competing at any level, but "desire and hustle" are human qualities that last. It is a funny flip-flop: with each passing year we want more "desire and hustle" and less "size" at least. I always appreciated Coach Carlisle's generous words, but finding them again after many years I finally get the depth of understanding and the accuracy of the predictions in his few words about my brother.

As children growing up in the neighborhood surrounding the school, Jimmy and my friends and I absorbed Murrah's traditions up close. We just had to get close to the power of it somehow. Home games and games against other city schools were played at old Newell Field, a concrete behemoth built from leftover white concrete used to construct Bailey Junior High in 1937, located about a quarter mile from Murrah. About forty-five minutes before 7:30 p.m. kick-off, a large crowd gathered around the team as it processed from the locker room at the rear of the school due west across Murrah's campus, over the curvy spur of Peachtree Street and the bottleneck of a narrow concrete bridge over our neighborhood's largest drainage ditch, up through the pine trees to the elevation of the field. We were inconspicuous among the large entourage that trailed the team, including scurrying team trainers and equipment managers, the cheerleaders (so beautiful up close they made us dizzy), doctors, dads and granddads, faculty and staff and other hangers-on. The thick odor of equipment sweated through hundreds of times, the sinus-clearing scent of a painful lineament called "Hot Stuff" used on sore muscles, mown grass and dust and faint perfume and, in those days, cigarette smoke, all lingered together to create a sense memory nothing else in my world has ever matched. The only sound was the breathing of the hulking players, heads down in full concentration on the task at hand, the clanking and clacking of pads, cleats on Peachtree Street and the little bridge, until the team, led by the cheerleaders, took the field. Then it was the loudest sound 5,000-odd white people in the home stands could strain to make, over the marching band playing the Murrah Fight Song—"Hail to the blue and silver, Hail to the Murrah Mustangs" based upon "The Victors," the University of Michigan's 1898 classic that John Phillip Souza called "The greatest college fight song ever written." In a time and place where there was little to support, let alone believe in, what we had as kids looking for something to aspire to was, at least for a little while on those Friday nights, the vicarious thrill of following King Arthur and the Knights of the Round Table onto the field of battle. There was just something so inevitable, so utterly unstoppable about the spectacle and about our team that winning seemed a foregone conclusion, almost a byproduct of the collective force of the team, its fans, and its traditions. In Coach Carlisle's years we were rarely disappointed.

And it was ours.

If that sounds inflated or in any way contrived, we respectfully contend that you weren't there, or here. For us, it *was* glorious—or at least the closest we could come to it. Not that high-school football, or any sport really, is always the best touchstone for the wandering idealism of youth, or the only worthy subject of the dreams that sustained kids then and now, particularly in the computer age. It's just that, in our time in that place, sports, best exemplified by Murrah football, were all that for us. Southerners, especially Mississippians, have always had to practice what the poet John Keats called "negative capability," meaning the ability to revise, sometimes even transcend, the context in which we find ourselves. We didn't know a damned thing about Keats, of course, let alone what "negative capability" could possibly mean in our lives; but that's essentially what we were doing given the options we had. Those nights experiencing Murrah football allowed us a way to escape the constraints that so consumed the energy of the grown-ups we knew or watched on TV: the threat of nuclear annihilation early in the decade; Vietnam later; and, above all and constant, race. Other than as part of the juggernaut of Murrah sports and the school's "overall pattern for excellence" as Coach Carlisle termed it, in what circumstances could a white Mississippi boy of that time expect to win, earn respect, or even matter? If there were others, we didn't know about them.

And because Murrah was ours, or would be absent tragedy in life or learning when we finally turned fifteen, its traditions of excellence created expectations for the future that nothing else available to us could possibly fulfill.

All of us, everybody I knew growing up, looked forward to Murrah with great excitement and the sense of hopeful expectation that is the best part of being young.

It took me years, long after our full integration experience, to understand that our black contemporaries felt the same hopeful expectation about their futures at Brinkley High School and, perhaps, other all-black schools in the city. At our first class reunion in 1983 my catcher on the baseball team, George Coleman, told me, "We didn't want to go to Murrah more than you all didn't want to go to Brinkley." It's always easy to miss the signals; occasionally, though, we are shown the depths of our own ignorance and blindness, and it always stuns us. After thinking about George's statement for a while, I found George and admitted to him that whites, including me, felt that we had paid most if not all the costs required by the desegregation experiment, mainly because what we knew about history made it our burden to bear. We assumed, without asking, that black people stood only to gain by being forced to abandon their old schools and neighborhoods in favor of Murrah certainly but other white high schools as well. We assumed, without asking and before we ever even met one, that black kids had nothing to lose in the desegregation experiment. George has always told the truth, even when I thought I was a good ballplayer and didn't want to hear it, but he does so with a wry generosity of spirit and a kindness he's never lost. When I confessed to George that my assumptions about what he and other blacks felt about being transferred to Murrah were not only wrong but racist, he smiled, then held my eye for a moment and said, "Why didn't you ask?"

Beyond all the history and politics and who was to blame and whether what we were being asked to do was in any sense justified, it was the loss of those expectations that caused the gut-punch pain and the quick responses: for whites, abandonment of Murrah and all that it and the entire JPS had meant to the larger white community; for many of the black kids we encountered in the first year of the experiment, anger to violent reprisal toward whites in general, particularly white administrators and teachers whose job was to discipline and instruct the black students on new educational requirements. When Coach Carlisle and all but two of his juniors on the '70 team fled Murrah the weekend after the last game and moved operations across the Pearl River and out Lakeland Drive to the new, all-white Jackson Preparatory Academy, the die had indeed been cast. Except for the dad of one of the juniors who stayed—Jeff Miller's heroic father, Dean, who actually had the gumption to confront Coach Carlisle and was able to rescue much of Murrah's equipment that had gone with the team—nobody in a leadership position stepped up to defend Murrah or JPS or to even urge restraint and caution in the face of such sweeping change. The people who left in that first year were gone, for good. At the same time, Brinkley ceased functioning as a real high school, lost all its sports teams and extracurricular activities, and beginning in the fall of 1970, became solely a tenth-grade center. All of that past, as well as the expectations of those who knew that past, were lost, and I don't recall anybody saying or doing anything about it.

For those of us who stayed, it seemed like the gloomiest predictions were all being fulfilled. Integration had terminated all sports and extracurricular activities at Bailey during the second semester of our ninth-grade year, but we had hope that some normalcy would return once we got to Murrah the next year. The federal courts weren't through, however, and in the summer of 1970 the Fifth Circuit ordered even more radical desegregation of the JPS. My class was diverted from Murrah and sent to Brinkley for the tenth grade. A formerly all-black high school with its own great traditions (Brinkley had won the state championship in basketball in 1968-1969 and the foreshortened 1969-1970 season) entirely sacrificed to desegregation, Brinkley was located in the northwest quadrant of the city that had been predominantly black since the Civil War. During the 1970-1971 school year, the school had no teams, no extracurricular activities sponsored by the school, and though athletes went on to the high schools to which they were zoned—I played baseball at Murrah in the tenth grade—Brinkley was essentially a holding pen from which we watched distant events unfolding at Murrah and our rival Callaway High School (Brinkley was also the holding pen for tenth graders headed to Callaway), as well as at Prep and the schools opening all over the city that year by a reawakened and totally reinvigorated Citizens' Council. Over six hundred black students attended Brinkley that year, with eighty-three whites: a model of a failed social experiment, representative of nothing in the black or white community. Some of our former classmates came back to Murrah for the eleventh grade after a disappointing year in the "seg academies" as they were called because they were invented and maintained to preserve segregation. At Brinkley, though, in the first full year of desegregation, we had no reason to expect that anybody would return, or for that matter any other hopeful news. I thought that Murrah would be a mere extension of the worst of what we'd experienced at Brinkley: isolation of those of us in the substantial minority; nothing to unify the students; fear fed by occasional violence and threats of violence; tightening security followed by loss of extracurricular activities and freedom to do anything not on the schedule; resignation to total ineptitude by many white administrators and teachers; abandonment. Except for what we learned about each other in that wild setting at Brinkley, which turned about to be critically important, what basis did any of us, black or white, have for hoping that things would get better, at least in the short run over the next few years?

But they did.

In the history of race relations in this country, sports have provided the first common ground. Athletic competition, where talents combine against common enemies, produced the earliest examples of cooperation between races, leading eventually to acceptance, even friendship. Sports have been used and overused as a metaphor for almost everything in American life at least since Jackie Robinson's time. Was there, though, a sports metaphor for what was happening on the ground during the first year of forced integration of the JPS? It seemed doubtful.

Before the opening of Murrah and her south Jackson sister Provine High School, both in 1955, the old Jackson Central High School was the only game in town for whites, and the dominant force in Mississippi high-school athletics since the first teams were fielded. Both of my parents graduated from Central, as did most of the parents of my white contemporaries. Located in the middle of downtown Jackson in a sprawling brick building with white fluting and filigree around the entrances, it looks to this day like the all-American high school, circa 1947, despite the closing of the school in 1977 and its present use as the central office of the state Department of Education and other administrative agencies. In its day it drew the best talent from all over the city and dominated the "Big 8" for decades. But after Murrah and Provine opened, Central lost many of its athletes, some of its brains and beauties, and, by our time, most of its former luster. I thought Murrah would suffer similar cruel attrition, but only if we were luckier than we'd been at Bailey and Brinkley and were allowed school sports and extracurricular activities. The best we could hope for was a Central-like slow decline: an *ad hoc* gathering of white athletes left after Coach Carlisle and Prep took the best, joined by the black athletes who were surely around us but whose skills we knew nothing about after a year and a half of full integration, leaderless, all stumbling around and under Murrah's traditional symbols of excellence.

Coach Bob Stevens coached the Central football team in the late '60s. He had been a great high school and college player at Copiah-Lincoln Junior College and what is now the University of Southern Mississippi. His assistant coaches at Central were themselves legends in Jackson sports history: Louis "Skin" Boteler, at 300+ pounds, nonetheless able to keep Central competitive by getting maximum performance out of 160-pound linemen; and Willis Steinhaus, the Trojan King Priam (with his shock of long white hair and pompadour stuffed under a tattered baseball cap) of Jackson baseball for a generation, still pitching for the semi-pro Jackson Cowboys into his fifties while spotting and steering the best high-school and college baseball talent in the city in summer ball. Out of necessity, those three came up with a technique that worked throughout the period of Central's decline: they identified and cultivated two or three superior athletes in each class, made them play every sport, and built each team around them. And it worked, year after year. In fact, Central would have beaten Murrah in 1970 but for Central's Bill Baggett drilling his last-second, 12-yard field goal attempt directly into the bottom crossbar, causing the ball to rise fifty feet straight up only to fall harmlessly into our end zone, sealing for us a 7–6 victory in Coach Carlisle's final game at Murrah. Central came within a game, a pitch really, of winning the district championship in baseball in my junior year, 1972, on the strength of Joe McCaskill's right arm and ability to hit under pressure unmatched in my experience, his sturdy catcher Dwight King, and their best basketball player, Clarence Johnson, who played right field using a catcher's mitt. Even before the full descent of radical desegregation of the JPS, Central's coaches were adapting, innovating, moving forward instead of whining over all they had lost, dealing with the way things actually were, abandoning nothing. The time had come for precisely that type of forward thinking and action from everybody in the JPS system.

Thanks to the efforts of Pat McNease, quarterback and co-captain of the second Murrah team in 1956, aided by Dean Miller and very few other white parents committed to integration, and to Murrah's extraordinary good luck, Coach Stevens came to Murrah as head football coach in the spring of 1971. Then in his early forties, Coach was 6'3", flat-bellied and handsome, with a cool car and a great-looking blonde wife. He was still the state handball champion, pounding younger players at the old downtown YMCA though he looked like he was going to keel over between points. He was funny, too, goofy and befuddled, clear-headed only while coaching. I once saw him pull a drawer all the way out of a teacher's desk, stare open-mouthed at the mess he'd made, painstakingly replace all its contents and, after five minutes of fumbling and mumbling without paying a bit of attention to the class he was supposed to be teaching, shove the drawer back in and nod at it, finally satisfied. Not two minutes later, he pulled it all the way out again, and then repeated the same process despite our giggling. I knew him well for two years, saw him often in later years, but I am certain he never knew my name. His absent-mindedness and apparent guilelessness were all a bit of a put-on in my opinion. He was, in fact, perfectly fitted for those times: completely without racial prejudice, instinctive, patient, not intimidated by the past at Murrah or anywhere else, willing to take great risks, totally unpredictable, and an offensive genius. He was exactly what Murrah needed. Following and improving on the example of Coach Skin Boteler, he possessed an almost supernatural ability to inspire his players to do things that were beyond their physical capabilities, to play better than they really were. Sports mythology holds that Knute Rockne, John McGraw, Vince Lombardi, John Wooden, maybe Chuck Walsh, and one or two more, possessed that quality, placing them on the highest pedestals in the coaching Pantheon. But given the players those coaches had, the attribution of such rare qualities in the context of Notre Dame football or UCLA basketball sounds more like the kind of sports myth-making that is inevitable when old sports successes are recalled. But Coach Bob Stevens, aided by his great staff, had it in truth. I know. I saw it that year.

In spring training, 1971, Murrah had exactly two players on the team who had ever played a down of Big-8 football. Coach Stevens was lucky to inherit the heart of the coaching staff from the '70 team: Coach Doug Clanton on the line and Coach Freddie Lee in the backfield, together they invented and operated the defense. Both declined invitations to follow Coach Carlisle to Jackson Prep, and the two of them became critical players in the drama that was about to unfold. Coach Orsmond Jordan, fabled basketball coach from Brinkley about whom more is told below, transferred over as an assistant football coach for two seasons before somebody wised up and made him head basketball coach. Yet even with coaches of such quality, nobody knew if Murrah could field a football team that fall. We had Wyatt Washington, a talented back and the only black player Coach Carlisle put on the field (on specialty teams mainly) in the '70 season, Jeff Miller, a tough lineman who had played in '70 and was counted on by Coach Carlisle, and our classmate David Hutchison, at 6'5" and 250 pounds and fast, a truly great lineman who went on to play at Ole Miss. One other player with actual playing experience came over from Central with Coach Stevens, fullback Dan Henley, but beyond that there was ... not much.

So, Coach Stevens improvised. After grabbing the best athletes from the basketball, baseball, and track teams, he scoured the gym, the halls, cafeteria, the boys' bathroom called "The Head" at Murrah, the rooms where students served detention, even pilfered from the band, and from such sources he pulled together a team. Following Coach Bear Bryant's rule that any team's best athlete should play quarterback, he put Wyatt at quarterback, though Wyatt, for all his talent and leadership abilities, had an odd, stiff-armed throwing motion and ... well, Wyatt couldn't throw the football. He persuaded our best baseball player, Willie Ray Purvis, to agree (they told baseball players back then not to play football) to play at 5'7" and 155 pounds, put speedster

Freddie Funches (the bard of our graduating class of 1973) at split end, and developed a rotating system of running backs that took advantage of the very best each player had to offer. Coach Stevens once asked me who among my peers was the toughest to tackle in sandlot football and a generalized mauling exercise we called "roughhouse." I told him John Mixon, from my neighborhood, a little guy with great balance and grit and one of the kindest guys to ever come out of north Jackson. John went on to become a fine high-school running back, rushing for 104 yards against Yazoo City in a key early season win, though John admits today that he would not have played for Coach Carlisle. When it came time to throw the ball more than 10 yards, Willie Ray got the ball on a reverse or halfback pass, or in came left-handed quarterback Terry Jones, who hit Funches on a key "bomb" that went for a score late in the year. But we had a great defensive team, especially in linebackers Craig Cole—a tough sophomore who could and would tackle a moving 18-wheeler if he could catch it—plus the dominant Willie Miller in the middle, and defensive backs Hercules Parker, Willie Taylor, and Victor Watts, to name only a few of Coach Freddie Lee's and Coach Doug Clanton's swarming hoard: guys out of nowhere who knew nothing of and cared less about Murrah's traditions but were scared of nothing and nobody and got better with each play. Still it was a hodgepodge of kids, some not even athletes let alone football players, so eclectic that I remember laughing when I saw some of them in uniform on the '71 team. But not for long.

The *Jackson Clarion-Ledger* predicted that Murrah would win one game: we'd probably beat Central. Every mention of Murrah football was followed by a summary of what the team had lost, variations on the theme that Coach Carlisle's departure had destroyed a Mustang team that was expected to vie with Callaway for the state championship, as if anybody who cared about that needed to be reminded. Coach Stevens played it to the hilt in his comments to the paper on the day of the first game, lamenting the loss of experience at every position, venturing only that "everybody will get a chance to help the team." He said that he and his coaching staff weren't scared of trying "things that might surprise some people," but beyond that he declined to elaborate. All of it fed the gloom most who cared about Murrah's traditions felt when school started the day after Labor Day. We hadn't a clue.

When the 1971 Mustangs took the field for the first game in Natchez, they were not wearing the classic blue-and-silver Mustang uniform drawn on the pattern of the Baltimore Colts. Coach Stevens had changed the "away" jersey, adding stripes and long sleeves rather than the small numbers on the shoulder pads and short sleeves with tidy blue trim. That was all the change the budget allowed, but it was enough. For people like me who knew and cared about such things, it seemed at first like the fall of great tradition very fast, and, worse, an unjustified usurpation. We thought we had a right to expect that the team would look the part at least. But our future was not going to be about recreating that past, no matter how glorious it was or at least seemed. It didn't take me long to understand what the coaches were telling us: this was a new version of the Murrah Mustangs, unmoored from all that past, ready for change. And exactly the right thing to do.

The 1971 team won seven, lost three, and tied one. Something happened that was beyond our fondest expectations. Our rival Callaway had kept their entire '70 squad and had the best team in the state that year, whipping us soundly 38–10. But in our other two losses, against Natchez and Wingfield High School from south Jackson, we were outscored by a total of only 15 points, and tied a strong McComb team 7–7. We finished the season pounding our more-inner-city rivals Central and Lanier, and were invited to play in the tenth annual Mississippi Bowl in Clinton, where we owned Mendenhall 30–0.

Of all the sports I've watched over an average-fan's lifetime, the "Cinderella" teams and "Comeback Kids" and "America's Teams" and "Dream Teams" and somebody's "Army" and another's "Machine," nothing was as exciting to me as witnessing that team and their coaches will themselves into playing like, and then becoming, winners. As fans we were very much a part of it. Many of the unexpected stars, like John Mixon, were my good friends, and I simply wanted more for John than I wanted for the great football players who had left with Coach Carlisle. It would have been easy, even understandable, to give up in the face of early difficulties, lay down to better teams on paper when we couldn't get our offense on track because that usually took a while, fulfill the predictions of the sportswriters and the low expectations that accompanied the team through the early part of the season, indulge in self-pity, and quit. We had an obvious and easy scapegoat. But our coaches, followed by the players, simply wouldn't allow it. And somehow, the sense of abandonment, coupled with the tension that came from ramming two races together in one place, did not combine to grind the thing to the dust; rather, that friction created energy and a kinetic potential that was better than the sum of the parts, and explosive. We saw it happening on the field as the team coalesced and figured out how to win in real time.

It took a while for the players to pick up the faith of the coaches, but gradually the team began to believe in itself. Success bred more success, and not just game by game or even series by series but play by play. We could *see* it from the stands when a play or defense worked according to design and the coaches and players fell all over each other in unrestrained joy and not a little surprise. None of the strutting, helmet-off dancing of today's players at every level, finding the camera or their fans or taunting other players, pointing at themselves when they make a good or even a routine play. When a player on the '71 Mustangs made a play, his expression was more like "Did you see that?" directed only to his coaches and team, his teammates responding with giddy gestures that showed how happy they were for their teammate because they didn't expect it, either. The coaches stuffed their own smiles, tried to act like they expected it, and, like all good coaches, quickly returned their focus to anticipating and plugging holes, cajoling or praising based upon what motivated each player, hammering the fundamentals. On that team, the players needed the coaches as much as the coaches needed the players. I can't think of another sports team where that linkage was so critical and so clear. It was a truly fine thing to see.

Teena and I went to Brookhaven in 2010 to interview Coach Clanton and Coach Lee, and I talked to Coach Clanton several times after that about memories and feelings he didn't want to share while we taped. He was head baseball coach at Murrah from my sophomore year in 1971 until his retirement in the mid-1990s, and we stayed close over the years. He died in October 2013, and his family asked me to speak at his funeral on behalf of his former players. Recalling his private words—Coach wasn't effusive; his wisdom was earned, limited to what he knew, deeply felt, brief—I shared his memory that the 1971 football team was his favorite coaching experience because of the low expectations, the success he and Coach Lee had in cobbling together a defense from "scraps" and making it work, and what it showed "to those people who left when the going got tough." Though I didn't share all of it at Coach Clanton's funeral service, he was the only participant in our project to address certain issues directly, and his wisdom is as relevant now as in 1971.

"We didn't coach those boys like that, and it made me mad. I'm still mad about it. They weren't taught that it was ever all right to tuck tail and run away from competition, from somebody who may be faster and stronger and wanted to take their positions, to not step up when things didn't turn out the way they thought they should. I don't know who had promised them they wouldn't have to deal with change. Who thinks that things will always work out according to plans? So black people were going to be a part of it. So what? You don't quit. You don't try to rig the game in your favor. No. You fight harder, especially when it's a new ballgame and it may be tougher and you don't know what the outcome will be. That is when an athlete proves himself. It's not enough to just have the talent, the raw speed or quickness or power, whatever. It's what you do with it, how you come out of a fight or competition you've not had before, win or lose, that you learn about real competition, about what you are made of. That's what sports is all about in the first place. Really and truly I was mad at all of them, for a long time, because that's not what we thought we were showing them about the game, teamwork, winning, losing, who we were as coaches, what all of it meant about growing up and being a leader. I just thought it was the wrong answer at the wrong time. I still do."

The 1972 Mustangs went 8-2. Still improvising, Coach Stevens and his staff started sophomores at quarterback and wide receiver, but the defense was back, a year older and tougher, bigger and faster, and all but dominated our opponents. I think that the transition from the Carlisle era to the Stevens era was completed in that year—just two seasons away from segregation. The paper no longer rehearsed Coach Carlisle's departure at the beginning of every story about Murrah football. Nobody, especially the coaches and players, looked back any more. And over the next five years or so, while the ratio between white and black remained at or near the 65 percent/35 percent black majority reached in our time, Murrah remained a dominant force in football. Coach Freddie Lee took over as head coach in the mid-seventies, and he recalls that his 1975 team was the best of all post-integration versions of the Mustangs. Coach Lee went on to coach at St. Andrew's and Madison Central and is a legend in Mississippi high-school athletics. He is also a highly intelligent, articulate, and funny man with a memory that, for me, made this period of transition in Murrah sports live again in acute detail. He and Coach Clanton came out of the wilds of Franklin County, played all sports together, and by another fortunate coincidence came together again in 1968 at Murrah. They saw it all—the last of the segregated Murrah teams under Carlisle, the special contributions of Coach Stevens and Coach Jordan during the transition period, the success of the integration moment from 1971 through the fragmentation and eventual loss of white commitment followed by total white flight by the end of the 1970s—and together they provide critical continuity to the story.

Coach Lee: "I think we proved something then about who we were and what we could do as coaches. When you follow a coach like Jack Carlisle the prospects are pretty bleak anyway. When you combine that with losing all your players or most of them, and don't know if you've even got enough players to field a team, what can you do? What you do is make do, and that's what we did in '71 under Bob Stevens. Later on, when I took over, we had a good mix of kids, black and white, who wanted to be there and were willing to put in the work and dedication that goes in to making a competitive team at that level. We had really good years, and I remember Doug and I and others thought we'd eventually start pulling back in some of the athletes who'd left for

Prep and the Council schools. It didn't happen that way. The white kids quit coming to Murrah—the white athletes anyhow. By 1977–1978, we'd reached the tipping point in terms of white involvement, enrollment, and after that it never turned around again. I don't know what caused white parents to pull their kids. We can see in hindsight that once white enrollment falls below 25 percent of the student body, you're beyond that tipping point and white parents just won't stay with it. And it's a shame really. We were over the toughest part. We had developed a good model, I thought, for what was possible in the first five years. And not just for what was possible, for what was very real and good and positive coming out of integration. It's strange to think that we pulled ourselves up after Coach Carlisle and his players left at the end of '70, when we had something to prove to our opponents and ourselves, even the coaches. Why we couldn't hold that momentum past '75, '76, '77 is a question nobody has ever really answered for me. There were two mass defections: one in '70 and another in about '77. Other than that tipping-point phenomenon, I can't explain it. Still, I think that what we did in '71, '72 had never been done before. In retrospect, I think it was desegregation's first real success story. And I'm glad all of us—Doug, you, me, Teena, Carole [Clanton—Coach Clanton's widow, who was a counselor at Murrah in our time and a favorite of all]— were a part of it. It should have lasted."

Coach Lee and Coach Clanton were right, both in what they said to us about the events of that interim between '70 and '75 when integration actually worked, and in investing most of their careers (for Coach Clanton, all of it) in the beliefs they expressed to us. They had no regrets. In fact, the '73, '74, and '75 teams were ever bit as dominating and accomplished as the best of Coach Carlisle's Mustangs of the 1960s losing a total of five games over those seasons with fully integrated teams.

The successes during that five-year interim weren't limited to the sports teams. The spectacle and much of the force of Murrah sports survived desegregation and was still present in our time, albeit in an evolved state. It had to evolve. The old clichés still applied, but alloyed with something foreign, unpredictable. The bright lines of social strata separating the students and fans from the players and performers, and from each other, were nowhere to be found. The new cheerleaders in '71, black and white, were every bit as beautiful as the legends from the old Murrah; for my money even more so. But they were also more with us, the common students of all colors and sexes, more *of* us than the previous groupings of north Jackson girls, most of whom were cheerleaders for every school they'd ever attended and occupied the highest strata; not exactly untouchable but they were accustomed to being worshiped from a distance and appeared to prefer it so.

The Murrah Misses were the dance troupe that performed at halftimes and marched with the band, attired in white cowgirl outfits with short, fringed skirts and white boots: the subject of great expectation and longing for us as kids. Now the Misses were black and white in roughly equal numbers, superior in talent and allure to the troupes of the past, still in the cowgirl outfits though the long-outdated cowgirl hats often had to be pinned to the tops of Afros. The new Misses supplemented the old high-stepping with synchronized routines and flourishes I'd never seen, and I always watched. Importantly, in the female faces of the spectacle there was no conscious effort to mimic the past or get away from it; they took the best of the old and new, came up with something different but more interesting, and appeared to be comfortable with the way things were, with the others on stage with them, with themselves. It was all part of the evolution, and a gift to the school and the fans.

The new marching band was about a third larger than the old Murrah marching bands. To our black classmates, playing in the band meant something entirely different than it meant to us white kids. The sense my friends and I brought to it was a function of stereotyping and elitism of some sort, but whatever it was we were not used to seeing band members enjoying themselves and giving so much to their performances. Coach Stevens even drafted a couple of big tuba-lugging and horn-playing guys out of the band to play football, only to lose them back to the band after a couple of weeks. Other black guys tried to play ball and play in the band, but that didn't last long. Those guys thought that their performances in the band was at least as cool, promising just as straight a path to the hearts of the girls they liked, as their performances in athletic competition. That was utterly new to us. But when the new band announced its presence through a massive percussion section that shook the old wooden bleachers of the Murrah gym during pep rallies, and then boomed out of Newell Field every chance they got, we got it. It was powerful stuff that drew all of us in. In my memory, the band actually mastered only the fight song and an old R & B number, "The Horse." I expect they had other numbers, but the band always nailed those two. The spectacle was augmented by the physical contortions and acrobatics of each member of the marching band, limited only by the instrument or equipment he or she played or carried, from the highly exercised drum major to the graceful baton twirlers to the big brasses and demur woodwinds, everybody swinging and dipping in step, particularly when the band member reached a turn at the end of his line during a routine and was out front for a few beats. It was still the juggernaut but vastly improved by a potent African American presence that could seem stereotypical until the fan was drawn in enough to become part of what was happening, stereotypical or not. The band's performances, no less than the evolution of the cheerleaders and Misses, were a critical part of what Murrah was announcing to its opponents and the people in the stands when the team took the field. It was all new, but somehow it was even more "ours" than what it replaced.

Among all the odd synchronicities and happy ironies at work in the early years of the desegregation experience, the most critical was again in sports. In 1971 Murrah lucked into a counterpart to Coach Carlisle when Coach Orsmond Jordan was named head coach of the boys' basketball team. He was already a legend, having coached Jackson's Lanier High School Bulldogs to a *national* title in 1963–1964 before moving to the new Brinkley High School in 1967. By 1968–1969 he'd won the state basketball championship for black high schools, and his Brinkley team was the top-ranked black team in the state again when desegregation hit in December 1969. At that sad point, Brinkley's championship trophies, support system, all the evidence of a superlative basketball program that under Coach Jordan stood above all others black or white in Mississippi at that time, were packed up with the uniforms and put away for good. Brinkley became a tenth-grade center in 1970, another failed experiment in desegregation that lasted only through 1972. It is now a junior high school.

In January 1970 Coach Jordan was transferred to Murrah as part of the flip-flopping of all but a select few members of the faculties of Brinkley and Murrah under federal court order. He thus lost his championship team to become an assistant to a white coach who coached at Murrah one more year before escaping to Prep. His Brinkley players—like Henry "Launchie" (my favorite sports nickname ever, and self-explanatory) Ward, who at 6'5" could pluck a quarter from the top of the backboard from a flat-footed jump, and Ricky Berry, who, with a Jerry West / Kobe Bryant-quality jump shot, went on to lead an invincible Lanier team in 1970–1971—were scattered by desegregation but showed white Jackson what was coming in high-school basketball. No more games where both teams together scored fewer than 100 points; no more freezing the ball for entire quarters to prevent a good shooter from getting the ball; no more rebounding battles at the base of the backboard. These were the best athletes in the city who, from a young age, played nothing but basketball, mastered their own style of play, and somehow shrank the size of the court by at least a half. Or so it seemed to little white guys like me. When Berry and his Lanier team rolled over Murrah twice in that first full season following desegregation, we saw sure proof of who and what we had in Coach Jordan: a coach who could harness and drive the overflow of basketball talent that has always come out of Jackson's black community.

Over his thirty-five years in coaching high-school basketball (with a 722-232 record), Coach Jordan was at Murrah the last twenty-two through his retirement in 1993, during which time he compiled untouchable records including but not limited to the following: winning four more state championships; Jackson *Clarion-Ledger* "Coach of the Year" four times; fourteen seasons with twenty or more wins; four seasons with thirty or more wins; one with forty or more wins; Hall of Fame member with every school, league, and organization with which he had contact; the coach and mentor of seven high-school All-Americans and eight pro players. What Coach Carlisle did for Murrah football in the 1960s, Coach Jordan matched in basketball from the 1970s through the early 1990s. In separate sports and in disparate contexts, but aligned in their focus on winning and a shared concept of how to develop championship teams, they brought Murrah to sports prominence and kept it there for thirty years.

Neither coach was a forerunner in the struggle for integration. The record shows that Coach Carlisle and Coach Jordan each won with players of their own race almost exclusively. Although desegregation was in its earliest phases during Coach Carlisle's last year at Murrah, Coach Clanton and Coach Lee told us that they did not think that Coach Carlisle was prepared to start black players at key positions, or center any team he coached around black players. Nobody we talked to accused Coach Carlisle of racism or anything like it; he never earned a reputation for racism and certainly should not be remembered as a champion for the old guard. His focus and his goals were all about winning, not furthering some view on race, and most of his players and fellow coaches understood that about him. Coach Jordan, who was an assistant under Carlisle throughout 1970—"I just stood around" on the football field he remembered—told us he didn't think Carlisle was "unfair to the black players. He got on white players easier than he got on the blacks." In truth, they had the same demands and expectations of their players irrespective of race. "Coach Carlisle, to me," Coach Jordan observed, "just meant what he said. He wanted you to do just what he said do. So did I. If you are going to play on our team, you do what we say do."

Coach Lee remembered a gifted black quarterback from Lanier who came to Murrah for spring training in 1970 but returned to Lanier the next year, not because of disputes with Coach Carlisle in football but because he failed to keep the practice schedule on the track team and was told to turn in his equipment. "The kid could play, and we needed a pure-drop-back-passer quarterback. The kid had a rocket arm, and fast . . . It probably would have been smart to encourage the kid and play him. But Coach Carlisle treated him just like everybody else. Nobody got special treatment. Ever. If you didn't follow the rules, you didn't play." In the end, all who were there, including Coach Jordan, remain convinced that black athletes of that time were not prepared to adopt the "Mustang Creed" or sacrifice their autonomy to fit Coach Carlisle's unconditional demands, especially the better athletes of whom both coaches expected the most because they had the most to give. The same was true of Coach Jordan.

Recalling the departure of Coach Carlisle and most of the juniors on the '70 team, Coach Jordan simply noted, "I could see why they might do that. They'd played together, and I didn't have any problem along that line." He added that every coach needs support from the school and the parents, which Coach Carlisle got at Murrah and Prep but he almost never received. "You go out there and look at Prep's facilities and look at Murrah's facilities. Hey! Oh, shoot! No, I understand all that. [Coach Carlisle] lived on the same side of the street his players and their parents lived. I didn't live on that side." Whatever spin one wishes to place on Carlisle's departure from Murrah in 1970—and everybody who remembers it has his own—the reality is that Coach Carlisle's son Mike, my age and my friend and a gifted quarterback, and the team that had grown up playing with Mike, were all at Prep. I understood then, and understand even better now as a father of sons who were athletes, why Coach chose to be with his son. Still, I wished then, and wish now, that they had stayed at Murrah—not so much for us but for them.

After a mediocre beginning in 1971–1972, Coach Jordan's 1972–1973 team won the city championship against Callaway and Lanier teams with more talent position by position. That team won with a smothering defense, always getting the ball to the right guy in the right place to take and (he better) make the easiest shot—in other words, through a constantly pressing defense and disciplined offense based upon, above all, passing the ball, picks and rolls and finding the guy open underneath the basket. There were no superstars; in truth, I don't remember a star or even who scored the most on that team I followed closely during my senior year covering the games for our student newspaper, the *Hoofbeat*. I do remember some of the players shocking me with a move or a shot when they were on a fast break or simply chose to ignore the offense for a moment, following which they were jerked off the floor by Coach. And I remember witnessing the best coaching I have ever seen in any sport.

A starting guard on that team was our classmate and my oldest friend since kindergarten (where, on the TV in our kindergarten teacher Mrs. Downing's living room, he and I watched the inauguration of John F. Kennedy), Kip Ezelle. The next white player who started for Coach Jordan was

Kip's cousin Travis Ezelle in the early '90s. Kip believes that, like Coach Carlisle, Coach Jordan was never willing to sacrifice or even temper his demands or his unrelenting drive to win in order to achieve racial balance or to make any point that didn't have to do with winning. When asked about the lack of many white players on his Murrah teams, Coach Jordan is unapologetic, explaining only that "some of the kids came there looking for favors, but I didn't have any favors to give out." Kip remembers that the rules were clear and simple, and nonnegotiable: no wearing of game shoes anywhere but in games; no dunking because it was illegal and Coach would not "practice things we couldn't do"; running the plays and defenses called, without exception; passing the ball; maintaining strict control on defense but especially on offense or "he'd give you that scowl and I knew I was fixing to come out of that game." Coach Jordan recalls that Kip had great "shooting touch, when I let him shoot," but also that Kip worked harder than anybody else on the team, and he "knew how to play with the other boys. He respected them, and they respected him." Kip agreed: "It really was about respect, giving it and earning it."

Now in long retirement of over twenty years, Coach Jordan remembers "the only thing I wanted them to say is that I was fair." But when we asked him if being fair and being successful, winning, were the same thing, Coach Jordan was honest enough to admit "probably not." Coach Carlisle would surely agree. Neither coach intended to make any political statements with their Murrah teams; winning was statement enough.

Off the field or the court, other features of the spectacle that was Murrah came through, albeit in evolved form, during the five years of the integration moment. The theater productions—especially *The Wizard of Oz* starring today's greatest female jazz artist Cassandra Wilson (nee Fowlkes) as Dorothy—came close in quality to the musicals directed by Karen Gilfoy in the 1960s. We were diminished in size and breadth but not in the depth of talent appearing on the various stages Murrah still provided. If we were held back at all, it was due to the lack of funding. We didn't have support groups made up of parents who, in earlier days and certainly now, ensure that kids' sports and extracurricular activities through high school never lack anything that money can provide. My parents tried the early PTA meetings and the few other gatherings of white and black parents with kids at Murrah. Those meetings reflected what was happening between black and white students. Offers for funding were regarded as efforts to control, which was true in part but counterproductive overall, and nothing was accomplished. There was too much history to expect "open dialogue" or other clichés for cooperation popular in those days.

The administration quite wisely tried to preempt these kinds of disputes among the students. I'm not sure of its origins, but in those years there was a requirement that everything with Murrah's name attached had to involve equal numbers of black and white participants. So we had black and white student body and class presidents, black and white this and that. The practice offended some, accommodated others, and was overall a harmless remedy intended to head off disputes over important matters like who and what fairly represented the school and the will of the majority. Once we got past those issues, anything that required, or encouraged, black and white students to interact and move toward a common goal was a great leap forward. The sad but honest truth about the early period of desegregation is that, outside those mandates that required black and white students to work together, and of course outside the galvanizing force of Murrah sports, there was little interest in "mixing"—to use a hateful old term trumpeted by the likes of Mississippi governor/US senator Theodore G. Bilbo but nonetheless descriptive—with each other socially. It was all too new. We didn't really hang around each other until our senior year—late in our senior year—because it took that long to put away the prejudices, preconceptions, and conditioned responses and get to know each other as individuals. We had to build a common experience base before it became easy to share ourselves. That took a while.

Before that happened, I knew my black male classmates only through sports: through Murrah baseball for me but more extensively in the day-to-day competition that occurred mainly in the gym or outside playing pick-up basketball. Everybody played basketball, or thought they could, and it was easy to get a game together. You learned who could play and who was all mouth, but it was a start. Later, when I played baseball at Murrah and had black teammates I wanted to get to know, I discovered that they weren't interested in anything but my performance on the field.

For two years, '71 and '72, I gave five or six black guys on the baseball team rides home after practice in a '59 Plymouth station wagon my father got me because it was built and drove like a PT boat and was far too slow for me to get hurt in the series of scrapes and collisions that inevitably follows the grant of a driver's license to a fifteen-year-old child. But none of them allowed me to see the houses they lived in; they made me let them out at the same corner between the Jackson Ready-Mix plant and Bailey Avenue, where Pleasant Avenue and Prosperity Street run parallel just south of Woodrow Wilson Boulevard, where parted and walked the rest of the way home. Of the range of reflexive responses white kids showed them early on, the black guys I first knew hated pity the most. They'd rather you sling a racial epithet at them and fight than try to be their "bro," act like you have a special friendship (including one formed out of respect for each other's talents in sports), or, worst of all, condescend in word or otherwise thoughtful deed. Twice I drove them to my house for my mother's spaghetti, and while they were appreciative and responsive to my parents' gushing, they didn't want to go outside and shoot baskets with my little brother, and they weren't about to go into the front yard and throw the ball around while the neighbors gawked. In truth I don't think they liked the experience; they were silent on the ride back to Pleasant Avenue and Prosperity Street. I didn't ask again. They just weren't interested in my life off the baseball field and resented my interest in theirs. More than that, my teammates were not about to be somebody's pet black friend, like a mascot, and none stood for false familiarity—like the term I heard white housewives use later in the '70s when introducing their domestic help: "This is my special friend." The only place where all those pretenses were dropped, where we supported each other in earnest without incurring any obligation, was on the field.

It was a start, really. We first had to change appearances, for appearances mattered. The alteration of the football uniform, the forced "equality" of black and white student body presidents, all the window-dressing somebody (not the students) came up with to try to symbolize racial equality and change, were for the sake of appearances and harmless overall. The old traditions we all knew, black and white, had to evolve, give way to new influences, include other traditions never before considered, or die. Most of all, we had to find a way to get past the prejudices and preconceptions that all of us, black and white, brought to new relationships we'd never had before and hadn't a clue how to develop. The key was, again, getting to know something about each other as individuals. And in that critical context, sports performed its historical function as the great leveler, talent on the field providing the common ground. From there we could commit to something we held in common, and, with enough time and constant contact, become friends. When late in my senior year we had a small function at my parents' house that included many of my black teammates and others from our class, the resistance and unease of the spaghetti dinners had relaxed but was still there to an extent I could not fully remove. That would take more time and deeper commitment, and we had neither.

Sadly, after we graduated almost everybody went back to the old repetitions of traditions, options, choices and paths to the future that were still based upon race: for me, Ole Miss and Millsaps, later to Law School back at Ole Miss, where I never again was as close to any black person as I had been with my teammates on the Murrah baseball team. I developed professional friendships with many black lawyers over many years, but the friendships are different because they developed from common experience in Law School and practice. We each know the other earned his or her reputation as well as our different strengths, our successes and failures, from roughly the same places, and I hold those friendships very close. Some of my black teammates at Murrah went to junior college for a year or two to play ball, a few went on to college, most of them went to work in jobs they rarely left. Very few moved out of the neighborhoods of their youth. And today, just as you cross the bridge over the Ready-Mix plant heading west, look to the left and you can see Pleasant Avenue, Prosperity Street, the ramshackle buildings and the tiny clapboard houses that populate that old neighborhood where my teammates lived, all in exactly the same condition they were during the integration moment of the early 1970s. The only thing missing is the large number of black children on those streets.

We didn't see each other for ten years after high school. When we reconnected, what we had in common was sports, those times we let each other down and the fewer times when we came through for each other, all of which we could both recall with empathy and a generosity of spirit that we could finally show to one another. Thanks to all our reunions, and our shared interest in seeing each other frequently, we are closer now than we were in youth. We reconnect through our appreciation for the unexpected successes of Murrah's sports teams during the first years of desegregation, and how those successes gave all of us the assurance that we had made the right choice to stay with the public schools. As George Coleman—the catcher on the baseball team and my good friend—finally made clear to me, it was an assurance that all of us, black and white, needed. We all needed to know that our experience during radical desegregation was not going to be about dashed or diminished expectations, embarrassing the school's traditions, disappointment, each of us with our individual talents getting lost in the crush of such massive social change. In the reality of what we experienced, and now in memory, we know that we found common ground playing ball. And from that shared experience we learned what playing ball under good coaches is always about: shaking off the past and all the politics because they just don't matter when you have the ball; learning who you can count on and who has the character and strength to do his job under pressure; commitment and giving up everything for a greater good; and, if only for a moment in the game when we are counting on our teammate to come through and wishing with him or her for the very best, getting past the irrelevancy of race.

School Spirit: The Murrah Cheerleaders, Misses, Band, Pep Rallies, and Homecoming

Narrated by Teena Freeman Horn

■

A Tale of Two Cheerleaders

Boisterous and spirited pep rallies were the trademark of Murrah High School in the 1960s and 1970s. There was such exuberance among the Mustang fans that they usually filled the home games and out-of-town bleachers to capacity. Undaunted by any opposing team, the fans wore their blue and silver shirts to rival towns expecting to win the game and party afterward. That was the idea that really set Murrah apart from all the rest of the schools in Jackson. They expected a positive result from players and students. Even the preparation for a Murrah football game was exciting. Signs painted by cheerleaders and others covered every inch of the Murrah gym. The band and the famous drill team, the Murrah Misses, practiced new routines in anticipation of a halftime performance that was always innovative! The football players trained in the hot Mississippi climate and during the rain. Regardless of the weather, the team looked fearless and powerful. The football team was almost always the Big 8 champion.

As an elementary school student at Power, which was adjacent to the great Murrah High School, I dreamed of becoming a Murrah cheerleader and wearing those starched gray shirts with a blue bib and skirt. The uniform beheld a Murrah "M" with a valiant, bold mustang raring up on its hind legs. At certain times of the day, I looked out the window up the hill hoping to catch a glimpse of the football team, band, cheerleaders, and the Murrah Misses practicing on the field. "Hail to the Mustangs valiant, hail to the blue and silver" were words to the fight song they practiced. I remember buying the Murrah football facts book to memorize the names and numbers of the handsome football players.

Some afternoons I rode my bike around the corner, from Power to Murrah, where the doors were unlocked, to glimpse at the grand trophy cabinet filled with the championship athletic awards and photos of winning teams. There was an article inside that boasted Murrah was one of the top twenty schools in the nation for having the most national merit finalists and semi-finalists. I remember how much I liked a sign that read, "William B. Murrah High School is dedicated to the pursuit of excellence." That mantra inspired a desire within me to be excellent at something, one day.

My Murrah was different from the one I evidenced as a child. They say that you never get over being a Murrah cheerleader—that is probably true.

Chryl Covington Grubbs, from the class of 1970, beautifully describes in an essay her cheerleading experience—at the Murrah that we idealized—before the integration process began.

Testimony of the "Old Murrah"

Murrah, just that one word conjures up memories that are as vivid as the moment they actually happened. Unless you attended Murrah High School it is hard to explain the energy, spirit and attitude that was there.

Having an older brother who attended Murrah just sweetened the anticipation of actually attending one day. I had one goal during the spring of 1967—to make cheerleader at Murrah.

My time finally arrived to try out for cheerleader at Murrah. In order to try out you were required to attend the cheerleading clinic prior to tryouts. I was so nervous the night before clinic that I only slept for a few hours. After surviving clinic the tryouts began. I still get butterflies just conjuring up the memory of that time. Finalists were chosen by a panel of judges a few days after the clinic. Lucky enough to have made the finals I now had to try out in front of the entire student body. People still don't understand (including my husband) the atmosphere that was there in the Mustang gym. The roar was so loud that I couldn't hear the person next to me. This was only a cheerleader tryout, and yet the energy was so tangible you felt as though you could touch it. After making cheerleader I floated around for weeks.

My first time to really realize the notoriety of Murrah was at the Ole Miss Cheerleader Clinic in Oxford during the summer of 1967. We were walking through the Grove and other cheerleading squads would be whispering and pointing—"There's Murrah!" Not: "There's Jackson Murrah" but just Murrah! I have to admit my height increased and my pride definitely swelled. I know I have written a lot about cheerleading but let me explain. In the years from 1964 to 1970 cheerleaders were the spirit leaders for the school. Murrah was all about "Mustang spirit" and as a cheerleader that was your job and in my case a love affair.

Another major part of Murrah during those years were the dances. I can still recall my first dance as a student at Murrah. I had a date with the late Bobby

Temple (cofounder of *Mississippi Magazine*). The dance was held at the Heidelberg Hotel in downtown Jackson. The memories are so sweet and vivid that I can even recall what I was wearing that night. I can still remember walking in and seeing guys and girls dancing to "Apples, Peaches, Pumpkin Pie, You Were Young and So Was I." When I hear that song even today it makes me recall that first dance as a Murrah Mustang. I still appreciate the effort of those core seniors who worked to make sure we had a place to dance to start another Mustang season. You see, the schools were not allowed to host dances. We were not even allowed to have dances in our own gyms. Can you imagine your children's schools not allowing them to host dances on their property today?

The first week of school was always so exciting. Students from the two [northeast Jackson] junior high schools (Bailey and Chastain) were merged to form Murrah's sophomore class. Over the summer we would get together to discuss any NEW BOYS that were being transferred from other schools to attend Murrah. As cheerleaders we would try and sneak a peak at the new guys on any of the athletic teams practicing during the summer. No matter what anyone says, high school was all about the dance woven between the guys and the girls.

Game days were the most exciting times at Murrah. I will NEVER EVER forget my first time to run into the gym for my first Mustang pep rally. I didn't realize that even the teachers and janitorial staff came to watch and participate. My hair stood up on my arms and I remember looking up into the bleachers at my classmates and seeing all of them chanting. I was overwhelmed. I remember actually praying, "Lord, just let me remember the cheers so I don't make a fool out of myself."

When the football captain of the week got to the microphone, the crowd would go WILD! I can still see players like Paul Dongieux, Mack Chunn, Win Foshee and of course movie-star good-looking Rod Taylor standing at the end of the gym wearing their blue and silver letter jackets. You understand that it might be 90 degrees outside with no air inside but they had on those well-earned wool letter jackets. Of course standing watch over his players was Coach Jack Carlisle. He was bigger than life though not big in stature. As a cheerleader I had a lot of contact with Coach Carlisle and the other coaches. I always felt his bark was much bigger than his bite (at least for the cheerleaders). He was always agreeable and helpful to the cheerleaders when we suggested a change. I truly believe that Coach Carlisle had a lot to do with Murrah's winning spirit.

Looking back at that first year in 1967–1968 I realize we had some very wonderful people in administrative positions. I don't think I really appreciated principal James Merritt (better known as Dopper Dan) and assistant principal Robert Oakes (better known as Teddy Bear). Our school had a fine reputation and scores to back it up as one of the best high schools in the nation. Through the years I have become very close friends with Mr. and Mrs. James Merritt. We have had lots of laughs about those years in school. Mr. Merritt has some fascinating and wonderful funny stories about his years at Murrah.

There were so many great things to be involved in at Murrah. Everyone could find something to be involved in. From clubs to musicals, from sports to offices held, everyone could find a niche. This is what made Murrah so great! The only negative memory I have is that Big Eight Schools (which Murrah was a member) did not allow girls to play basketball. Some interfering mothers decided that it was unladylike for girls to play basketball so it was prohibited in the Big Eight schools. I can remember going to basketball tournaments at Forest Hill and being mesmerized by the girl's teams. Yes, county schools could have girl's teams but Murrah could not!

The school year would begin with football, basketball, baseball and tennis in that order. Each week several things would take place that would build up to the "big game." Sign painting parties would usually take place at three different houses. One each for sophmore, junior and seniors. NO MIXING was allowed here! It was pretty much taboo! Then on several Thursday nights during the season we would have a bonfire under the Pearl River Bridge. The cheerleaders might lead in several chants and a football player might say a few words to fire us all up. The bonfire was mainly just to get together and show our independence away from the school environment.

Each week there would be a victory dance, win or lose during the football season. We won more than we lost, but the losses were devastating. I took the losses personally and felt the sadness in our coaches, players and classmates. I still remember one game like it was yesterday. We traveled to Meridian to decide who was to be the Big Eight champion. Meridian High School beat us 35–7. I even remember the quarterback's name was Straus and he kept passing to a very small receiver named Guilet. They beat us up and down the field. For a woman of fifty-seven years to remember the name of the quarterback and receiver says a lot. I was devastated and my bubble was burst. Our winning season was over! I really took it personally as did everyone else. That was the Murrah I knew.

Our victory dances usually would be at one of two locations: Costas Lodge or Cedars of Lebanon Lodge. Everyone would go and most everyone would actually have a date. The dances were always fantastic and everyone danced. I really don't remember people not dancing. It was a time to dance and a time to be happy. Even on nights we would be defeated in football we would dance until they closed the place down. Of course our losses were few in number. Saturday was usually a downer because another Friday night of Mustang football and victory dancing had come and gone.

Other memories of Murrah still conjure up feelings of laughter and maybe still a little uneasiness. At Murrah there was a bathroom for guys and girls that was OFF LIMITS to anyone but seniors. They were called the "boy's head" and the "girl's head." I had heard stories of girls' heads being flushed in the toilet if they ventured in and weren't seniors. I went out of my way not to test the truth of those stories.

Another memory of that first year as a sophomore is as vivid as if it were yesterday. I received a phone call from a friend saying she had heard she was on the "senior girls" black list. Whether real or not I was panicked. Word was that if you went out with a senior boy then the senior girls would put you on the list. I was toast. I had been out with several and had my eye on several others. I immediately went to my brother, who was a senior, with tears in my eyes. I told him about my friend's call and my concern. He just happened to have been talking to one of the "cool senior girls" that he was dating. He called her back and told her about my worries. He asked her if I was on the list and she said I should have been but she was taking care of me. Thank goodness she liked my brother! I have never loved my brother more than at that very moment!

My sophomore and junior years were wonderful with the Murrah Mustangs bigger than ever. My senior year looked promising as I had been selected to be co-head cheerleader with one of my best friends, Jane Thompson Barnes. We were rolling through the football season way too fast when rumors starting flying around about our school being shaken up . . .

Chryl reflected, "Murrah, that one word still brings joy to my heart and makes my soul sing. Hail to the Murrah Mustangs!"

My Murrah Cheerleading Experience after Integration

The big day for tryouts finally came at Murrah, and I was successful, along with my two friends from Bailey and Central: Nancy and Susan. At that time, Murrah was denoted an eleventh- and twelfth-grade school. We had practiced together at home in the streets for several years and our dreams became a reality. In the first round of competition we performed a cheer in front of judges who were teachers and old cheerleaders. The second round involved selection by the "old Murrah" student body. Not one junior (eleventh-grade) cheerleader was returning to Murrah, which I found to be odd. They were going to private schools or graduating early. I wondered why they would miss their senior year at such a fine school.

Entering the world of cheerleading was exciting and humbling for me. It was a privilege to serve the school; an opportunity that I honored and cherished. Being one of eight Murrah cheerleaders in a school of over a thousand people was probably the biggest thing that could happen to a north Jackson girl. We later had nine cheerleaders. The school added the first black cheerleader, a senior named Gloria, sometime before the season began. I do not remember the circumstances, but she did a good job.

The old Murrah was known for bonfire pep rallies, that were spirit boosters on the night before the game, and big victory dances after the Friday night football home games. Bands like the "Crackerjacks" might have been the entertainment. I was lucky enough to go to a few of those dances, which were so much fun! The Murrah Booster Club and parents lavished the money on the team and the students.

Being a white cheerleader in the 1970s meant entering the closed inner circle of northeast Jackson women and society. Perhaps there was an invitation to the Sub-Debs and the Sub-Deb Ball, which was the high-school version of pre-debutante. It meant getting to know the Murrah football players. People could wander around downtown Jackson (the main shopping center in the seventies) for years and never find much to do . . . until they were invited to select society gatherings. The north Jackson women (that I knew) were and are today very conscious of style in every aspect: their clothes, homes, and especially their nails and hairdos. There were deigned dress codes in schools and social functions that befitted the rules of southern social etiquette. My mother, always a fashionable dresser, told me to "take those blue jeans off and put on something more feminine." But in the seventies, blue jeans were new and we wore them in a hippie or bellbottom style at my Murrah.

I enjoyed a few moments of social fluttering and then—again—misfortune continued. Jackson Prep and a few other private schools were built. The football team left with their coach to attend Jackson Prep along with the weight equipment, which we were informed belonged to the booster club, and not to Murrah High school. All the money was gone, and the big parent-sponsored victory dances ceased! We were cheerleaders with no football team. Was Murrah High School going to perish? I walked into the gym and saw the emblem with two horses standing on hind legs touching an "M," then turned to the empty stands, remembering the roar of the crowd that had existed before. Paper signs like, "Go Murrah, #1," once hung from the rafters and covered all the gym walls. How could we ever be #1 again, without a team? Old pieces of confetti floated across the floor, like torn-up memories. The spirit of past sporting events was almost tangible as I walked across the polished wood surface of the basketball court, and I could imagine the vocal magnitude of pep rallies. It was so loud that it gave me chills! Now it was strangely quiet, empty, and void. I sat down on the floor and cried.

Murrah hired a new coach, Bob Stevens, who had previously been at Central High School. I knew him. He was accustomed to team building, so the task placed before him was nothing new. He was a quiet, strong, and able man who went into the gym during physical education practice and formed a team from boys who had never stepped onto a football field. Coach Stevens told each of them they could be good ballplayers, and he encouraged the boys to work hard. Someone left a sign that said, "Traitors" by the gym. We assumed that it was meant for Coach Stevens, Susan, and me, because we had left Central High school to come to Murrah.

"The biggest coaching challenge in the Central Division of the Big Eight Conference awaits Murrah's Bob Stevens. He has the unpleasant task of replacing 42 lettermen off of last season's 10-1 pony team," wrote Sue Nables of the *Clarion-Ledger*. Only one letterman remained.

Integration had happened in stages to Murrah before this school year, so it was already home to many black students. Some of them were quite unhappy about the new school home. They had dreamed of playing for Lanier or Brinkley, the former all-black schools. As luck would have it, we inherited these football players. For the first time, we saw the power of black ball players, and young white boys who had never played ball were encouraged to participate in sports.

That first year we practiced cheerleading four hours, at Riverside Park or Murrah on weekdays, all summer to get ready for that much-anticipated season, and for the traditional Ole Miss summer cheerleading camp. Our squad did not have full attendance for the cheerleading camp or daily practices, even though they were mandatory. "Mandatory" events tended to go out the window at Murrah, along with the dress codes.

It occurred to us that our job was far greater than just cheering. We had to build confidence in that brand-new Murrah team. We stayed up all night writing each player a "happy" letter of encouragement, telling him how valuable he was and what it meant to hold the title of a Murrah Mustang. Statements, such as "Ya'll are so good; we are going to beat Callaway [our rival]," were messages we wrote to get them fired up. Being a Murrah Mustang simply meant (to me) being the best, because it had always been about mastery of academics and sports. We wanted to continue the champion tradition. Somehow things had to work out this time.

The cheerleaders worked late into the night on Thursday before the football games. We filled the rafters with signs and listened to songs like "All Right Now," and "Fire and Rain," while trying to make everything perfect for the pep rally. We prayed for our team and expected them to win! We told them excellence was expected of them; it was as if they put on a shining, imaginary coat of armor before the game. At that time, the purpose of the cheerleader was to support the team and the school. There were not any female sport teams during my high-school years. Although I had always felt that cheerleading was a sport, my job was to encourage the players. The pep rallies were amazing and loud; each class competed to win Mr. Curtis Hall's coveted spirit stick, which he threw to the most enthusiastic class. (Students were positioned in the bleachers by graduation year.) In my lifetime, I have never heard another school pep rally with as much volume as those at Murrah. It was a great challenge to blend and form a unified school spirit, but we did it with the help of Mr. Hall, our teacher and fervent booster. I loved planning the pep rallies, mastering the cheers, representing my school, and building faith in the players. That first season (fall of 1971) the football team had to work hard to find the best within themselves, to produce a result that was deemed impossible, according to the local papers.

As the season progressed, we won most of our football games, and integration continued to go well with few conflicts. We lost our first game on a rainy night in Natchez. At this game, I fell down onto my face while trying to do a "round-off" as I was running out onto a wet field. A large black football player (I cannot remember who it was) scooped me up out of the mud into his arms and gently put me down on the sidelines, so I would not be trampled by the rest of the team. I cheered with mud in my hair, uniform, and shoes, the entire game. My friend, Susan McBroom, laughed with me all night about my muddy burst into cheerleading. Even though we lost that rainy Natchez game, we still had hope in our hearts.

The other teams' run-through signs usually read, "The ole gray mare ain't what she used to be." That saying just made us angry. We retaliated with a crash sheet against Callaway that read, "No Fruit Sucks like the BIG ORANGE" (this was a nickname, as their colors were blue and orange). This sign was not a good idea; it just motivated Callaway to beat us. Mr. Merritt told the cheerleaders how unprofessional the sign was and he expected better art in the future, if the school was to continue paying for the crash sheet supplies. Freddie Funches (football player) told me that Callaway used to throw oranges out on the field and he tried to eat one, but the coach made him drop it. He also mentioned that Callaway students brought a makeshift coffin to our school with a fake "ole gray mule" in it before a game. He was tickled by the stunts of this rivalry.

During my senior year many of the white private school students returned to Murrah. Jackson Prep ended up beating all their small opponents, who were no challenge. Many of them came back to watch our games and wondered how the once all-white band, which in the past marched in rigid fashion, now boogie danced and swirled while they played the traditional fight song, "Hail to the Mustangs Valiant," and "The Horse." The black students taught us, you got to have soul when you move. If you had "soul" you were considered "cool." We had different views about music, dancing, and clothes. I remember that one of the black cheerleaders would not wear the traditional bobby socks that went with our cheerleader uniforms. She wore knee socks, and we wore bobby socks until the white girls just gave up and wore knee socks, so we would all match. It was hard for us to change little parts of tradition, but we did and things were still good.

Our basketball season went well. I rode with the team and a few cheerleaders on the school bus to out-of-town games, with one white player, Kip Ezelle, the rest being black. Coach Jordan's players were well disciplined, so I felt comfortable traveling with them. Coach was a man of high integrity. It was a more pleasant drive going to the games than from the games, when the guys were soaked in sweat, traveling on our old non-air-conditioned bus, but I enjoyed going to support the Mustangs. In appreciation for my interest in the basketball team, and attending the out-of-town games, Mr. Jordan gave me a trophy on basketball awards day. I was surprised and cried as I went forward to receive it. It was one of those impact-moments that I remember about a great teacher—Coach Orsmond Jordan. He noticed the efforts of those that worked hard, including cheerleaders.

After all these years, I had forgotten just how serious I was about maintaining "Murrah spirit." It was my first keen interest and vehicle to show the capable activism that Mrs. Ainsworth, my teacher from Central High, had engendered within me.

Coach Orsmond Jordan: Interview

"I really enjoyed coaching. My only thing is I put in too much time, and what I mean is by the day. I'd get home sometimes, finished at 8:30. Some parents would say, 'Y'all just finish practicing?' Yeah, we just finished, because I want to go over everything every day. When they walk through that gym door, we did what we call free shoot. I never said a word. You practice shooting where you get your shot . . . The boys loved to scrimmage and I loved to see them scrimmage . . . [If] I was disappointed with practice, I'd light my cigar and say I am gone, run y'all until my cigar goes out. We used to practice in the heat." Coach Jordan said that he did not have any problems. "I had the advantage, because if you're gonna play on my team, you do what I say do."

The Pep Rally

Robert Hand said in an essay, "I still smell the sweat covering my back and coating my underarms, dripping down my forehead onto my advanced math textbook after returning from the pep rally in the gym to Mrs. Tramel's advanced math class. How we could work up so much energy in a thirty-minute period escapes me now. My voice would be hoarse from the screaming and cheers led by the football coach and cheerleaders."

John Mixon became a really good football player under the supervision of Coach Stevens. He recalled, "We loved those cheerleaders, and those Murrah Misses. They were very inspirational. They were really behind us." *John remembered the "happies" that the cheerleaders gave him before the ballgames. I told him that we stayed up late at night writing one to each player.* "Yeah, I've still got them . . . They wrote the nicest things whether it was true or not, to all of us. You could tell they worked real hard."

Freddie Funches, *remembered for his beautiful smile, was good natured with keen football skills.* Freddie said he loved his time as a Murrah student and really enjoyed the pep rallies, "Mr. Hall was a great inspiration . . . he was a fireball. Mr. Hall, he tickled me when he entered the gym, he threw his hand up and that was it. Hall was our mascot. It was the cheerleaders, the majorettes . . . You didn't want to get out of school because it was so fun . . . because you caught it, you grabbed it. Everybody gave each other an opportunity and a chance to be who they were, to prove who you were." Freddie said he had never heard anything that loud before. "That makes a big difference when you are happy. That's how loud you get." Freddie remembered the "cheerleaders that flipped all over the floor."

Coach Stevens asked Freddie to give a pep talk at the rally. Freddie was reticent to do so. "Coach Stevens was saying, 'Funches, you always talking on the team. You get up here and talk.' I said, 'Coach, please don't make me go up there.' And I think I said a few words . . . We always had to say something before y'all took over, to just kinda rally the troops around, said, 'We playing Callaway tonight and we expecting a big crowd and we wanta go out there and mash some heads in and we need y'alls support so, let's go get 'em' and here y'all [cheerleaders] would come. It would get quiet for a minute and that door from the hallway would open, and there'd come Hall. He'd look over there at that crowd. He'd throw his head over there, and they'd holler. He'd throw his head over there, and they'd holler. But it was fun. You can't do anything like that without having pride; Murrah was a very prideful school. Our rival was pretty much Callaway."

Freddie talked of the activities that went on before the football game at Newell field. "You know, y'all would get to fix our signs for us that we used to run through when we come out on the field. Y'all would be out there jumping around, flipping, and everything, and y'all would hold the flag for us. When they said 'The Murrah Mustangs,' . . . we would bust up through there, and y'all would run in front of us, flipping around. We didn't know where y'all was flipping, just having a bunch of fun. But it was good; it was fun because we always had something going on, some kind of activity . . . We couldn't wait for Friday to play that game because the anticipation. We looked like we was doing something that whole week preparing for it, at least you all was." Football practice was held at the same time as cheerleader practice. "You know, we couldn't practice for looking at y'all. He [Coach Stevens] said 'that's why we can't get nothing done for y'all watching them cheerleaders!' He changed our practice field from y'alls and put us over there on the other side. But I'm just saying, it was a lot of fun, no kidding."

The Murrah Misses

Lindy Stevens Clement from the class of 1973 talked to Johnny and me one afternoon about her experience as the captain of the Murrah Misses. Lindy was much disciplined in her leadership style with the Misses, who performed in (what I remember as) perfect unison.

I asked Lindy what it felt like to go out on the field, as a Murrah Miss, with a new integrated football team, band, and drill team during those first ballgames.

Lindy replied, "I will sit here and just cry. I can't talk. I just wanted to prove everybody wrong. I wanted to go 'na na boo boo,' that this can work and we can do this and we are going to all get along. I should have brought my scrapbook, 'cause I wrote a letter . . . was in the tenth grade and we had just had our homecoming dance and Teena has heard this; Johnny, you haven't. And so he wrote in the dance, 'had a great time, blacks and whites together had a great time.' Well some 'power that be' man from north Jackson wrote a letter in and alluded that integration was mongrelization. Well, I wrote a letter back—I've got it and I said, 'How dare you compare high-school kids having a good time at a dance to mongrelization?' We are just trying to make it work, I was real . . . offended, because I felt like he attacked me personally. I felt like sports helped a lot, and cheerleading helped a lot, and the band helped a lot."

I said, "And the band, you remember how the band used to march real straight then all of a sudden they started dipping?"

Lindy: "And they would teach me to dance and we would shake everything we had, and the pep rallies! My children never ever saw a pep rally like that!"

I asked her to describe it.

Lindy: "OK, we want [Mr.] Hall. He would come out. We would all start screaming and he would come out. First of all, the Thursday night before we would all be up there painting signs. We would paint a hundred signs. I guess Mrs. Bennett [the cheerleader sponsor] was up there, there had to be somebody up there but I never saw them. I bet we had fifty kids every Thursday night, painting signs, tearing up confetti, black and white, painting, hanging signs from the rafters and then the players had their jerseys ... I had 73, with Stevens on the back, or sometimes I would wear my Murrah Miss sweatshirt and jeans or sometimes we would get to wear our uniforms made for homecoming, which I love that because that skirt was so short and I loved that and you would just scream the entire time and be soaking wet when you got through, and you couldn't hear anything."

Johnny: "At the pep rally?"

Lindy: "Yeah, Mr. Hall would get on the microphone and he would kinda holler and he would point to the sophomores and they would go nuts, then he would swing around and point at the juniors and they would go nuts and then he would do the seniors last and we would be going nuts and crazy, and then the football team would get up there and I can remember thinking what leaders Hutch and Willie Miller were. And I can remember my parents going to every football game."

Lindy: "The Murrah Misses were great, my first year ... they wore white cowboy boots and white, short (*too* short) skirts with white fringe and a white cowboy shirt and white gloves and white cowboy hats. We were a dance team, we would mainly kick."

She explained that the rigid movements were challenging to learn her junior year, when there were no experienced senior Misses returning to teach routines. "We were doing all the straight line drill type stuff and [one of the black Misses] started crying one day and said, 'black girls just can't move like this.'"

Johnny: "I guess it had all been worked up for white girls?"

Lindy: "All for white girls, we were all real stiff and so the next year I tried to shake it up a little bit, you know, but I had never had any problems, and when I was a senior my Misses were just great, they were fabulous! They were just great!"

I remember that the Murrah Misses put on an incredible show at halftime during the football games and at a few home basketball games. It was the highlight of the evening to view their performance. The girls danced and kicked in perfect unison to "The Horse" and other songs performed by the Murrah Band.

The three Murrah Miss officers wore blue inserts on the lateral scapular area of the white shirts.

Randy Robertson from the class of 1972 enjoyed watching the Murrah Misses in 1969. He sent a poem about them.

Murrah Misses 1969

My lord they were untouchable mystic
icons powder rouge in white
their half boots snug over smooth

short skirts cowgirl fringe barely
cloaking the mystery innocence oh
many throng of virgins!

It was halftime high school
the cotton panties posing
in unison with drums and hats

cocked neatly, straps
snug round, poised as one
fantastic chastity

belt in posture perfect
impenetrable, marching
to the one voice purity

Betsy Grimes Triggs from the class of 1973 wrote of the Misses, "When you talked about the Murrah Misses and Mr. Barksdale, it sparked several memories. I'm pretty sure our junior year was the first year for the Murrah Misses to be both black and white. My sister, Julie Grimes Dolci, would remember. I definitely remember the buzz in north Jackson that we had ruined the Misses by integrating them. Somehow the idea in the white flight community was that the school was integrated, but surely, we would not integrate such a sacred institution. I *loved* being a Murrah Miss. I felt so cool in that little white skirt with my cowboy boots. Lindy Stevens really rocked the whole thing; she was definitely in her element, and it was contagious. I loved the practices, the dance routines, being part of a group, and marching into a football stadium with the band. Nirvana."

Margie Cooper Pearson from the class of 1973 was a Murrah Miss that Alan noted had been famous for her perfect afro. Margie said in an interview, "Yeah. It was very trimmed, and you know why? Because that's another thing—I spent my summers in New York."

Debra Lindley Ruyle's recollection was that "the Murrah Misses, an interracial group, used to hang out together and go to each other's homes preparing for school functions together. After leaving Murrah we didn't remain friends."

Mary Al Cobb Alford wrote that "Murrah High School had an excellent reputation both academically and socially and I was thrilled to be a Mustang! My good friend Lele and I participated in the Murrah Misses for a while but it was apparent that my kicking and high-stepping abilities didn't quite meet the expected requirements. Our end of the line was referred to as the 'bad end' and we could never quite give 'The Horse' due justice."

Carol Sanders Bailey ('75) wrote: "By my senior year, I was very involved in the Murrah Misses and we had four officers. I remember Mary, who was captain, and I, first lieutenant, would pray together constantly about leading the Misses and being good role models and for our time together. We prayed all the time for the Misses. I went to Rangerette Camp at SMU during both summers (after tenth and after eleventh). When Mary and I were officers, after eleventh, we roomed together at SMU. I learned so much during that time. I didn't think anything funny about it, because I wasn't raised to think that way. My parents were not prejudiced, at least not my father. My mother, who was from the North, was more prejudiced than my father, which I've always found interesting. But when Mary and I roomed that summer, we learned so much from one another. I learned how different our cultures had been, but not our souls. Mary and I were Christians at heart, and we were very close friends. I loved her dearly, and still do, although I hate to say we've really lost touch except for class reunions. But when I see her, I still feel the closeness we had at such a pivotal time in our history. I sincerely don't think she and I were aware of what a big deal it was for us to room together at SMU. We thought nothing of it. I remember a couple of strange glances, but blew them off. We had a great time together."

Lenda Taylor Brown remembered a play-off game, "with St. Joe, unusually cold Thanksgiving and the Misses marched on an icy like field; we lost, but it was a great game and team. Remember 'The Horse.'"

The Murrah Band

The Murrah Band was an awesome organization with cutting-edge movements that played new music from the seventies.

Robert Gibbs ('72) recalled in an interview, "A lot of the band members ended up on campus before school started, so we ended up knowing some of the students, knew the band director, Mr. Dollarhide and we kind of integrated in a little easier maybe than some because we were there several weeks before school started. So I mean it was no apprehension. I don't think any of us, or very few of us felt that we could not succeed there. We were good students at Brinkley, so we were not bothered by the challenge of academics. It was the changes in culture because the biggest thing was . . . certain things that we were used to doing at Brinkley were just different, you know pep rallies that they used to do and Mr. Hall. Yeah, we never did anything like that at Brinkley so it was unique to see that type of school spirit. Being in the band, the songs that we played at Brinkley were totally different than the songs that they played at Murrah. The cheers from the cheerleaders were just totally different than the cheers we were used to. You know we had a much more lively, more upbeat way of doing things and we had to learn to be a lot more subtle and—"

Johnny: "And uptight."

Robert: "And uptight. [laughs] That's quite right!"

He said he played the drums. I noted that the band evolved and began "moving around a lot." I asked how that changed.

Robert: "It was hard. It was hard, that was probably one of the biggest challenges we had because when we came out Mr. Dollarhide, you know he was deep in tradition and he was used to marching very traditional styles and we were used to the more upbeat style and trying to become disciplined enough to do that was a challenge, and you know he would have to constantly get on us about our lack of discipline . . . There was one thing that kind of brought it to a head. Mr. Dollarhide had designed this halftime show with a ship and the song that we was going to play was 'The Good Ship Lollipop.' [laughs] And we kind of rebelled on that."

Robert said the band "just decided we can't do that. We just can't do it." They ended up playing the song once, after which Dollarhide agreed to include "more upbeat" songs in the band's repertoire. "When we played Lanier, he let some of the band members—African American band members—help him develop the show for the halftime show and that was probably the most upbeat band performance Murrah had ever done. And I often thought that when you think about integrating schools and the decision made to send blacks to integrate into a white culture how we were probably able to do that easier than doing it the other way if you had made whites try to integrate into our culture. I just don't see them being able to dance at a halftime show or play the songs that we played. I think it would have been very, very difficult. You know, we learned how to be a more disciplined regimented band. I don't think they could have done it the other way."

I said to Robert that I remembered that at the start of the school year the band "walked straight and all of the sudden they started dipping and everybody was like, WHOA! It was like really exciting to see that new way."

The band and Misses worked together with new motions, movements, rhythm, and sound. A totally original style and sound emerged on the football field and in the halls of Murrah from 1971 to 1973. The combination of white and black music was an epiphany for me. I knew that our class, in our time, was creating something magical in music and dance. I have noticed that wherever I have traveled, that beautiful music and dance are a universal language that all cultures can appreciate and understand, regardless of words. I recall seeing the Jackson Prep players and cheerleaders sitting in the bleachers, watching our game and halftime performances. I believed it may have been a revelation to them—that perhaps they missed something important.

The Homecoming Queen, the Dance, and Traditions

Homecoming was traditionally a time for the alumni to come home to a special football game. Usually the new freshmen from college came to this game to tell the Murrah students about their cool new life and studies far from home. They would dress in the latest university styles sporting a new haircut to let everyone know *they had grown up*. I noted that the alums from the previous year, of the old Murrah, did not return to see any of us for our homecoming. My junior year it was obvious that we were in this boat alone.

The week of homecoming had several added school activities. We dressed like rednecks one day and had a bonfire at the school on Thursday night before the game. Some guys put on Murrah Miss uniforms and did a hilarious kicking routine at the pep rally. The band and the Murrah Misses put on a special musical-dance show in dressy uniforms. The Misses wore black top hats, instead of the white cowboy hats, and a sparkling vest. At halftime a court of popular and pretty girls in long glittery evening gowns paraded with their escorts onto the field.

Debbie Horn Bondon was the homecoming queen, my junior year at Murrah High School. I can remember when they announced her name on the loud speaker. Debbie was the first black homecoming queen ever to be elected at Murrah.

Debbie Horn Bondon: Homecoming Queen

Debbie Horn Bondon submitted her story in an essay form:

> It was 1971 in the midst of racial tension in the country. In my community in Jackson, Mississippi most of my friends and classmates were focused and

disappointed that with the integration of schools. Longtime friends were being split up and not able to attend and graduate from high school together. Many of us had been together since elementary school and were looking forward to attending Brinkley High School together. It's amazing what young minds think is important.

There I stood, in 1971 on the grounds of Murrah High School, crowned the first black homecoming queen. Who would have thought it? My friends, family, and definitely not I ever imagined I would win, it was just enough that I was nominated. Never in my wildest dreams did I believe I would receive the most votes. My competitors were one White girl, and several other African American girls. They were pretty, smart and much more popular than I. No, I wasn't one of the Murrah Misses, I wasn't a cheerleader, I wasn't on the debate team. I was an introvert by my own definition, or maybe I was just a quiet soul, but by all accounts I did not participate in any extracurricular activities, I was not asked out on dates on Friday or Saturday night. So who was I . . . I was eighty-five pounds soaking wet, barely 4'11", an average student, raised in a destitute single family home—to think, I would be crowned homecoming queen of a school that was recently all white!

Willie, a football player who was a junior at the time cast an unprecedented nomination: African American, Black, non-White, Debbie Horn, nominated to become part of the Murrah Mustang Homecoming Court, and then receiving the coveted crown of most high school girls, homecoming queen. Yet, there I stood, freezing cold on the outside, due to the late fall chill in the air, but quite cozy and warm on the inside and not because of the hot chocolate that was oh so good.

Hours prior to the game, I was quick stepping it to the laundromat with pillow cases full of clothes to be washed; all chores that had to be done before any homecoming game. (Funny what sticks in your mind over thirty-nine years ago). Although overwhelmed with excitement and disbelief, it became clear why a White classmate and member of the student body that I did occasionally converse with in class began to quiz me on the certainty of me coming to the game, and what I was going to wear and if I would be wearing my signature afro, which I proudly wore regularly. The day before the homecoming game, this student's overzealous questioning contributed to the fact that he was in on a little secret that history was about to unfold on the grounds of Murrah High School, and I could not have been more clueless. Strangely odd, I remember thinking, but clueless all the same. The band was playing loudly, although I can't remember what was being played. The excitement was as palpable in the air as the heart beats in my chest. I was so happy, as I stood there in my lovely royal blue velvet dress trimmed with silver piping. I knew I wanted to wear my school colors and I distinctly remember the feel of the soft blue velvet fabric upon purchasing it. The gown was meticulously made by my best friend's mom, who was a seamstress, it fit me perfectly! I don't remember if we won or lost the game but I do remember the pride and joy I felt that night.

The years 1971–1972 were some of the most turbulent times, however, this tiny black girl who lacked confidence and [was] unaware of her abilities was crowned the first black homecoming queen of Murrah High School. Racial barriers were crossed that night, which was an amazing feeling. I remember reading a surprisingly supportive article from the *Clarion-Ledger* newspaper about me winning the crown. I'm sure my classmates, family and friends were all in awe that night, but no more than I, Debbie Gail Horn. I learned a very profound lesson that magical night . . . to have confidence in myself and my abilities . . .

"MMM UR . . . RR RAH, Murrah Mustangs Fight . . . Yeah!" Debbie said, remembering one of the cheers.

The Homecoming Dance

In the days of the old Murrah—there were expensive dances with real bands. We did not experience this extravagance. I remember that I personally paid (from afterschool jobs) to front some expenses for a homecoming dance that was held in the gym. Someone played records for the event. We sold tickets, but I don't recall ever being reimbursed. We didn't break even. I am not sure why there was not as much interest in organized dances during our tenure.

Cy Rosenblatt of the class of 1972 remembered the dances in an essay, "One of the more intriguing aspects of this period was how the students chose to associate with each other after the custodial staff locked the doors each weekday. Presumably during the freedom of choice period that preceded court-ordered desegregation, the administration of Jackson Public Schools frowned on school-sponsored dances. The assumption may have been that these social events would lead to fraternization of boys and girls across racial lines. However, there were Friday night post-game dances at the Knights of Columbus meeting hall. Interestingly, these dances were organized by entrepreneurial individuals who operated outside of the purview of the school's administration. Admission was by ticket, which created an economic barrier to less well to do students attending the functions. Consequently, the dances were attended primarily by relatively better-off white students whose parents did not mind paying for their children to socialize, but poorer students of all colors were left out.

"A year plus under court-ordered desegregation allowed the Jackson Public Schools to favorably consider a request by the student leadership of Murrah to have a school dance on campus. Homecoming 1972 witnessed the gymnasium being used as a dance venue. The crowd was completely mixed. There were no problems. A social barrier had been broken."

One Wild Night

Alan Huffman

■

Memory isn't fixed. It's not like a framed photo that fades a little but otherwise remains the same, so that the younger you is still there, exactly as you were, on the balcony of that motel in Daytona Beach during your senior class trip. It's more like a jpeg that can be photo-shopped, cropped, forwarded around, or accidentally deleted.

Our brains constantly update our memories with new information, such as something we hear on the news, or a story someone else tells that gets incorporated into our own. At the same time, we may discard details that are crucial to someone else's recollection, without even realizing it. The result of all these adjustments is that it's possible to remember the entire musical arrangement of the instrumental "The Horse," and the scent and feel of the autumn air the night Murrah played Callaway, but not our high school teachers' first names or the fact that we hurt someone's feelings in biology class in a way that haunts them to this day.

All of which makes probing the disparate memories of a large group of people, forty years after the fact, a complicated endeavor, especially with the added variable of a charged subject such as race.

At a late-night gathering of alumni from the class of 1973 at Johnny Jones's law office, the pitfalls of memory were on full display. The meeting was supposed to be about sharing memories and comparing notes about integration, but it became clear that the memories themselves, as well as how we interpreted them, had changed. There were shared recollections, yet at times it felt as if we had inhabited parallel universes. Cassandra Fowlkes Wilson had no recollection of one event that was very vivid to me, which was all about her, and she remembered an unrelated episode involving a group of classmates who insisted it never happened. Some things sounded familiar, but it was hard to say if it was because they actually happened, or because they were merely plausible. At one point, one of the participants accused another, saying, "You were always a bigot," which led to a spirited, ultimately hurtful exchange. Those of us who were putting this book together decided that it is enough to acknowledge that the exchange took place, without quoting it verbatim, because the allegations were so damaging and impossible to prove or disprove.

In some ways, integration was designed to create shared experiences, which would naturally lead to shared memories, and despite that one dispute, it did. At our reunions, it has been obvious that both black and white classmates share many similar vantage points—not necessarily in the political realm, but as people who had been on the cutting edge of racial integration in the Deep South. During our senior year, we had been required to vote for both black and white class beauties and favorites, in equal number, which had been an eye-opener if only because it revealed to us that black and white students often had different ideas about who was beautiful and favored. We had voted for black and white co-class presidents. But when it came time to select the top honors, the bilateral selection process was abandoned—whoever got the most votes for Blue Knight and Silver Lady won. The result was that Fred Sheriff, who is black, was picked Mr. Murrah High School, and Nancy Powell, who is white, Miss Murrah High School. Seeing them posed together in the *Résumé*, like some interracial couple in formal attire at a 1973 prom in Jackson, Mississippi, was mildly provocative to some of our parents. But that was who we were. It was who we still thought we were. But the details encompassed in our respective memories varied—widely.

Life at Murrah was mixed, in every sense of the word, including in the school production of "The Wizard of Oz," in which Cassandra pioneered the role of a black Dorothy. At football games, both black and white players took to the field, with black and white cheerleaders on the sidelines, and both black and white Murrah Misses strutting to "The Horse" at halftime. There were racially mixed parties after the games. As our senior year drew to a close, we held our graduation party at Charles Irby's family house in Eastover, the most exclusive, all-white neighborhood in town, which no doubt scandalized some of the neighbors in that our group encompassed the largest contingent of black people who ever visited Eastover at one time, and not one of them was a maid or yard man. And so, regardless of where our lives had taken us in the intervening years, we shared a lot of common ground. The hope was that our individual and shared memories might help explain what had happened in Jackson in the years since—what had gone right, and what had gone wrong.

But forty years is a long time to account for, and even our first class reunion had illustrated a gap in how black and white students remembered their time at Murrah, and how they viewed what had happened in the decade since. At the organizational meeting of the tenth reunion, two white alumni had said they could take the lead in planning the event because they didn't work and had maids who could help them. Hearing this, I thought: Wow—someone has forgotten how freighted such a comment would be. And in fact, silence fell over the room. Both of the women who offered up their privileged lifestyles for the cause had been open minded about race, but somehow, in the intervening years, had forgotten how it sounded to brag about having a maid. The result was that a group of black alumni decided to hold their own all-black reunion, without telling the white alumni. The official reunion was mixed but, owing to the rift, predominately white. Subsequent reunions have been more racially mixed, though always more white than black. Getting together—like discussing integration—seems to matter more to white than the black alums.

The reunion that landed us at Johnny's office had been organized for "all classes" of Murrah. Teena, her husband, and her sister and I had recently attended another "all classes" reunion, with a younger crowd that was, aside from us, all black. This one was the opposite—older, and predominately white. Both reunions were held in bars, and after the older, predominately white one, a group of us adjourned to Johnny's office, where we might talk more freely, without having to shout to be heard. A few former classmates who attended the group interview session declined to allow us to use to their names or words in this text. We have followed their wishes.

Otherwise, the group included the following cast of characters:

Johnny, a staunch liberal who saw integration thoughtfully, more or less as the white man's burden, yet who sent his own children to private schools.

Teena, a conservative Republican who believed forced integration was unfair, but who was glad she'd been a part of it, and who sent her own children to racially integrated public schools.

Me, the writer in the bunch, who had initially objected to forced integration but joined the effort after spending time in the bowels of the beast—a year as a student in a segregationist academy.

Cassandra, a successful jazz vocalist who had been a cheerleader and had served as a kind of bridge between black and white students, though she occasionally suffered for it, but who declined to be quoted directly in the book.

Steve Jenkins, a rocket scientist with a nerdy sense of humor who had been among the very few to befriend a black classmate during the early years of desegregation—a period known as "freedom of choice," which preceded full-scale integration.

Laura Ashley, who, as an army brat, had attended numerous schools in different parts of the country, and so was not overly concerned with the shifting dynamics of integration in Jackson public schools.

Betsy Grimes Triggs, whose mother had been extremely liberal, and who was, herself, equally liberal for a time, but who was now more conservative.

Katie Barwick-Snell, who was liberal through and through.

And Randy Robertson, an erudite upperclassman—he was a year ahead of us—who was white, and had dated a student who was black, in high school.

In summary, the group was comprised of several white alumni and a single black one.

Teena recorded the conversation, and later typed up a transcript, which is excerpted here. Johnny started things off by explaining the process of compiling our experiences for a book, through interviews, essays, and Q&As.

"What we've done so far is talk to people about what they did before they got to Murrah, what was happening when desegregation hit in December of '69, what school they went to, and then what Murrah was like and what they learned from it. Pretty simple." he said. He then called on Laura to give a thumbnail history of her education.

Laura said she had attended about nine different schools before arriving at Chastain Junior High in 1969. "And then this thing came along we had to change schools," she said, referring to court-ordered integration. She was among those who completed the year at Chastain, after integration during the Christmas break. The change in the school's student body did not have a profound effect on her because she was accustomed to changing schools, she said.

At that point, I said I remembered two things about Chastain: That during desegregation the school received a couple of black students, and that I had felt sorry for them because, though there were no problems that I knew of, no one talked to them, including me. And then after integration what I remember was being resentful that we didn't get to have ninth-grade class day.

By having interrupted Laura's narrative, I caused the conversation to veer away from her personal history, and a classmate who did not want to be mentioned by name, but said he was fine otherwise being quoted here—we'll call him Wildcat—saw his first opening. He said he had experienced some racial trouble at Murrah, but only during our senior year. "It was bad," he said. "It was just . . . people wanted to get in fights and whip asses." The episode, which took place in the seniors' men's room, included interracial violence that ended, Wildcat said, when a teacher entered and said, 'OK, boys, it's time to get out of here.'"

During our senior year, Murrah had three classes, though during our junior year it had had only two. Wildcat's position was that the addition of a tenth-grade class had upset the balance and caused a lot of fights. I didn't remember this, nor did several of the others, but Wildcat seemed to know what he was talking about, and Laura seemed to agree.

"When we were there as juniors and it was just the two classes, I felt so close," Laura said. "It was great! I felt like we were all one big class . . . And the next year when we were seniors and there were three [classes], I didn't feel that way anymore."

Katie said she felt that the class had bonded during the year that Brinkley was the tenth grade.

Wildcat then recalled another interracial fight, this one behind the cafeteria. A white football player, David Hutchison, who was respected by both black and white students, had broken it up. Wildcat said Cassandra ended up giving him a ride home because he was afraid to go out to the parking lot to his car.

Johnny observed that some black students had told him they had not been thrilled by the idea of being transferred to Murrah, which was something of a revelation to white students who, due to their comparatively privileged upbringings, thought they alone had sacrificed for integration.

"The catcher for the baseball team, said, 'We didn't want to go to Murrah as much as y'all didn't want to go to Brinkley,'" Johnny said.

Other black classmates had observed that not being able to attend Brinkley High School (beyond the tenth-grade center) had been a disappointment, because Brinkley was held in the same high esteem in the black community as the old Murrah had been in the white.

White Jacksonians were generally oblivious of this fact, in part because they had limited knowledge of the black community other than that black educational facilities were considered unequal to white. As it turned out, the way the lines were redrawn for integration, the students from the best black schools ended up going to the best white school, which was Murrah.

"So the question we were debating," I said, "and I don't know how you would answer it, but, whether or not this was done by design, whether or not they chose to bring—obviously, they had the whole city to choose from when they were drawing these lines for these school districts, and so they took what was basically the best white school district, and it looks like they took the best black school district and put those two together. It's an idea I had never really thought about. I had no idea. We still don't know if it's true, but it just seems logical based on what you're saying."

Steve observed that, "it would be hard to say exactly what was behind any of those plans because they were actually three, right? So, I mean, one plan would go into effect in the interim, and then there would be litigation . . ."

Yet it was clear that while black students were in the majority at Murrah, it felt to many of them as if whites were, including what Steve described as "that co-president type deal with—I mean, if the black people are in the majority and they want to elect the black president, go ahead on."

Randy said that he, as a white student, had been harassed in the men's bathroom by black students for being close to Cassandra. "They raked me over," Randy said. "I got threatened a lot." He said he'd be in the bathroom, smoking Kool cigarettes, and a group of black guys would enter and corner him there. He said he actually liked the controversy surrounding his relationship with Cassandra.

Teena asked, "What did they say to you? They just pushed you... or what?"

Randy said the students mostly just insulted him and badgered him with personal questions.

I then asked if it was clear that Jackson was the first court-ordered school integration. Johnny said Little Rock, Arkansas, had integrated its public schools in 1957.

"But that was just allowing black kids to go to school; that wasn—" Steve began, but got drowned out by everyone talking at once.

"Are you saying this was the first school district in the country that was truly integrated?" I asked.

"Forcibly," Johnny said. In fact, several other school districts in Mississippi were forcibly integrated the same years, but he said another two years passed before integration was enforced in many parts of the south.

Steve said he now lives in Los Angeles, and integration came much later there, that it was "in litigation for years and years and years."

Johnny said the federal justices were angry at Jackson Public Schools "because they knew it was just run by a bunch of damn racists."

Steve responded that the problem wasn't solely with the Jackson school system. He said the state of Mississippi "had just much more explicitly and vigorously said we deny the authority of the Supreme Court and we are going to fight it."

"And we were the center of massive resistance," Johnny said. "But the [Jackson] school system particularly was horrible."

He asked Betsy to tell her story. She said she "had really liberal parents, especially my mother," and that she had attended Brinkley. She said her grandfather, who was white, had helped blacks register to vote in Memphis, and her family had moved to Jackson from Tennessee when she was in the seventh grade, and while living in Nashville her mother had driven the kids to Franklin, Tennessee, specifically so they could swim at a newly integrated public pool. "I mean, I'm sorry . . . it was a little weird," she said. "But anyway, I thought I was helping the cause [at Brinkley], and I was so excited when all of a sudden there were all these black people in my school, you know, because there were 20–30 percent at Bailey, and then after Christmas there were a lot of black people. And one thing is, I loved that things loosened up, and I met Cassandra. I mean, I remember you [speaking to Cassandra] smarted off in French class or something, and I thought, 'I like that girl!' And from there, you know, a lot of the snooty kids left." She said she wasn't worried about attending Brinkley. "I loved it."

Johnny asked Betsy if she had any problems and she said no. "I mean, people were mean," she said. "But: High-school mean."

Johnny asked Betsy if she considered herself as liberal as her mother. She said no, that she was much more conservative now. He asked when she realized she was more conservative.

"When did I wake up?" she asked. "I remember in, I guess, in eleventh grade, in art class, Kelsey Garnet was there. I was so guiltily liberal. I thought I had done something wrong because I was born white. And they kept goading me and goading me, and I finally said to Kelsey, because she was going to beat my ass, and I finally said, 'Well, just beat my ass. I'm sick and tired of hearing you talk.' And then she laughed and said, 'I wondered when it was going to happen.'" Betsy laughed at the memory. "When I was going to break, because you know, because whatever she wanted I would do, because she was black and I was white. I was having to prove to her that I was worthy . . . And after that I just, you know . . . I started taking people as they came. And again, my mother is just, 'If you're black, you have been discriminated against. If you are a woman, you have been discriminated against, and if you are a black woman, you can't do anything wrong because the world has been against you your whole life.'" Betsy said she often votes for Republican candidates, though she voted for Obama.

Teena said very emphatically, concerning Betsy having voted for Obama, "I did not!"

"Are you cheering now, Teena?" Steve asked, somewhat mischievously.

Wildcat interjected that his wife had attended formerly all-black Jackson State University, which had been a beacon of education in the black community in the days of segregation, and sent graduates to Exeter, MIT, and Harvard.

"You know, it's so interesting because people in the white community used to think they were the ones who sacrificed," I pointed out. "You know, that was the way it was sort of perceived in the white community . . . that we were sacrificing things in order to bring the whole system up, and I don't think it ever occurred to white people that black people were sacrificing anything to do it. It's like, we were helping you . . . And it's so interesting and it's so funny that we all have been together this whole time, and I've never—I never picked this up at all."

"Well, I'm curious, because I was always told that the black schools had textbooks that didn't even mention Alaska as being a state," Katie said. "In fact, is that some P.R. thing that was given to us?"

"Well, I think, I have read a lot about the history of the civil rights movement since I left Jackson, and one thing I think is very interesting is that even when black people were really getting the raw deal, they still could have bought the American dream," Steve said. "The upward mobility—based on education. And they still really believed these lies we were telling them that, you know, you go to school and everything's going to be fine . . . you could become a minister, you could become a teacher, or if you really sort of went out of state or something, you go to dental school or become a doctor or a pharmacist or something, but the things you could do without really leaving the area was to become an educator or a preacher, and those required education, and it was really considered an accomplishment to do that, and I think if I were growing up in that environment, I think I have the kind of personality I'd be saying, 'This is bullshit. I'm gonna throw some gasoline or something,' you know . . . I think it is remarkable that they hung in there . . . You think about a guy like Medgar Evers [the civil rights leader assassinated in Jackson]. I mean, Medgar Evers served in the military, defended our country against its enemies, and came home, and they said, 'Boy, go to the back of the bus.' Now, I think I would've said, 'I want to shoot yo ass right now!'" He laughed. "I don't know how they were so brave . . . The people I admire most in life are the people who just will not be moved, you know. They just stand and take it and take it and take it until they win. I don't have the patience for that. I would've just shot somebody and gone to prison and been a sad case, you know. But a guy like Medgar Evers, I have nothing but admiration for these people who just stood firm, you know."

The conversation segued to segregationist leaders in the South, and Betsy recalled that she and Cassandra had once gone trick-or-treating at former Mississippi segregationist Governor Ross Barnett's house while students at Murrah. "One year we said, 'Let's go to Ross Barnett's house and trick-or-treat and see what he does,'" she said.

I asked what happened, but before she could answer, Teena's tape again ran out, so while we were waiting for her to reload the recorder I brought up the time a group of us were driving back from a football game in McComb, Mississippi, and Cassandra had gotten into the car of a friend who attended a segregationist academy. "We were a little worried about it because we knew that it was the first black person that had ever been in [his] car—"

Cassandra did not remember the episode, so I recounted it. "Anyway, so, Cassandra was game," I said, "and we were just, 'OK, whatever.'" The guy who went to the segregationist academy was a notoriously fast driver, and our group, which was following in another car, lost sight of his car, a Plymouth Roadrunner with a hemi engine. I said we had later come upon his car, pulled over on the side of the interstate by a highway patrolman, the hood of whose cruiser was open, with the engine smoking. We pulled in behind. The trooper had clocked our friend going 142 in a 70 mph zone.

"And Cassandra was in the back seat . . . This was in Hazelhurst, Mississippi, in 1972 . . . And, we're like, 'OK, this is not cool,'" I said. "It's bad enough that he got caught doing 140 mph. When they pulled over, we caught up with them, and we got Cassandra, and we took Cassandra to Jackson because we were afraid that—we did not want her going to jail in Hazelhurst with a [white] guy who was going 140 in a 70."

Steve then went back to the trick-or-treating episode at Ross Barnett's house. "I don't think Ross Barnett had . . . I don't think he had an ounce of animosity in his heart," he said. "He was a pure politician. He said what it took to get elected, and if suddenly the population had wanted everybody to be integrated, that's what he would've been for. I think he was the perfect example of a demagogue."

Wildcat asked, "Now y'all did go trick-or-treating, didn't you?"

"Yeah, we went to the door," Betsy said. "He opened the door and was a little surprised but then he said something like, 'I don't have anything but maybe there's some doughnuts in the kitchen,' and . . . we said, 'No, thanks.'"

"I bet he was a bit flustered by two girls trick-or-treating," Steve said.

At that point the conversation took another abrupt turn, to an alleged episode involving a dinner for white cheerleaders at River Hills Tennis Club, which got divisive, and which none of the former classmates involved in the discussion agreed to be quoted about here.

Wildcat said he couldn't imagine any of the cheerleaders participating in such an event. Who was right, then? Both sides were adamant about their recollections—either that it did or did not occur.

I said I'd never heard about it, "But I also do know that some things that white people didn't think anything about meant something in the black community. I mean, it's very possible that there was some episode that was just totally innocuous to the white people, that represented something completely different in the black community."

The subject of the Mississippi state flag, which contains the Confederate battle flag in its canton corner, came up, and after a short, inconclusive discussion, Betsy said, "Well . . . I'm getting tired, and I want to hear the other people who haven't spoken yet, and then we can talk about the flag."

With that, Johnny turned the floor over to Katie, who said she had also gone to Brinkley, then to Murrah. She said she had enjoyed both, and was glad she didn't have to attend the old Murrah, where female students were subjected to something similar to sorority hazing by "these snobby socialites." She said her mother became more liberal after the three civil rights workers were murdered in Neshoba County in 1964. "It was probably the turning point for her, so, you know, that probably influenced me staying in public schools." She said she never had any bad experiences at either school, though she heard "words in the bathroom between black girls and white girls."

The conversation moved to tales of white girls being molested or touched in the halls of the school and the "teachers not doing anything to stop it." No one mentioned whether anything similar happened to black girls. Of such episodes, Teena said, "My sister said once you learn to confront it, it stopped. But, you know, girls, southern girls, have a harder time confronting, but you learn to do that, and then just back off."

"I remember going to New York, I was sixteen, on a Belhaven tour and some guy did that to me," Betsy said, amid the excited chatter. "I was so shocked, and my first thought was, 'What did I do?' And then as you get older . . . you're like, 'asshole!'"

Steve was up next to talk about his experiences. He said he had made his first black friend while in elementary school, after the first round of desegregation. "We sort of bonded on the universal boy theme of 'farts," he said. "We found we had a lot in common in that area, the physiology being sort of universal and everything. So, we're friends, and I had him over to my house one time, which, I mean, I was not post-racial. I mean, indeed this was the only black kid in the class but I think I was probably making an effort. I had this really overdeveloped sense of fairness and stuff that's just not right and pisses me off, you know, so I invited him over to my house, and I remember that my parents were OK with it, but I wonder if they were worried. I mean, this was 1968, '69, and our next-door neighbors, who I'm not going to name, who were prominent contributors to the Citizens' Council and, you know, I don't think we were worried that we were going to be firebombed, but I bet there were some people looking out the window going, 'Who's that little black boy down there playing with Steve?' You know.

"But I remember at the time thinking freedom of choice is the right thing and I have sort of libertarian instincts, you know. People should go where they want to go and do what they want to do. And I went to Chastain. I loved it except for the fact that I was just sort of a late bloomer, so I was always kind of a small, not very grown-up looking boy, you know, scared of all the other boys and really scared of all the girls. But I sort of felt like I was going through life the way I was supposed to go, and Chastain was just the best place ever and we just kicked ass on everybody in football except that one game to Callaway." He laughed. "And then in the middle of the year it was announced that I was going to have to go to Bailey, and I can remember feeling so wronged by that, you know, that I should be able to go where I want to go. This is America, damn it. Plus, we hated Bailey, you know, for no good reason at all. You put these kids in one school and they just immediately 'hate those bastards!' Bailey, you know . . . But I went there, really kind of, again, nervous. But I had great fun at Bailey. It was just, it was so raucous compared to Chastain. I mean, Chastain people practically walked in straight lines down the hall, you know. It was very, almost militaristic. I mean, I wrote in my essay that I remember I wore a peace sign emblem to school one time, and one of those dumb-ass coaches, you know, grabbed me and really kind of threatened me, like, you know, and I thought, I mean, 'This is what gets you worked up?' But when we got to Bailey . . . I don't know whether Bailey was different like that fundamentally, but they had a whole new set of issues to worry about, all these kids just thrown together, and I can remember it was just a lot louder and more raucous, and again, kind of intimidating, but I had great fun at Bailey, and you know, met a lot of new people."

He said one black student had tried to pick a fight with him, "going through the sort of escalating rhetoric, you know: 'Yeah, you bad, ain't ya . . . you bad!' And I'm going 'No, I'm good!'" He laughed. "I didn't know what the protocol was, and he was really trying to get me to escalate so he could kick my ass, and I just, I didn't know I was supposed to [do]. And then finally, Robert Kelly came and saved me. He came over and put his arm around me and goes, 'He all right, man . . . he all right . . . he all right.'" Again he laughed. "It was only later, after Murrah, that I realized that I had sort of just skated past an ass whooping. I don't know why anybody thought it would be any accomplishment to whoop my ass, but . . . I don't remember any violence or anything. I do remember being threatened the way boys do, and I don't know that it was anything racial, but every once in a while, somebody would threaten you to watch you cower, and I could cower. I could do that. I do remember seeing that there was a pecking order on skin color among black people, and I remember being surprised about that. I had to learn to stop using the N-word, the way we used it all the time, to other white kids, you know, somebody did something. The same way you'd say, you know, 'you jackass,' you didn't mean you were a . . . four-legged, mule-like animal, you'd just say 'you jackass.'"

Steve said he skipped Brinkley because he had earned advance credits, and went to summer school. Instead he went straight to Murrah. He said there was no real discussion in his family about whether to stay in public school, that his parents "had a very well-developed sense of fair play and they left Saint Luke's Methodist Church because they were turning black people away, but they were not crusaders and they were not risk takers and they were not, you know, going to be out there on the front lines and get shot at, so, I should ask them sometime, you know, what their thought processes were. But anyway, I went to summer school. I showed up at Murrah as a junior there, and kind of scared to death because I was young looking and not very big ... I was afraid the white guys were going to kick my ass."

He said he remembered being in downtown Jackson with Cassandra during high school, acting affectionately toward each other, "trying to get a rise out of passersby, and they just weren't interested. It was like, 'Do you not see what we're doing?!' But, so, to try to answer your question, 'Did it work?' I think it did something really important, and that's to show that it's possible to do this. I still don't know whether it's the right thing overall. I mean, well, I like living in a society with less coercion, you know, and I'm not really a libertarian, but I like the kind of society where you go to school where you want to go, not where some jerk says you have to go ... But, I also know that that method wasn't going to remedy the inequities, just was never going to, and I think there were people who thought this couldn't be done, and we did it, so, you know, that answered that question, and now we can talk about whether it's a good policy and how much and where and when. We don't have to wonder whether it's possible; we know it's possible."

Johnny asked if Steve had any opinion about why so few white students now attend Murrah, which was at the time 98 percent black. Steve said he left Mississippi after college, "and one of the things that I am kind of sad about is it seems much less progressive now than it did when I left." He added that, "What's happened, though, is that everybody who's got any money, black or white, has left town ... I'm not saying I'd blame anybody; I'm just saying that, you know, if the city, if the productive, educated core of the city is moving out, then what you're going to be left with is this sort of, not so well functioning, and if you don't have that community that ensures that people go to school and get an education, then what you have left is what you got ... I think some day ... people will look back and say, 'How did they let their education system collapse the way they did; how did they do that?'"

"Somebody's got to get a handle on Jackson, period. That's it," Wildcat said. "It's not going to be the white folks, because the white folks aren't there."

And with that, everyone decided it was late and time to go home.

Life Lessons of the Murrah Experience

Narrated by Teena Freeman Horn

■

The hero's journey was eloquently described by Joseph Campbell in his book, *The Power of Myth*. Campbell defines the hero as "Someone who has given his or her life to something bigger than oneself . . . The usual hero adventure begins with someone from whom something has been taken, or who feels there's something lacking in the normal experiences available or permitted to be members of his society. This person then takes off on a series of adventures beyond the ordinary, either to recover what has been lost or to discover some life-giving elixir. It's usually a cycle, a going and a returning" (J. Campbell and B. Moyers, *The Power of Myth* [New York: Doubleday, 1988], 123).

I always thought that some of our class and special teachers took Campbell's hero's pilgrimage of departure from the known to fulfillment of a full experience and now a return forty years later to tell the story of our unusual adventure. During a time of uncertainty and even danger, some classmates protected other peers, teachers kept us busy—engendering competition and friendship. We went from living a normal teenage life of fitting into a group—wanting to be like all the others before us—into a situation of chaos, then deciding to be what we wanted regardless of what the others around us thought. We learned to make the best of change and go with the experience of something different, and then celebrate these original notions while finding a secret strength within ourselves. Let's not try to be like the rest of the city. We are unique. Our class motto went, "We are the best that will ever be. We are the class of 1973!"

What began as a quest for Murrah during the mass integration school switch became a discovery of an inward mystery for me. No matter what happens, I can reach down into my soul and pull out what is left and be anything, survive anything. That was my life lesson from the mass integration experience. Looking back, I was not happy about the method and procedures that took away our liberty in making school selections. The initial process in Jackson, Mississippi, in 1970 could have been done better. I was afraid of new things, and new people, but then later—it turned out OK. My mixture of new friends, for a few years at Murrah, was like a "Camelot" (many have made this comparison). Both races were on equal footing (in my view point) pulling for one team.

What did my class learn from our educational experience in the Jackson, Mississippi, public schools during our formative years? Was our education more than the curriculum required by the state, as compared to any city or town in Mississippi or other areas of the South? The consensus of many of the participants is that we learned much more in a social interaction sense and perhaps became more tenacious in our search for a deeper meaning of life, looking harder to find the truth about human relationships. Most of those interviewed stated that they enjoyed their time at Murrah. The opinions vary as to whether we filtered much from the actual classroom situation, which left some of us underprepared for the rigorous academia of college. But, we learned to hold fast, to endure and to hope that things could change and work out over time.

Some classmates and teachers at Murrah and those in other schools we visited along the way shine through in our memories after all this time. It has been forty-plus years since my 1973 high-school class graduated. A few great teachers, parents, and coaches stayed with us during a frightening period of upheaval. I will never forgot how grateful, and for some reason safe, I felt when I saw Governor and Mrs. William Winter at our high-school events; it affirmed to me that I was in the right place. Coach Orsmond Jordon watched over me and the other cheerleaders that rode the bus with his all-black basketball team and his sole white player, Kip Ezelle. Coach Jordan was in control of his environment and his players; he was a professional. His calm demeanor was one to emulate, as was that of Mr. Merritt, our principal. Coach Bob Stevens and the football coaches were like heroes in the way they put together a winning season. Coach Lee and Clanton told us that it was not heroic, but just a coach's job to turn a team around and make the statistics work.

Classmates Reflect on Special Things They Learned or Experienced at Murrah

Doug Levanway wrote: "I finally got to go to Murrah . . . After the detour to Massachusetts and the lost year at Brinkley, I got to a real high school, and it was great. It was the school of my brothers, only different. We had our academic and athletic heroes, our leaders, our popular kids and everyone else, and our achievers and under achievers; the difference was that now some were black and some were white. We had cheerleaders, the Misses, national merit finalists and semi-finalists (lots of them, in the Murrah tradition), the Murrah singers, plays (one with a future Grammy Award winner singing the lead), pep rallies, proms, the *Hoofbeat*, football on Friday nights at Newell Field, parties at McBroom's house, and endless drives at night on the loop that always went through Riverside Park. We had everything that makes high school high school, and I remember it all with great fondness and pride."

Michael Bounds *told us, in an interview, that he joined the army after finishing high school.* "Mr. Curtis Hall [Murrah teacher] was such a great influence on my life. I knew I didn't have enough money to go to college . . . Mr. Hall said, 'you need to go in the army or some sort of armed forces . . . the Vietnam War is winding down. Don't worry about it. Go ahead and go.' Well five months later, I was arriving in Vietnam. I was really kind of pissed at Mr. Hall. But it was an eye-opening experience. I went from being an eighteen-year-old, not knowing anything; to by the time I came home from Vietnam I had seen and done it all. It was a wonderful maturation. I just grew up in that period of time that I was there." *Michael was later stationed in Germany, where he ran into his Chastain Junior High English teacher named Joe Moss. Michael said he enjoyed theater while at Murrah and actually was cast in a play with Joe in Germany.* "My experience in Germany was a dream. I loved it; I saw all of Europe, compliments of Uncle Sam."

Susan McBroom *was my best friend in high school and we are still very close. She wrote,* "I think I was influenced more by my parents and the people who helped raise me more than the situation at school. I was more upset that so many of my friends ran away to private schools and we were not as close anymore. I think I got a great education in public school and in state colleges. My views on issues today are formed more from my pocketbook and my resentment for government trying to run my private life than it has to do with anything that happened back then. . . . Nothing 'happened to us'; we lived in a time period of change and upheaval and it made us who we are today and I don't think that is a bad thing. All generations have their trials and tribulations to deal with. We end up where we are because of a lot of factors not just what happens to us at school."

Myra Stevens Myrick, *Lindy Stevens Clement's younger sister, was a sophomore cheerleader when I was a senior.* Myra recalled, "The only incident at Murrah that might have been race related was in Mr. Campbell's art class. There were two sisters, Big Iris and Little Iris. Of the two, Little Iris was the trouble maker. She started picking on me for some reason and tried to get me in trouble with Mr. Campbell. When I complained Big Iris got mad and thought I was getting Little Iris in trouble. Both girls wanted to fight and we had to go to the principal's office to sort it out. I never went to the principal's office for any reason, so it was a big deal to me. Looking back, it was really funny maybe it was because I was white, we'll never know. I am thankful to the principals, teachers, and coaches who looked out for us. It was all a big experiment and I think it was more interesting and educational than anybody realizes."

Freddie Funches *said he enjoyed all of the extracurricular activities at Murrah including square dancing. He recalled that Cassandra* "was in 'The Wiz.'" She played Dorothy. But I'm just saying, that was some hidden talent there. We had Lele Winter, the governor's daughter over there, so we had a mixture of a lot of people in that school at that particular time. We had Mr. Merritt's son [Greg], who went on to be a doctor." *Freddie remembered another classmate,* "Yeah. He would dress up in the little lady's, girl's, he had y'all's uniform on. I'm just saying he didn't mind being silly . . . We went to Riverside Drive after the game, and we hung out over there having fun, and it was just a great time. Those are the times that you put into a little shell and you look back on them and some people look at you and you're smiling and they don't really know what you're smiling about. But, it's lonesome times that you think about it and you say, that boy knew he was silly." [laughs]

I too remember a few very masculine guys dressing up in the Murrah Misses' uniforms and performing a routine during homecoming spirit week. Like Freddie, sometimes I daydream about these nonsensical things and just start laughing.

Freddie said, "I'll tell you another person that I really loved and I love her today and I always will, I admire her, and that's Lindy Stevens . . . That young lady didn't have a prejudiced bone or whatever in her body." He mentioned that their mutual friend and classmate Charles Irby had contacted Freddie after he lost his two sons. Charles "called me, come by my house." . . . "The man was there. He was so comfortable. That's why I love him today . . . All he saw was a person's heart. He saw the inside. The outside didn't matter, and that's why today I have so much respect for him, his family." *Some students, Freddie said,* "couldn't fit in because they didn't even know what to do. People was trying to keep them from folks they didn't know nothing about, but was what somebody else projected who they were. That was very frightening to some kids because most people, when you growing up, you learn from their ancestors . . . But that ain't really what life is all about. Life is all about you and I right now, sitting next to each other, the best of friends. We don't have to be with each other every day. We don't even have to call each other every day. But you know what, when you called me, I was just as happy to hear from you than I was if I was listening to you every day. That's what life is all about."

Freddie recounted of Murrah, "It was a fun time . . . You didn't want to finish school, because you caught it, you grabbed it. Everybody gave each other an opportunity and a chance to be who they were, to prove who you were." *Freddie believed that his friends at Murrah looked at "your heart instead of your color."*

Margie Cooper Pearson relayed to us in an interview, "One thing I have learned, because I did think that you were so much different than us, culturally, in what you had versus what we had, or how we grew up. As I've met people and experienced things and traveled, the thing that stands out more to me than anything else is we're more alike than we are different, and I just can't even imagine how I was thinking that back then, because I really did see you guys as something foreign, because you're growing up . . . I just saw you as having everything easy, too. So, as I've lived this life, I really see we are truly, truly more alike than we are different, even with the cultural things."

Robert Kelly said, "One of the things that I learned about integration and it's carried over to what I do every day here in business and from a civic standpoint as well, is that diversity is so important. You look at our organization. It is very diverse. If a person walked into this building and they didn't know anything about our company, they wouldn't know if we were white owned, black owned, female owned, or whatever the case may be. I know for a fact that me having an opportunity to finally get a chance to meet white folks and develop relationships with them put me in a position where I realized that we are all the same, we just have different backgrounds. With diversity brings a lot of strength. That is one of the things I preach throughout this entire community. Sometimes people want to hear it and sometimes they don't want to hear it . . . Birmingham . . . is much better than we were thirty years ago. Jackson, Mississippi, is as well I think. One of the things I notice about Jackson it is amazing how all the white folks have left. They're like let's get the hell out of Dodge. I think that hurts a city. One of the things about Birmingham is that has not happened. You still have a lot of white folks that live in the city of Birmingham and a lot of white folks that are looking to move back into the city of Birmingham, especially in the downtown area. In Jackson it is really different. Are there any white kids at Murrah now?"

I told Robert that I had learned there were not many white students at Murrah now (compared to the 1970s) or in the other city of Jackson public high schools.

Robert continued, "I think what helped going to Murrah was the year or two years before we were at Bailey and we experienced integration. We found out that white folks, they are OK. It is not as bad as we thought it was going to be. The other thing that a lot of us sensed, and speaking for myself, is that the white folks that were at Murrah, the majority of them were at Murrah because they wanted to be at Murrah, and the white folks that went to Jackson Prep went to Jackson Prep because they did not want to be at a school with black folks. That was our thinking. That was my mindset and if I would talk to a lot of my black friends now, I think they would think the same thing. It was one of those deals where, you know hey, I wish that I could have heard the conversations in some of the white churches and some of the white homes and this type thing.

"I also noticed that the white kids that were at Murrah, for the most part, in my thinking, they embraced the situation that we were in—integration. There were some that you would never feel too comfortable with and I could always sense that. It is kind of like . . . we have some Hispanics that work with us and probably half of them don't speak good English. I speak very little Spanish . . . but I can do greetings and two or three little sentences and stuff like that. I was with this guy one time, a friend of mine, who is a white character in the construction industry, he was outside with one of my guys and he said, 'You don't speak Spanish, but how does he, it seems like he is really happy being here.' I said just because you don't speak someone's language does not mean they don't know when you are treating them fairly. People know when it is a warm feeling. I said this to say, there were some situations when I was at Murrah that you could sense the white folks that didn't want to be around. It wasn't a lot of them, but I think there was a few and it was bad for them, because we ended up having some really great times."

Kathy Wilson Phillips *wrote that she enjoyed her Murrah years and had fun.* "I think at the time I didn't think going to school with blacks was such a big deal, they were just people. I didn't understand why everyone was making such a big fuss over it. At Murrah, I don't recall the blacks getting special treatment because they were black. In today's world it seems they think we owe them. I resent that, because everyone should pull their own weight in society." *Kathy recalled an incident of conflict at Murrah,* "Once while walking down the hallway alone three black guys came over to my side of the hall walking straight towards me, being cool. I said, 'excuse me' twice trying to get around them but they kept blocking me, so I jabbed my binder into one guy's ribs and said, 'I said excuse me!' And I walked through them. Another time four black girls cornered me in the locker room and sprayed 'Skinny Dip' perfume all over me. Yuck!"

Ken Allen *believed that friends Joey Oliver and Mike Carmichael made his transition at Murrah easier. He admired Coach Willie Heidelburg,* "He picked me out of the gym class and put me on the track team. I was small but could always run and while on the track team I met many interesting young men who also happen to be African American . . . actually they were all African American as I was the only white on the track team and I ran sprints . . .

It was a good time and I was accepted because of what I could do . . . not only on the track . . . or tennis court or soccer field . . . or the classroom, but because of who I was at the time. During that period I learned that there are no differences between black and white humans. We have the same feelings (our hearts break when we lose a girlfriend) the same wants (we all want to impress our friends and families), needs (we all need positive attention and reinforcement) and desires (we all want to be successful . . . in our own way . . . and build a better life for our children.) I saw life from another side . . . a side that was different than mine . . . but oh so the same." *Ken said he carried the lessons he learned at Murrah* "from Houston, Texas, to New York . . . from Miami, Florida to Seattle, Washington . . . relating this story as I go and passing it on to my children." *Ken is the director of Development for the Mississippi Children's Home Services.*

Williams (Bill) G. Lewis *was asked a question about his expectations of high school before radical desegregation. He wrote,* "That they would be somewhat different than they were. I expected to continue attending school with most of the people with whom I attend elementary and junior high school. That changed. Most of my friends left public school and never came back; I left for junior high, but came back for high school." He said that Murrah, "mostly met my expectations. I did feel that the academic curriculum was a bit lacking, which is the reason I skipped my junior year, moving up my graduation by one year."

"I mostly enjoyed my experience at Murrah. It opened doors to everyday living that I might not have otherwise been exposed to. I met people from all walks of life, which helped me gain an understanding of how to deal with different people. This has certainly been of enormous benefit in my professional and personal life . . . There is no question that my Murrah days help to shape my social views of the world today . . . If I had not attended Murrah, it might have taken me longer to develop a necessary sense of propriety about some things."

Betsy Grimes Triggs wrote: "Because of Claiborne Barksdale, I learned to love reading. Not directly, of course, but because I thought if I read all the assignments and did well on the tests, I might catch his eye . . . Anyway, along the way, I started liking what I was reading and have kept it up ever since. (Have to give some credit to my mom, too. She liked that I was reading for Mr. Barksdale, but wanted me to push myself and read some of the classics. She started me with *The Decameron* by Bocaccio because it was full of sex. She knew that would keep my attention)."

"In general, I look back on those two years at Murrah as a golden time. Before integration, I was not even close to popular. After integration, things loosened up and there were more ways to be accepted. Clothes, cars and money didn't seem to matter as much. Rarely did anyone meet at Jackson Country Club. It was finally OK to be smart. Also, I felt like we were part of an important change in our country's history, sort of a part of living history. That might just be what absorbed from my liberal parents, but I still think that today. I think if things had stayed the way they were, I would be a much different person."

David Flanagan ('75), *brother of my classmate, Mark wrote:*

"I learned that the most important thing about being born is to have loving parents who care, as there were a lot of students who didn't even know who their daddy was and those who did have a daddy that told them, 'You ain't shit, boy,' and they either believed it or made it a point to make it become a self-fulfilling prophecy. I learned you can get an education anywhere you are if you really want to but you have to want to as most teachers are dull, boring, and burnt out. I learned that it would have been nice if the teachers could have had control of the classroom; most didn't and were clueless ...

"Regarding the academics, there were some wonderful teachers—Mr. Hall, Herr Lowe, etc. The teacher who had the greatest impact on my life was Pauline Tramel, the algebra teacher. She cared and she demanded respect. I wasn't a scholar and therefore I am not going to tear down the teachers as I did as little as I had to to make the grades. I was there to have fun, meet the girls, and enjoy high school. Regarding integration, three years had passed and most products of the public school system had learned to go with flow and get along ... I give Mrs. Tramel all the credit in the world. I made a 'D' in her class and she challenged me to take it over. I told her 'Mrs. Tramel, the last time I checked, a 'D' is a passing grade.' She said, 'David, if you're willing to accept less than you are capable of doing, you will accept less the rest of your life.' What a guilt trip. But she cared! She was the first teacher ever to confront and challenge me to be the best I could be. I admired that! I took algebra over and missed an A by one point. However, in college, I made an A in Algebra and I give Mrs. Tramel the credit."

David Flanagan *sent us four situations he encountered,* "I've shared these stories because it describes the way life was at Murrah."

David's First Incident: He wrote that when he was in the tenth grade, a black girl tried to "cheat" from his test paper.

She got up and tried to bite me on my arm. I pushed her away and Mr. Harper tried to restrain her and she tried to bite him, said some serious cuss words, and bolted out of the room ... I went and sat down and about five minutes later two

6-foot-seven black guys walk into the classroom and ask, 'Where is the white guy who jumped my sister?' I sat still. Mr. Harper told them to get out and they pointed at me and said, "You're dead, boy" . . . Mr. Harper sent a girl to the principal's office. Right before the bell, Mr. Merritt and assistant principal Mr. Carey came and escorted me to the principal's office. When we walked outside I kid you not there was a sea of black. The whole portable building was surrounded. I walked to Mr. Merritt's office, told him the situation, and he said I needed to go home. They called my brother Mark, who was a senior, had a car, and told him to get me out of there. How did I feel? I felt like this is another world, not a school, but an episode of "Survivor."

The next day I went to school and learned that a red head kid had been jumped and beaten up because they thought it was me. His older white brother wanted to fight me because he thought it was my fault. My only way out was to talk with . . . a guy nicknamed Wolf, who was a gang leader, and also played baseball. I told Wolf the story and he said not to worry because he had my back and would be my slack. Luckily, things went well and there was no more fallout from the incident. [The girl] never came back to that class and I don't really know what became of her. This was all because of the fact that I would not let her cheat on the exam.

"Let me hold a nickel," *David's Second Incident*

Using the bathroom at Murrah was a joke. You learned that if you needed to use the bathroom the best place to go was by the gym as coaches were always around with physical education classes and you didn't have to worry about altercations. On the other hand, the one place you didn't want to go to use the bathroom was the second floor head. Why? Because I went in there once and there were a lot of black guys smoking and they had their belt in their hand and were swinging the buckle. A belt buckle can hurt! In addition, instead of saying, "May I have a nickel or quarter please?" they would say "let me hold a quarter!" Or "give me a quarter so I don't pop you with this belt buckle." If you said, "I don't have a nickel or quarter" they would question you or confront you. Went to the second floor head one time and that was enough . . . used the bathroom by the gym if I needed to go.

"Swamped," *David's Third Incident*

One day as a senior, I was walking down the hall between bells, and I saw this black guy haul off and hit this sophomore white guy in the face for no apparent reason. I mean sucker-punched him and he was just walking down the hall. Shocked, I went over and asked, "What was that for? He didn't do anything to you. You know you can beat him up. What are you trying to prove?" "Hey man, you better watch your ass, we'll swamp your ass!" I told him to pick on somebody his own size, etc. He said we're gonna jump you and I said come on. He didn't do anything so I went to class and thought: This is barbaric, a guy is walking down the hall minding his own business and out of nowhere he gets punched in the face. My thoughts! Aren't public schools conducive to learning.

"My Down," *David's Fourth Incident*

There was a ping-pong table down by the gym. The rule was that if you lost, whoever had Down, got to play next. A friend of mine, Chris . . . , a small white guy, had the right to the table depending who won. Chris was watching Wolf play and lose and he walked over to Wolf and said, "My Down." Wolf reached in his pocket, pulled out a switchblade, punched it open and said, "My Down." Chris said you're right, "Your Down." A simple game of ping-pong and a very scary situation.

Willie Miller *spoke to me a few minutes at a class party at Sal and Mookie's in Jackson. I gave him the tape recorder to hold, as the music was loud at the event.*

Willie said, "Hello to each and every one of you. We the classmates, of that extraordinary class, if you look back on the things that we encountered and the situations that we were in during that era, I might be a little prejudicial, I might be a little boisterous, but I think we were a unique group. I don't see people now pulling off what we pulled off, because we were strangers and we gelled into a united class. Here it is thirty years later and we still socialize, we cherish, God knows, I cherish every day I was at Murrah and we had a ball. Socially, academic, religion, any aspect of education that you want to talk about, we were a united group at Murrah. I used to keep tabs on Murrah, you know, after I left and went to college and what have you. It seemed like, here it is again, I might be prejudicial about this, but it seemed like the classes that came after us, they separated. They were like water and oil, they did not mix well for whatever reason. People I met at Murrah, life experiences I had while I was at Murrah, I cherish! There isn't a day that goes by that you have those times in your life you just have a flashback of your youth . . . and it always puts a big smile on my face, some of the things and some of the real fun things that we did. And I think it had a lot with the sign that use to hang up on the wall in the gym, "PRIDE." We took a lot of pride in our school we took more pride in ourselves as individuals. You cannot put a value on that feeling of pride because you are either able to develop it or you don't have God in your life. You know that is the way I see it."

Steve Jenkins *wrote,* "Academics had its high and low points. Twenty-four years later I was proud to present Ms. Tramel with a bound copy of my doctoral dissertation as a way of saying 'thanks for getting me off on the right track.' She said, 'I'm gonna hug your neck' in her unmistakable style, and did. Ms. Tremaine from Chastain got one too. She teared up a little.

"What I remember most of all, however, are the friends. For better or worse, we found ourselves there, and most of us made the best of it. We did what high school kids do and had fun doing it. I think we were all aware, as well, that we were minor players in a major national drama, and that we could actually contribute in some little way to grappling with the issue that has bedeviled our country since its inception. By 1973, I could hug Cassandra on Capitol Street and get nothing more than a stare. In 1965 one of us might have gotten a billy club, or worse. So we weren't heroes, but we were on the right side of history.

"By the time we graduated, I was ready to move on. I left Mississippi in 1977 and don't expect to live there again. But in those two years I made friends, had experiences, and learned things that I treasure to this day. I wouldn't trade them for anything ...

"In the early twentieth century, psychologists put a lot of effort into using race to explain intelligence. Nowadays we know that race as a biological concept is empty. The characteristics that have defined races for centuries are now known to be mere chance associations of surface appearance that have more to do with mate selection than adaptation. To oversimplify, Scandinavians have blond hair and blue eyes because Scandinavians think blond hair and blue eyes are attractive. There's no gene for 'black' or 'white.' As a cultural construct, however, race is anything but empty. Black and white Americans are different because we're shaped by different experiences, and we have different experiences because, well, we've always had different experiences. Segregationists used to argue that races need to be separated because we're different. Now we know that the only reason we're different is that we've been separated. The Murrah High School class of 1973 did our little bit to fix that. That feels good."

In a questionnaire, **Velma Robinson Chisholm** *wrote,* "I liked my time at Murrah. We had fun. We worked through the prejudice and it was there but we knew who harbored those feeling so you steered clear of those people. Some things change, some don't, but that's life. I never lost any sleep over it and still don't. It is what it is ... I honestly was not brought up to dislike people because they are different. I learned through history that black people were perceived a certain way. If nothing else was accomplished it was that nothing is absolute. All black people are not bad and all white people are not prejudice.

You have to deal with each individual based on their own merits, good or bad, and judge how you will deal with them."

When asked if the steps to achieve integration were worth the upheaval, Velma answered, "I think yes, because it leveled the playing field, so to speak. Now people who didn't succeed were probably not going to anyway, black or white, so you can't blame that on anyone or situation. But the experience was worth it."

Alan Huffman wrote, "I'm not someone who obsesses about race, but the benefits of having attended Murrah became particularly evident to me on two different occasions—once, at one of our class reunions, when I realized how similar our group's reference points were, whether we were black or white. We may have had very different experiences, and we may interpret those experiences differently, but as I listened to people talking about their lives now and how Jackson had changed, what struck me was how much we had in common.

"The second occasion was less feel-good, but equally illuminating. In that case, I was in Washington, DC, and found myself lost in a ghetto. The farther I walked the worse the neighborhood became, and it was too late to turn back, so I forged ahead, hoping to come out on a well-traveled street where I might get my bearings, or perhaps hail a cab. As I walked through blocks of tenement houses, many with broken windows, I could sense the tension that trailed in my wake. People saw me as an unusual and potentially trouble-some apparition in their neighborhood. At one point I saw a group of young black guys in hoodies on a street corner up ahead, watching me. Everyone I'd passed in the last hour or so had been black, so that was nothing new. But these guys were different. They looked like gang members, and seemed to be organized around some street-corner purpose; they also eyed me with keen interest. I was a lone, lost, middle-aged white man approaching them on their own turf.

"At this point several options presented themselves. Two seemed like bad ideas: Crossing the street to avoid them, or turning around. Both would illus-trate my fear. The third was to proceed toward them, making eye contact. This was perhaps easier for me than it would have been had I lived in a segregated world. These guys were guys, after all—just a group of human beings who may or may not have had bad intent. I'd run into a few hostile black guys in the halls at Murrah and had learned that what they usually wanted most was acknowledgement, something white people typically denied. I'd also learned something about myself while researching a nonfiction book, *Mississippi in Africa*, in the West African nation of Liberia during a civil war: I could forget that I was white after days spent among people of another race. I also live in a predominately black area, and sometimes forget that other people are black.

"The point being, the guys on the corner were a potential menace, but they were also just a group of guys, so as I approached them I didn't feel particularly white, didn't see them as particularly black. There was something else at work that required me to make eye contact with each of them, acknowledging their existence, until I landed upon the leader, who would nod his acceptance, or not. Most people choose acceptance if you engage them in a nonhostile way, at close range. So that is what I did. I nodded to each of the guys, and eventually recognized the leader, who hesitated, then gave me the nod. I walked through the middle of the crowd, no problem. Eventually I made my way out of the ghetto, thinking, I'm glad I didn't graduate from Jackson Prep."

Debra Lindley: *The upheaval experienced by our class during the seventies* "was worth it. I'm sure it affected everyone to some extent. I was much more prepared for the 'real' world and my professional life having been through the experience . . . It is my opinion everyone learns to adapt no matter what . . . I will never forget the day that Anne had driven the carpool and after school we kept looking for the car and couldn't see it in the parking lot. Turns out, all of the tires had been stolen and it was sitting on the ground. We laughed so . . . hard it was unbelievable . . . then riding in Alan Huffman's Karman Ghia with no shocks after school (occasionally hitting a garbage can here and there). And who could forget going to Riverside Park after the football games and drinking Schlitz beer out of a quart bottle until we would get run off by the cops. I believe I remember a little smooching in the back seat of cars too." *Debra referred to Murrah as* "the most carefree time of my life."

Lele Winter Gillespie: "Although a lot closer to home for me than Brinkley, it was certainly not the Murrah of my expectations, the Murrah that I had been looking forward to attending. We had taken a detour and with this detour came a lot of sudden changes and life experiences. Time does funny things to people and some years, whether it be in school or in life generally, you hit a snag. For me I hit a snag and my two years spent at Murrah weren't the positive ones that I'd hoped for, academically or otherwise. This is not to say that those years weren't without some very fond memories, though . . .

"Looking back on our school years—1969–1973, I am saddened to think that so many of the friends that I'd made in my early elementary years would choose (or have chosen for them) other paths to take in their school careers. I have often wondered what those classmates who left us at that crossroad missed, not having stayed with us on this journey. I also wonder how they have coped without the advantage that we had of learning to work together as friends and classmates a long time ago. And the people that they missed knowing! Karen Bell, Joni Brown, Freddie Funches, Cassandra, Fred Sheriff, Victor Watts, just to name a few—I think back with fond memories and warm regard for these people and many others that touched my life.

"The lessons we learned from those years are many. I would like to think we learned to be less inclined to judge folks by their skin color, that we are hopefully more tolerant of people who don't look or talk or, most importantly, think just like we do, and that we possess an earnest desire to strive for fairness and justice. These are lessons, having been learned in the halls of Bailey, Brinkley and Murrah, that we've hopefully passed along to our own kids—those of tolerance, respect and kindness. Having grown up in a political family I'm not sure if I can separate or sort out the source of these lessons because I see them as intertwined, but I'm sure that in the public schools of Jackson and on the campaign trail for my dad in the small towns of Mississippi—in both venues—I have hopefully learned the value of treating all people with respect, knowing that we are all God's children. I've always thought that one of the kindest and most generous compliments that can be given someone is to refer to them without referring to their skin color—a kind of color blindness that is a result of getting to know and respect people for who they are as a person—of seeing 'the content of their character,' in the words of Dr. Martin Luther King, Jr.'"

Laurie Propst Ware expressed, "Murrah was a wonderful experience for me. I remember being very happy, and had friends in all grades. I never felt threatened or that I was not getting a good education. I still feel that way. I feel proud that I was part of what I call a 'successful transition' into desegregation . . . I realized that we are all people, even though we are different. I love learning about different cultures and backgrounds . . . The goal for me was that we would all be friends and socialize and that our children would not think twice about having friends of different races. That racism would END with our generation. I don't think it has, but I am proud of the progress that we made starting with our experience at Murrah. As I said above, I would hate for our work to be in vain, and for us to be in the same situation in twenty years, with all the schools being segregated again."

"You might say I have pent up anger . . . not really," wrote **Amelia Reagan Wright**. "What I have is a raw (un-retouched), realistic view of what it was and is. I wouldn't trade my public school days in Jackson, but considering the climate in Jackson now, never would I allow my children to attend public school there . . . Today, society is a two-edged sword. We want reality and equality, yet we are afraid to actively pursue either. Reality is scary. That fear can fuel a crippled future society . . . one unable to function. Equality . . . that is elusive and probably will never come to fruition. I don't know what the cure is, and I'm very concerned."

Fred Sheriff: "At Murrah High School I continued to try to do well in school (something demanded by my parents), was involved in the marching band my junior year (1971–1972) and began to have more interaction with white people outside the classroom. During my senior year (1972–1973), I was elected co-president of the Murrah student body; at the time there was one white co-president and one black co-president. Friendships and relationships with white people were forged through getting to know them better in the classroom, going on school trips with them and attending parties together (in 'their' neighborhood and in 'ours'). Really, isn't this how you get to know anyone—being around them, interacting with and talking to them? Overall, I look back fondly on my years at Murrah (I had a blast!).

"As I look back, I don't think integration changed my views regarding other races that much. I have always basically tried to relate to each person as an individual, and deal with them accordingly, regardless of race. It didn't seem to make much sense to me to judge people or treat them a certain way just because of the color of their skin.

"The thing that has most impacted my views regarding political issues, how I see other races, etc., has been my relationship to God. As a result, I am neither Republican, Democrat nor Independent; neither conservative nor liberal. It seems to me that millions of people have put their trust in an individual or a political party, somehow hoping that he/she or they can address their concerns. Our pride makes us think that our generation can solve problems like insuring equality in education, poverty, drug abuse to name a few, by legislation, organizations, conferences, meetings, etc. Think about it. We are the descendents of those who have gone before us; they tried and failed using this approach. How can we expect to do the same thing and get a different result? Are we wiser than they? Can one be wiser than the one whence he came?"

Carol Sanders Bailey: "It seemed to me like the sky was the limit. I never felt like I couldn't do something. I remember that I loved meeting people from all walks in life. I became very close with some people that I would have never known otherwise. I also became aware of our differences, but in a good way. I learned not to take things for granted. I learned to be open to other religions. I don't remember prejudices, although there were probably some there—I just wasn't privy to it. The only prejudice I do remember that stands out thirty-five years later, was a religious one. A guy friend of mine, who happened to be white, was picking on a girl friend of mine, who happened to be Jewish. And he did it all the time. I remember not liking the fact that he sought her out in a crowd to embarrass her. But as far as black and white, I don't remember anything blatantly right now. Being a Christian, I loved the idea of expanding what I had known up to that point, and learning to love others the way Christ did, not that I always did. But I was aware of it. I don't remember being afraid for my safety, and I think that's because I wasn't. In the beginning of tenth grade I was, but like I said, things calmed down by Christmas.

"Not only did I receive an excellent education, book-wise, but street wise, as well. I learned who to trust and who to stay away from, and I'm talking about all colors—blacks and whites . . . We were children of the seventies, in all that it means. It was a changing time in our history. We didn't know what to expect because we were all going through it together, for the first time."

Owen Patterson Phillips: *Owen was with our class during the junior year, but graduated early. Owen wrote,* "My daughter's high school friends were a diverse group with kids of all races and religion. Interestingly, it was at a private school. So the discriminator now appeared to be socioeconomic and not racial. I would like to think that there were small advances in liberalism towards race made by my generation in Jackson, Mississippi, in the 1970s and the fact that my daughter places no emphasis on the color of one's skin is the positive fall-out."

Reginald Rigsby: "I was a popular student leader at Murrah and that contributed to my self-esteem yet it didn't make me self-centered. For that I am grateful. My high school experience was so well rounded as a result of being a Murrah Mustang. It definitely contributed to who I am today. I am a productive citizen in my community, a good provider to my family and a Christian who works every day to be the best person that I can be."

Mary Al Cobb Alford wrote, "I believe there were attitudes of resentment at Murrah toward those who fled to Jackson Prep and other private academies following integration. However, their flight afforded many of us leadership opportunities that might have otherwise been unavailable. In some strange way this was perhaps the redeeming quality of integration from my vantage point. While the departure of several outstanding teachers left an academic void at Murrah, our practical life skills were enhanced and those of us who stayed behind formed a unique bond. I feel gratitude and an element of superiority for having participated and prospered in this dramatic experiment.

"I am occasionally asked where I went to high school and it is fascinating to witness the reactions when I respond 'Murrah, class of 1973.' My commitment to public education has been tested when I have pondered whether or not I would have sent my own children to today's Jackson Public Schools. Would I have been as brave as my parents? I hope that I would have been and have continued to follow Murrah's success with pride and optimism."

Bill Patterson: "I hadn't liked being stereotyped. So, I didn't do it to other people. People were good and bad, lazy and full of energy, funny and morose, dumb and smart, kind and mean, fat and skinny, beautiful and handsome and ugly, and all of the other adjectives that can describe mankind conversely. And that applied to all people, regardless of race and regardless of gender. I learned that it is very difficult to live up close to people and make judgments based on skin color.

"And, I have tried to remember it. I have tried to remember all the people who allowed me a new beginning. I have tried to remember the change in a school system that allowed me a new beginning. I have tried to appreciate these personal and societal beginnings and make them part of not just what I did years ago, but how I live. Like most folks, I would guess, I do a pretty good job of it some days and a not so good job of it other days. But, I know this. This powerful three-year experience at both Brinkley and Murrah has made me thoughtful about how I walk this earth and relate to its inhabitants. I also know this. That three-year experience was no accident. I don't believe that God has accidents. That three-year experience, for me, was a sure sign of God's Grace. Heaven sent changes in which we all played a part. Remarkable."

Doug Minor: "As unusual as it was, that first year of desegregation served as an invaluable transition to life at Murrah (1971–1973). By then, the black student leaders from Brinkley were well accepted by the white student leaders, and vice-versa, and we worked well together. My high school experience was very positive, and my base of black friends continued to expand. In general, I believe the two races slowly became more comfortable with each other, and more accepting of each other's differences. Now that the black students were on our turf, in our school, with long-standing white traditions, I'm sure there was some resentment, but I didn't see it or feel it.

"Looking back, I am surprised at how well the two races got along during those days. There was very little black/white conflict. I guess the main reason is that most of us (white kids) wanted to be at Murrah, and had been raised to accept all people, regardless of race, as equal. The white racist/bigots were off at the white-flight schools . . . they missed out on a life-changing experience. The mission worked for those of us who were engaged in the change, and sought out the inclusion of blacks as friends. An unintended consequence of this experiment, which should be acknowledged, were the very close friendships and strong bonds we (the white kids) formed with each other. We chose to go through desegregation, we went through it together, and we not only survived, but thrived as a result. I count many of my Murrah classmates as my closest friends (white and black). Even though we may not visit each other's homes, or socialize at the same events, I would welcome that opportunity any day of the year. When we gather periodically at the high school reunions, reacquainting is easy and comfortable, and fun."

Johnny Jones said, "I think my experience at Murrah changed everything about the way I view the world. At some point I quit thinking about the future as a recreation of the past; indeed, I looked on the future as something critically important but ultimately up for grabs. In high school we saw both the past and the future come and go in a moment. Time was compressed for us because so much was being challenged, the old processes for handling so much change no longer worked, and there was no grown-up that would step in and make everything okay. If it was going to be okay, we had to do it. We learned that kids are instinctively closer to the answer than any set of grown-ups; and the power to decide the future doesn't belong in old hands and must be passed along."

Foster Dickard *noted that he enjoyed Murrah and made the best of the situation into which he was placed. When asked if he thought the steps that were taken to achieve integration and upheaval was worth it, he wrote,* "Absolutely not; whatever the goals of integration were, the process forced on the students and teachers was draconian. While I am certain there were disparities that needed to be addressed, the students and teachers should not be sacrificed to serve a political ideal. Any benefits from an applied educational perspective were largely indirect or in spite of the social engineering efforts of the government and educational bureaucrats that spawned the forced integration plan. I also have to give some credit (blame) to the hardheaded local and state politicians that resisted reasonable approaches to improve racial parity in education resources (not to be confused with racial balancing) . . . The forced integration experience at Murrah taught me the first of many lessons that you cannot expect the federal government to effectively manage any program, particularly social programs at the local or state level. Not that state-level government is smarter but there is more accountability closer to home.

"Whatever good intentions, government either fails or at best is inefficient and/or excessively corrupt in managing projects/programs against any free market (cost benefit) standard. My experience shaped my worldview today in that the government's primary role is to provide for the national defense and facilitate international policy . . . besides that, the smaller the government the better. As far as race relations, I saw then (and now) that the main differences and resulting issues between the races (all, not just black and white) are primarily based on cultural differences and not just color differences. Skin color just makes it easier to differentiate and more prone to prejudge others . . . My year at Brinkley was when there were race riots at Jackson state which led to even more agitation with black students at Brinkley. I would like to think that there were some experiences that led to some positive results in race relations at the personal or some level . . . It would be a shame to think that we all were put through that for nothing."

Richard Sanders: "The experience was disruptive but overall a good one. I think the mutual tolerance and respect adjusted my value set a bit but not a significant amount . . . We needed to do what we did. It was for the overall good. I appreciate the Murrah experience and the prospective it gave us all . . . YES! We, the southerners, had to take the steps for the greater good of our state and nation. I know it was court ordered on short notice, but we had had ten years to do it and we had not made a serious attempt to follow the court orders . . . I can get along with anyone and find the common ground and issues while exploring those areas not in common. I was never much of a biased Mississippian, but this experience further opened up my mind to respect and celebrate the differences that make us all individuals. Religion, sexual preferences, differing life philosophies, etc., are to me, things to celebrate and explore."

Mark Flanagan: "Perception is everything. I tried to treat everyone equally and enjoy every day at Murrah High School. I am so grateful for the opportunity to graduate with the class of 1973. I was really proud of that beautiful blue class ring with the mustang in the stone. The greatest lesson learned was the experience of being a minority."

Joe Reiff: "I am proud that my family chose to stick at Murrah, and that experience remains a central part of my identity as a Mississippian and child of that era. It is my most direct involvement in the incredible changes of those years and symbolizes the death of the white supremacist, Closed Society past. I do not pretend that we solved all the problems of race relations then, in spite of our senior yearbook's idealistic theme of everybody getting together. Seasons of change are unsettling, but I believe that compared to where we were in 1968, we ended up in a better place by the mid-1970s as a result of school desegregation. Personally, I credit those experiences with helping me learn to accept myself and stop trying to live up to some imagined elite northeast Jackson standard.

"My experience at Murrah was mostly good; I remember those years with a lot of gratitude for the personal growth and community movement in the right direction, mixed with some regret for missed opportunities and my failure to know my black classmates better and some anger about other failures. I have no easy answers for how things might have been done differently, but again, I wish more white families had stayed at Murrah."

Robert Hand gave some additional insight: "I knew integration was something forced on us for the better and even though I knew I did not like authority, I accepted it as a grand experiment. I did not have any other option, as we had to attend public school. I now see my parents had it good. I have to pay $18,000 a year for my son to attend private school in New Orleans, and I have paid that since kindergarten . . . So, looking back, was integration worth it? It helps to know how deep in the racist well you were to appreciate getting out. My church was First Baptist Church. It was the largest church in town. The governor went there. One day CBS national television captured the church deacons turning black people away from worship. What did I do about it? I called up the black lady who was turned away and went to her house and knocked on her door. We spoke through the door at first. I said I was sorry she was turned away and hoped she could worship with us. Murrah's experience gave me the courage to do that. I thought I was righting a wrong. Later my pastor sent word to me that I was undoing all he was trying to accomplish. I still am not sure what he was trying to accomplish. But I still am righting wrongs today.

"I never was a racist, I just did not have black friends, nor any friends whose parents were engineers or doctors or attorneys, so I never thought of getting into any of those professions, but I did see racism—not in students, but in adults. My dad was a racist. Eventually, we brought him around, but it was only after the Murrah experience that I knew it was important to stand ground. I since have witnessed many adults in my dad's age bracket and WWII experience hated black people and also Japanese. Doesn't make it right, but that's the crowd they hung around. That's what integration did for me: It allowed me to hang around black kids which I never would have hung around otherwise. It shed light of knowledge about getting along with black people so we did not have to fear what we did not know."

Charles Miller: "My main emotion upon graduation was relief that I had crossed the finish line after all the angst of the past three years—Vanderbilt seemed like living at the Jackson Country Club for four years in comparison. There has been a lingering bitterness about my white peers who betrayed me and my close friends who stayed at Murrah and never gave integration a try by enrolling in private schools. Their collective failure of will made it that much harder on the rest of us and this still is a part of my makeup. (At a wedding reception in Texas several months ago I met a young woman from Jackson and the first thing I asked her was, 'What high school did you go to?' as if to determine if she passed the litmus test of being a Mustang.) When it came time to enroll my own kids in school in Fort Worth, I could not force myself to look at the private, independent schools in Fort Worth without being reminded of Jackson Prep and my resentment of its success in luring away so many peers."

Laura King Ashley: "All of Jackson was permanently and negatively affected (overall, I mean—there were positive effects, I know) by that December 1969 event; I understand that events happen, like rivers flooding and friends dying, and permanent effects exist. But this was manmade and did not need to come down in the manner in which it did—obviously, the decision-makers were middle-aged, pudgy political males that not once considered the toll that this huge and abrupt change in the middle of a school year would take on adolescents and their families. As hard a thing to imagine that this endeavor would be in this very segregated city, and with such impressionable young people directly involved with this huge culture shock which would surely follow, some wise thought should have been applied to the logistics and implementation of the plan so that the least possible amount of stress and strife would be felt by these young people, the parents, the families, the entire city, and to make this modification as smooth as humanly possible. Yes, I think back on the madness of the method and it really angers me. It was so not necessary to be this mean-spirited—no one was really caring about the shock of it all and how it went down . . .

"The education went down while I was in school there. After I graduated, people moved out of Jackson to go to better public schools WITH BLACK PEOPLE. Going to school with black people was never an issue to me and to others; it was the smack-in-the-face culture shock to everyone involved, black or white, who were forced into such an abrupt and massive change, whether they wanted or agreed with desegregation or not, whether they thought providing better and equitable educational opportunities to all was worth the risk. [I] just don't think it was worth the risk of trying or doing this in the manner in which it was done.

"Integration is a good thing. Forcing it on people does not work . . . What did the government betray young people's, black and white, hopes and dreams of going to 'their' high school when they came of age? Hardworking moms and dads. The government betrays society as a whole when people are forced to relinquish certain earned freedoms such as attending school where one chooses." Laura said, "It's like kiss my ass and like it!"

Art Minton: "Hearing and agreeing, that the federal government was meddling somewhere they had no business and that the segregated public school system in Mississippi was a good thing; it simply never occurred to me that black people were being oppressed. My segregationist sympathies made me a part of the problem that was making progress for equality such a difficult quest in Mississippi. For many years, when I thought about it at all, I thought the integration process was the work of, and only favored by, the 'outside agitators.' I wasn't consciously aware that it was the right thing. About fifteen years ago, when I was around age forty, the reality of the negative consequences of Mississippi's dual system had on black society started to occur to me."

Lenda Taylor Brown: "My favorite teacher was Mr. Barksdale for teaching me the love to read; all year we just read the classics. I loved my Latin teacher too—he took us on a hike to the nature trail at Riverside Park to read the tree labels in Latin and trusted to take us to Nashville; we had so much fun . . . Today when I see Freddie Funches, he stops, hugs me and asks me about my family. We learned life skills, allowing us to be productive adults who I hope care about mankind. I do.

"I think the blacks and whites at Murrah worked hard at liking one another and making the very best of what we had. I really think for those years at Murrah we did not look at color. We may not have been the most advanced with our learning skills but because of our experiences, as a whole I think our class may look at situations in a better light and work hard at getting along with everyone not just a few. But, have we progressed? I have to say no; it is so sad. I know most people do not want to hear my opinion but I have to blame the ones that left the public school system and the city of Jackson. Growing up in Jackson was the best; you could not go anywhere without running into people you knew. Murrah is a great school today but almost all black; Callaway is the same. My sister, Janie Hildebrand, has been teaching in the public schools in Jackson all her adult life and it is rare to have a white child in her class . . . The white flight killed our public schools in Jackson and the only person to blame is the ones who ran. If everyone had continued attending the public schools of Jackson and stayed in their neighborhoods, Jackson today would be a great city but no, the voice ran and left the city of Jackson and the public schools. How far can you run? You can't. I really have to say what we fought for and did in Jackson may have been in vain, my old neighborhood looks like—I can't say it makes me want to cry. Murrah may not have the tradition it should have; it is a shame that prior Murrah kids are not sending their children and their grandchildren to Murrah. That is where tradition comes from."

Adrienne Day: "While it was a shock to both black and white communities, I believed school desegregation of the public schools would never have happened voluntarily and it had to happen. I don't think it could have happened without tremendous upheaval. Something new was being born. Times were changing and it was a necessary step to bring Jackson into the twentieth century and prepare us (the students) for living in the real world outside the borders of our state and region . . .

"Today, with many years of hindsight, I realize how important this experience was at a critical period in Mississippi and American history. I feel honored to be a part of a positive aspect of desegregation in Mississippi. My remembrance is that it happened relatively smoothly and peacefully in the most ridiculed state in the country. Perhaps the particular group that stayed in the public schools, graduating in 1973, was simply a remarkable group, embracing change and growth."

Katie Barwick-Snell: "I am very proud now to have been involved in making societal changes in Mississippi. I had a lot of great adventures with classmates and was able to do things that I otherwise wouldn't have done. I can remember going to an all-black church with friends, seeing Martin Luther King march on State Street, and experiencing 'walkouts to protest the war' on the Brinkley campus. I now have an experiential exercise in the classes I teach at Oklahoma University in human relations that encourages students to go outside their cultural comfort zone. I firmly believe that educational experiences broaden culture awareness. And I think that my life experiences are interesting to my students also when we discuss social problems today."

Katie remembered some teachers at Murrah: "Mrs. Rogers, the faculty advisor my junior year, made me examine many social issues and rewrite, rewrite, rewrite. I was in Claiborne Barksdale's honors English class and really enjoyed his teaching methodology—not just straight lecture!"

Kip Ezelle *said that Coach Bob Stevens helped his students and actually let some of them live with him if they were down on their luck.* "He never turned his back on any of his old players. He always seemed to be trying to help them out, even when I was talking to him, had to be in his seventies." **John Mixon** *added*, "Yeah, he got me a job that second semester of my junior year when I didn't go to school—at Central School Supply. He let us use his houseboat out on the reservoir."

Lindy Stevens Clement ('73) talked to Johnny and me:

Johnny: "All right, well, did you, at Murrah, did you ever have any trouble with black people?"

Lindy: "No, never. No. I felt like Freddie [Funches] pretty much would have taken care of me if I needed him to."

Johnny: "When did you meet him?"

Lindy: "In the tenth grade."

Johnny: "Why did y'all form a friendship?"

Lindy: "We just did, I just loved him, still do."

Doug Levanway wrote, "What did I do when it came time for me to send my own boys to high school? Did I stand up for the public schools as my parents had, and insist that my sons go to Murrah? No, I sent them to Jackson Prep. And while I struggled with the decision a little, the truth is that it wasn't that difficult. When I made that decision I didn't know a single person who was sending their child to Murrah or Callaway. The reality was that Murrah at that time wasn't the same as our Murrah. Things had changed, and not for the better, by the time my boys were going to high school.

"As for the moral imperative to support the public schools that nagged at me then and still does, I have to admit that, deep down, I felt that I, and all of us, had done our part to satisfy that moral imperative when we put our high school years at risk by attending a school that was 70 percent African American. It worked out great for us, and I believe we are all better people for having gone to Murrah when we did. But things didn't turn out as we had hoped for the public schools in Jackson, thanks in large part to the lack of support from parents like me. (I don't know much about the public schools now and hope that no one is offended by my characterization of them. I read good things about Murrah in the paper and hope that it is once again the great high school we knew, but that wasn't the case fourteen years ago.) If it seems like I am using my having gone to Murrah during the infancy of desegregation to justify a socially desirable and convenient decision, that could be the case. I just wanted a great high-school experience for my boys. Whenever I've been troubled about that decision, I remind myself that they wouldn't trade their high-school experiences for anyone's. And neither would I."

Epilogue

Alan Huffman

■

Someone stole Angie Baxter's yellow Toyota from the Murrah parking lot one day, then brought it back and parked it in the same spot. She figured out what happened because the gas tank was empty and there was popcorn on the floor. We had to laugh. For most of us, that was about as bad as it got at Murrah. Some students did experience truly traumatic events, but overall, ours was a remarkably smooth transition, considering what was at stake.

It's true that some students—black and white—were harassed now and then. I was harassed, but it was really just a test, a way for a group of guys to show dominance. I was nervous walking the halls for a few days because there were four or five of them, but it wasn't like I could hide, so I ignored it as best I could and eventually it went away. It was just garden-variety bullying, the kind that happens in any school. In a way, it helped prepare me for minor conflicts later in life.

In hindsight, most of the bumps we experienced seem inevitable, yet they pale in comparison with racial crimes that had been committed before, or with violent crimes that are routinely committed in Jackson today.

Our experience illustrates that integration could have and should have worked. Even Barry, Amelia, and Cassandra recall enjoying much about their time at Murrah, and learning from it, which has something to do with the fact that we were in it together, exploring new territory. But for a variety of reasons, enough white parents pulled their kids out during the coming decade that integration eventually failed at Murrah, which is something we did not foresee. Today, Murrah is basically a black school. It would have been interesting to see where the school would have gone had the dynamic we experienced continued.

As it was, the black/white ratio of the student body went from 60/40 in our junior year to 65/35 during our senior year, and by then, the writing was on the wall. Kip Ezelle, who played basketball for Murrah in 1973, was one of the last white starters on the team.

"I think if all of us had stuck with the public school system it would not be in the shambles it is in today," said Susan McBroom, a cheerleader whose mother hosted many late-night parties for students at their Belhaven home. "If the affluent whites in this community supported the public schools we would not have such a problem, and by support I mean send your kids to school there instead of running to private schools."

Among the students, faculty, and supporters we interviewed during the course of our research, some consider the entire enterprise a failure. If integration means racial diversity, then it would be hard to argue otherwise, because all graduating classes in the city's public schools are today close to 100 percent black. Does that mean the school system itself has failed? Not according to those who are familiar with Murrah today. There are problems, but lack of white participation does not preclude a quality education.

The question, of course, is why our experience at Murrah was so different from the experiences of those who followed. George Schimmel, a physician in Jackson and, at the time of the interview, the only white Jackson public school board member, said white enrollment has been dropping since integration occurred. Asked when the tipping point occurred—when white enrollment reached a point of no return, he said it dropped 3 or 4 percent per year, and once the white makeup of the student body fell to around 20 percent, began to drop rapidly. It's now 2 percent in JPS, he said. Parents for Public Schools, in which Schimmel is also involved, originally sought to hold on to "a nucleus of white participation" in the schools, he said, "to hold on to some diversity in JPS." The organization's mission changed over time, and it became "not politically correct" to court white participation, he said. Now the group simply advocates for public education.

In our interview with Governor Winter, he mentioned his desire at the time to get white parents to go on local television to announce their support for the schools. "I think if we could have organized the Parents for Public Schools or an organization like that, sooner, before the massive desegregation took place, I think that would certainly have diminished the white flight," Winter said. "It might not have stopped it, but it would have diminished it. But now I am afraid except for a few kids, there is not going to be much moving back."

Winter said he sees glimmers of hope in contemporary efforts to redevelop Jackson's downtown area, which is attracting younger residents. And he said the loss of racial integration in the schools today does not mean it failed, because it created a generation that learned to live together. He recalled an essay by Louis Ruben about getting off an Amtrak train in rural South Carolina and entering a restaurant where "there was a table of six or eight women sitting having lunch, about half of them white and half of them black, laughing, staying in conversation, and obviously enjoying each other's company. He said, 'I thought to myself, you mean we spent a generation to keep that from happening?'"

There are many explanations for why whites abandoned the schools, with some attributing it to racism, others to crime. "Parents to a very large extent will send their children where their friends and neighbors send their children, and as more friends and neighbors are sending their children elsewhere, it becomes a snowball effect, and that would be the primary reason, probably, for 90 percent of the movement," Schimmel said. "You know, there are other things that parents will consider, and certainly rigor of curriculum and perceived strength of the teaching staff, but to a large extent, parents will send their kids where they believe the student body is attractive, and part of that attractiveness is: Are a significant number of my friends and neighbors sending their kids there? I would say that would be the primary reason."

Claiborne Barksdale said he had been at a dinner a few months before when the wife of a prominent white Jacksonian told him, "Well, you know, integration didn't work—we should never have integrated." He said he told her, "From whose perspective are you talking about that it didn't work? Who is it that wasn't better off as a result of integration?"

During our discussions about all of this, it occurred to me that the reason the schools are no longer integrated is primarily that white people don't want to be part of a small minority. Once people begin to fear that eventuality, they tend to flee. Jackson was basically racially balanced for a long time, but around 1990 it became black majority, and soon after that the black percentage rapidly climbed. Now it's in the vicinity of 80/20, black/white. And it happened in a single decade. At a certain point, the minority sees its control evaporating, and people leave who would not have left before. From that point on it's self-fulfilling.

"Nobody wants to be powerless," I said. "And if you live in a city where your vote is completely insignificant, it's not pleasant, whether you're black or white, and I think once you get to be a small enough minority that you're not ever going to have any power again, then you may feel the need to go someplace else where you can have some power, and people just have to leave and do that, and I think that's the problem: When people recognize that it's not going to get any better and is actually going to get worse, then they give up. I think that's what happened in Jackson."

Johnny said that there was a period—our period, and for a while after—when integration in Jackson worked, but, "The reality is, I don't know that we will ever in our lifetime see any effort made toward achieving any kind of integration in public schools by white people or by anybody else. It's just, we're stuck where we are now, despite the predictions of everybody, that the white private school system would end on its own very weight after a few years."

The public schools in the Jackson suburbs are sound, and they're racially mixed. Teena pointed out that the city of Jackson is only part of the story now, that the suburbs are at least as populous, and other cities, such as her home in Houston, Mississippi, have integrated schools. In such places, she said, "Integration is so normal that what's happening here, people probably couldn't even believe."

In fact, whites aren't the only ones who have left the Jackson Public School system—so, too, have many affluent blacks. And even the children of some of our comparatively liberal classmates—including Johnny—graduated from private schools. As Johnny pointed out, that may be viewed as a kind of vindication by those students of our age group who opted out back in the seventies. He imagined people our age who left for private schools saying, "Look at the Jackson Public Schools now. We just had the sense to get out early, and y'all tried, y'all thought something was going to happen that didn't. You were wrong."

Still, he said, there was no real reason to leave at the time, if the issue was quality education. Instead, "I think there was a fear of the unknown . . . that base fear that all white people in Mississippi had about black people," he speculated. "But I think whatever justification they come up with today, that's the reason that Prep exists, and we know the reason the Council school [existed]."

Claiborne said he didn't realize at the time just how well integration was working. He said that during one of his classes a student was talking about integration, "and I said, 'You don't have integration here, we have peaceful coexistence.' And he looked at me like I was an idiot, and he was right. I think considering the mass of people that had converged, of two essentially foreign cultures, it was incredible that there wasn't any [controversy]. I don't remember any." The only thing that he remembered that approached violence was when the black student was doused with white paint—"whitewashed"—by black students who thought she was too chummy with white students.

Johnny said that other than a few such racially charged episodes, he remembered remarkable tolerance, though there wasn't always much interaction. "I remember black people at Murrah being pleasant," he said. "Like, Margie Cooper was a pleasant individual, but she had no interest at all in talking to me. That was the majority of the response. I was amazed at how peaceful it was because Brinkley wasn't peaceful. I mean, there was a lot of active hostility going on."

At Murrah there were interracial parties, homecoming dances, and proms, the latter of which took place on the roof terrace of the old Heidelberg Hotel in downtown Jackson. Though many of us have continued to stay in touch for forty years, and still get together for reunions, for most of the students the extent of our interaction was two or three years in the seventies.

Despite the diversity of viewpoints and backgrounds that we experienced, most people in Jackson today experience diversity primarily in the workplace, where personal interaction may be limited by the fact that the employees don't have that close familiarity, that backdrop of having grown up together. The status of the schools is open for debate, but what matters to those of us who participated in this book is why students in the Jackson public schools no longer benefit from the kind of educational experience the class of 1973 had.

Teena, who spent a lot of time polling our classmates about their lives today, said she doesn't see much evidence of prejudice in her daily activities in Houston. From her own perspective, public school taught her to be open to people of different backgrounds, which remains true today, though she is politically conservative, Teena said.

In her essay, Teena wrote, "I want to say that by selecting not to go to public schools, the white people are missing something that our class learned. The black students are missing that opportunity to broaden their horizons, by not getting that chance to share a lifelong friendship like Freddie Funches and Charles Irby. Robert Kelly, a successful businessman, told me that he saw a new part of the world through his Murrah interracial friendships, which helped him to reach out to his Hispanic and white employees in Birmingham, [Alabama]. Susan McBroom, a physical therapist at the University of Mississippi Medical Center, treats people of all races, and teaches them to endure and have hope in the future after difficult accidents. Did she learn that by writing [happy notes] to the football players at Murrah? My sister Tricia Freeman, a nurse, says that sometimes she is the only person in those last moments with a dying patient. She attributes her shared empathy with her patients to her God and to learning about people at Murrah. Willie Miller says his mother told him when he was a teenager, 'If you do right, everything will turn out good for you. So you can throw that race card out of the equation.'"

At our reunions, it has been apparent that despite all our differences, our class members in many ways see the world from similar vantage points. Like it or not, we were there together. The argument could be made that we have more firsthand knowledge of interacting with people of other races at close range during our formative years than do most public school students in the

United States today, which has influenced how we have interacted with others since. We do not always fit neatly into prevailing racial paradigms.

Roz Clopton told us, "After graduating from Murrah, I enrolled at Belhaven College, where I was, in my sophomore and junior years, the only black student living on campus. Believe it or not, those were some of my most memorable years. Go figure." She noted dryly that the Belhaven basketball team's name was the Clansmen—"yeah, like it matters that it was spelled with a 'C,'" she said—and that the administration buildings were fronted by stately white columns reminiscent of an antebellum house. "Guess who was first runner up to Miss White Columns, 1974?" she said. "You guessed it!" Her point was that she moved freely through what might otherwise have seemed an alien world.

Katie Barwick-Snell, who is now a college professor in human relations at the University of Oklahoma, wrote in her essay, "Being of service is something that the Jackson Public Schools tried to incorporate into classes and extracurricular activities. I remember tutoring the elementary kids at the school across the band field [from Murrah] and realizing that I wanted to teach one day. I feel strongly that we are a product of what we have seen modeled to us."

Fred Sheriff wrote that after Murrah he graduated from Southern Methodist University in Dallas with a degree in mechanical engineering, then worked in the oil industry in Alaska, California, and Washington. Along the way he earned an MBA and became a devout Christian. "As a result my priorities and perspective were radically altered," he wrote. He began ministering to inmates in Alaska prisons and eventually moved back to Jackson to take care of elderly family members and work with Mission Mississippi, Promise Keepers, and the Gateway Rescue Mission / New Life Center.

Some classmates have become more liberal over time; others, more conservative. Bill Lewis wrote, "I consider myself a social liberal and a fiscal moderate. My political beliefs have moved to the left since I left Murrah. I believe attending Murrah certainly played a part in that drift." Kathy Wilson Phillips, who is now a conservative Republican, worked for twenty years in a nuclear weapons facility in Tennessee, where she was also a foster parent for children of different races. When her family moved back to the Jackson area a few years back, she said she was "saddened by the state of things."

Claiborne is involved with the Barksdale Reading Institute, which focuses on elevating literacy among poor children in Mississippi, "trying to give them the fundamental, essential skill of reading," he said. "We are making progress, working with chronically underperforming schools in poor, predominantly African American towns in Mississippi. We are putting strong principals into the schools, along with a lot of other resources, and the schools are improving."

The key, he said, is "to put really smart, empathetic teachers in front of the students" and to hire what he described as "transformative principals."

Robert Kelly, who was a favorite at Murrah because of his blunt humor and snappy clothes, now lives in Birmingham, and told Teena, "When you have the socioeconomic disparity and differences, the parents that I would say have the underprivileged or free-lunch kids, they are not as articulate about the things that they want for their kids, like you and I would be, because of our educational background and because of our social status or whatever the case might be. One of the things that I have found out is that they want the exact same things for their kids that we want for our kids. They are just not that good at figuring out how to hold the teachers and the principals and the school administrators accountable, whereas we are. We realize, hey, you work for us, whereas those students' parents would go into a school somewhat intimidated."

To address that problem in Birmingham, he said, the schools have created a "parent university, where those parents, who maybe work at the factory or in fast-food restaurants or [as] the help, they will come in those universities and get, number one, how the school system works and how important it is for them to be a big part of the school system, and how they can have an impact, and how they can hold those principals and those teachers and those people in those tall administration buildings accountable for what goes on in the school system."

When Teena asked Kelly—the name everyone used for him—how important it is for whites to be a part of the public school system, he said, "It's very important! Just imagine if all the white folks who have left Jackson, or all the white folks that live in the city of Jackson, Mississippi, right now and send their kids to those private schools, just imagine if 50 percent of them came back to the school system, imagine how much better that system would be. Am I right? It would be much better and it is going to give those kids, the black kids in the public schools in Jackson, Mississippi, the exposure that I got a chance to get. Because one of the things about it, when you are over there together, you start finding out that, hey man, white folks are pretty cool people. And I think white folks say, you know what, these black folks are pretty cool people."

"White people," Kelly said, "moving back into the city, not only in the city, but getting involved in the community, in the school systems, in the government systems, in civic things . . . it will truly enrich the entire community. It's going to make for a much better community. That diversity is so important. If you look at some of the nicer cities that I have been to throughout the country, I love watching the diversity. If you go to San Francisco you see it, New York City you see it, Chicago you see it. There is still some isolated pockets where segregation is just as prevalent as it was at some point, as when we were growing up, but the communities that really thrive and survive, they have embraced diversity and understand the importance of it."

One of the surprises of the responses we got from former students was how some developed a strong distaste for forced integration. Foster Dickard, who got on famously at Murrah, said in his questionnaire that "even the courts and the activist judges are forced to realize that engineering an artificial assault of 'racial balance' and forcing it on the regional populations fails miserably. But has anyone admitted that is was wrong or a failure? Don't hold your breath!" While it is true that forced integration ultimately had the opposite effect, Foster went a step further, arguing that even during our time it was a failure.

"What happened to us?" Foster asked. "We were socially violated by our federal government in the name of racial equality and were told then and now that it was a noble social experiment to correct a terrible wrong. The experiment was not noble and any wrongs that have been corrected were few and came at a terrible price. The fruits of desegregation can be seen in the aptitude scores of these public schools today compared to before desegregation. If you correct for cost per student then it is even more dismal. Our experiences at Murrah reflect what hopefully was all of us (black and white) making the best of the situation."

In closing, Foster wrote of the student questionnaires, "Thanks for sending this out. I guess by now you know if you wanted someone to gush about how great desegregation was for our education and social healing . . . you got the wrong guy."

Charles Miller, who was in the class ahead of ours, was equally dissatisfied, looking back. "I think school desegregation was not worth it for Jackson," he wrote. "I saw a show on TV years ago (either '20-20' or '60 Minutes') about Lanier High School in Jackson and its problems. Nothing has changed, as Lanier was 'the bad school that you never want to go to' back in the sixties and seventies as well. My politician friend there told me (and I think he is right) that the lingering instability within the school system and attendant problems of school desegregation sped up white flight to the Reservoir and Madison County by whites. With my analytical skills from being a lawyer over the past thirty years, I now see something inherently racist and stupid in the courts promoting desegregation as a per se virtue in itself—presumably, on the notion that nothing made a black kid smarter than the privilege of sitting in a school next to those smarter white kids . . . School desegregation did not help me make black friends later in life or in any way 'improve me' the way later events in life would—e.g., international travel, marriage, being a parent. Ours was such a unique experience; nothing I have read or seen in thirty years approximates our Murrah experience other than the movie *Remember the Titans.* I don't regret going to Murrah. The education there was as good as available in Jackson; [I] just think life as an adolescent was already hard enough without the difficulties caused by the desegregation. I have not attended any class reunion events and never intend to."

Williams Lewis, on the other hand, wrote, "I believe there must be close scrutiny of the issue of racial diversity in schools. Unfortunately, a level of racism still exists in our society, and many times that can spill over into the political system. Examination of the distribution of resources for public schools should [have] been constant. On the whole, my experience was a good one, and was definitely worth it ... It was a different day and time. It was important that action be taken then to achieve some sort of racial balance. As things have certainly taken turns for the better, I cannot sit here today and say, 'It happened to me forty years ago, so it should still happen to you.' I think we have to see what the next generation brings. Most high school students today seem much more tolerant and accepting of 'different,' which cannot be anything but good."

For Lele Winter Gillespie, whose father was governor and a strong supporter of public schools, the experience was a mixed bag. She was painfully shy back then, and Murrah in the early seventies was not an easy place to fade into the background. But, she said, it was worth it. Lele, who now lives in Oxford, Mississippi, with her husband, Guy Gillespie, and their children, noted, "A few blocks away from where we live, on the campus of the University, the William Winter Institute for Racial Reconciliation has just celebrated its tenth year. I'm so very proud of the efforts of the Institute (which bears my dad's name) and the exceptional work it is doing in communities across the state and region to promote racial reconciliation. Part of the institute's mission statement reads 'individual and group respect, equal access and opportunity, and justice are inextricably connected to and essential for community wellness.' This statement reflects the 'mission' that was put before us as the court called for desegregation of our schools in 1969.

"I will be forever grateful to my parents, who saw the importance of standing tall in the face of the unknown, of embracing the situation that was presented to us, of joining with other parents, both black and white, who stood by their convictions and allegiance to the public school system in Jackson. Although those days of uncertainty and a murky vision of where this experiment would take us are long passed, that hope for racial reconciliation and promise of greater respect for all people hopefully defines all of us who were graduates of the class of 1973."

Laurie Propst Ware wrote, "As I have said, I love the idea of neighborhood schools, but not if one has advantages over the other. The perfect situation would be a diverse neighborhood and community that attended a neighborhood school. Some redistricting may be necessary to achieve some kind of balance if there is none in the neighborhood. I would hate for all the work that has been done over the last thirty-plus years to have been in vain. It is a complex question and one I cannot fully answer."

Fred Sheriff found some middle ground between success for us and failure of the experiment as a whole. "It does seem that the goal of achieving equality of education for all through the integration of the Jackson Public Schools has for the most part failed," he wrote. "Maybe, for a moment, there was a 'shadow' of equality in the public schools for the first few years. Today, however, the Jackson Public Schools system seems to be largely re-segregated. And public schools in Jackson (now made up of primarily black students) face the same dilemma they did forty years ago—the need for adequate funding and resources. We have indeed come full circle. Was there then any value in what we went through in the 1970s? Yes. It was appropriate for those laws to be passed, for public schools to be integrated. As a result, if we didn't know then, we know now that this approach can only have very limited success. Clearly to have any real success, another approach must be sought; therein is the value. What did I learn? Probably something my parents already knew— that if people don't want to be around you, they will find a way to get away. It's a shame so many people had to be beaten, threatened, and killed—both black, white, and others—in an effort to achieve equality in education, hiring practices and the like. It seems the fight for equality is still going on today after all that suffering. Why? Because unless a person's heart is changed, they won't see you as equal and so won't treat you as equal. There will continue to be hatred toward those that may have a different skin color, culture or traditions than you do. This hatred may go from the overt to the covert, but it will still be there, whether one is in the city or suburbs, in public or private schools.

"One thing I have noticed, however, since I became a Christian, is that racism is only a result of a deeper problem. The same root that produces racism also produces sexism, pride, hate, gossip, etc. The Bible refers to this root as sin; sin is like a cancer that has infected the entire early race (now referred to as the human race) and unless the root of any problem is addressed, it cannot be effectively solved."

Carole Sanders Bailey was among the white students who both enjoyed her time at Murrah and lamented the loss of the old world. "Well, on one hand I'm sad that I lost out on the great experiences my two older siblings had, when Murrah was one of the top five high schools in the nation," she wrote. "When neighborhoods supported their neighborhood school, and thought nothing about it, all over Jackson, in all areas. It's just the way the neighborhoods were. Kids walking to school together or riding their bikes, all to the same school. Today, you might have five different schools represented on one block. But, on the other hand, I also feel like I got a better education in the sense of dealing with people and relating to others and thinking outside the box. And none of that would have happened to me without integration. I guess I'm torn because in my family, we had two that graduated before everything changed, and two that graduated afterwards. And there is a difference in how we think, and look at things, and what we all went through.

"What I remember is, I loved my life at Spann [Elementary], then Chastain. I loved the people I went to school with, and never thought anything different about it, other than they were my neighborhood schools. They were great academic schools and I loved my teachers. Then everything changed, and was never the same again. Was this a good change? In the big scheme of things, I guess so. Seemed to serve its purpose. Yes, it was good to go to school with so many different kinds of people. Did it serve its purpose? Yes, but on what level? Educationally? I would have to say no. I don't think the schools have ever been as strong as they were before. And I'm not sure why. To pull people out of schools where they were happy, and bus them across town to prove a point? Yes, we needed to have integration, but at what cost? Education? Busing for thirty minutes to get to a school across town? Everyone was bused across town, just to mix everything up. I'm not sure what the answer is, but thirty-five years later, the public schools in Jackson are still struggling. Some are better than others. Private schools are still here and growing, and educationally better."

Mary Al Cobb Alford wrote that when her husband, Tim, completed his medical residency in Columbus, Georgia, the couple returned home to Mississippi with two young children. "Our primary goals were to find a community with strong public schools where Tim could apply his medical skills successfully. During our search we saw firsthand the devastating economic effect that a splintered school system had on small communities in the sixties and seventies. In 1986, we moved to Kosciusko, Mississippi, and all three of our children graduated from the Kosciusko public schools. Kosciusko was an exception in that its public school system remained intact following integration due to the courage and foresight of many leaders in Attala County.

"Throughout our years in Kosciusko we have been involved in a variety of projects related to public education including establishing an Education

Foundation to supplement local school programming and teacher scholarships. We have chaired the PTA and Band Booster organizations and have sold pizzas, Brunswick stew, T-shirts, cookie dough, candles, magazines, all but our souls in support of the public schools. I even stood in front of the Kosciusko Lower Elementary School every Friday morning with a life-sized Teddy Bear collecting pennies to air condition the schools in 1989. We were successful!

"Tim is a member of 'The Club,' an interracial group with no set agenda and no dues. They meet monthly to develop friendships and relationships between the races. I have been privileged to serve on the Oprah Winfrey Boys and Girls' Club Board of Directors with a diverse and committed group of individuals. Regretfully, our church, First United Methodist, remains segregated on Sunday mornings, as do most churches in the rural South, and perhaps this is an indication of the failure of desegregation to sufficiently succeed.

"Tim and I were determined to instill in our children the importance of public education. Timothy, Leah and John Paul were minority students in their own right during many political races as their parents were two of the few white Democrats in Kosciusko. They were subjected to ridicule from teachers and classmates alike due to our yellow dog commitment. While sacrifices were made to live in rural Mississippi, I am thankful that through these experiences our children learned the value of commitment to others regardless of race or creed. I pray that they maintain this spirit and attitude throughout their lives."

Doug Minor wrote: "Desegregation may not have accomplished all of its goals, but, for us, it was a big step in the right direction . . . I am still a believer of the benefits of a public school education, and I am proud to say that my boys all attended public schools, and two graduated from public schools. I know they are better prepared for the real world, as a result of their interaction with kids from all walks of life."

In his interview, Robert Gibbs, who graduated a year before us, said he had a son at Murrah at the time we were writing this book, and a daughter who graduated from there. He said he chose to send them to public schools, and if he felt that whatever school they were attending was failing them, he would go to the principal and say, "Listen, I can take my kids and put them wherever I want to because fortunately I'm blessed enough I can afford it. So you need to be responsive, not only to my needs, but to the people who don't have any choice."

In 2011, Robert's wife chaired the board for Parents for Public Schools. When it came time to enroll their kids in school, he said, the couple "just made a choice because public school was good to me. I did well in public school even though I think if I had graduated from Brinkley I would have probably graduated in the top ten of my class. If I remember correctly when I graduated from Murrah, I think there was 210 people in my class, and I think I was number 37. So that was pretty good, but you know it was not where I would have liked to have been and I think some of it probably had to do with the fact that I had Mrs. Ruff." He laughed to recall the most notoriously hard—and aptly named—teacher who had been a hold-out of "old" Murrah.

Both of Robert's children were in advanced APAC classes at Murrah, he said, adding, "I often tell people that I got a private education at the public expense." He said it's easier to keep tabs on the schools, to be more involved in your children's education, when you are able to take time off of work, if necessary, which isn't the case with many parents. "So I think you need people of means to be in public schools just to keep the public school teachers on task."

He noted that Murrah's student body was, in 2010, 97 percent black. Some of his son's classmates at Chastain had continued on to Murrah, but most white parents pulled their children out of public schools after elementary school. He mentioned, during his interview, to Johnny, "I know you told me your kids ended up going to private schools."

Johnny said, "They did, after eight years in public schools."

"And that is what happens," Robert said. "There is something we have got to deal with in our middle schools so that parents will feel as comfortable going to middle school as they did in elementary school. I do not know what we are losing there, when I would go to Chastain sometimes and I see how unruly some of the kids were, I can understand. I still felt that I needed to keep my children there to send a message. And I could go talk to the principal and tell him, you know, that if you don't keep a lock down on this school you are going to have people that are scared to send their kids here."

Robert said his daughter was a cheerleader at both Chastain and Murrah. "Some of the white cheerleaders at Chastain matriculated to Murrah, but after being there for about a year they left," he said. "And I always wondered why. I never found out why. I don't know if they felt unsafe or uncomfortable or whatever. They were all friends. Usually when you come over with friends, you stick together, but why they left, I do not know. Her senior year in school the cheerleading squad was all black, but when she went over there it was three or four whites on the cheerleading squad. So I am not sure why they left. It has not changed. You know, we have got to figure out a way for white parents who live in the city of Jackson to start going back to the public schools. Until we can figure out a way to make that happen, the school is going to stay segregated, because Johnny is not going to have his child as the only white student in a predominately black school. He's just not going to do that. I would probably have the same problem if my child was the only black student in a white school. But we have got to figure out a way . . . once they go to Casey and go to McWillie [elementary schools], we've got to figure out a way to keep them matriculating up through Chastain and Murrah, and we just haven't figured that out."

Johnny responded, "That is one of the things we were interested in exploring. Because it really worked. We did not get to that tipping point where you had a massive out-flux of white people, really, until about '75. Freddie Lee was a coach at Murrah; we interviewed Coach Lee and Coach Clanton. They said they had basically the same school that we all went to. Claiborne went to the old Murrah. But we all went through until about '76 or '77, when it went from a 30–35 percent white involvement, white student population just down dramatically and never, ever came back."

Johnny asked Robert to explain what he sees as the legacy of our experience at Murrah. His answer: "That I think black and whites can live together peacefully in society. It doesn't matter where you come from, your background, your experiences. You put people in a common place, particularly where learning takes place, you, and the future, is whatever you want it to be."

In his essay, Johnny said that despite what he considers the ultimate failure of school integration, for our class, "I think it worked. Given what happened before and since our high school years, there really is no question that it worked. It is unrealistic and wrong to dismiss or minimize what actually happened and what was achieved, which is nothing short of historic. Our experience is one of the very few success stories that exist in the extensive record of race relations in Mississippi. I know of nothing that compares to it. That it worked out at all is nothing short of miraculous."

"There was less than no assurance that it would work," he wrote. "Many times it teetered on the brink of utter failure. We really were the first [major] school system in the entire nation to be flung out into the storm alone. There was no script and no set of instructions. We had to survive without experience on what worked and what would not, without support in the general population and certainly none from local politicians (with the important exception of the greatest statesman Mississippi produced in the last century or, in my view, since statehood in 1817, William Winter . . .) and without an enlightened or even competent leadership among the people who ran the system. With very few exceptions, [white] Mississippians in our time disagreed with the goal of integration and were adamantly opposed to the process selected for achieving it. We students were seen as helpless pawns in the ongoing struggle with federal intervention in Mississippi affairs, the same struggle that brought us the wars and retrenchment that dominate our wretched history. The wrong side of that old struggle won, again, and integration of the public schools ultimately failed because it became another battle for the forces of massive resistance, meaning old white people who were no different from the white politicians who thought the right way to respond to *Brown* in 1954 was to privatize all public schools and abrogate mandatory school attendance laws. Those of us who stayed with public schools were engaged in a struggle that most of our fellow citizens desperately wanted us to lose.

"The strangest thing to contemplate [now] is: Integration was the victim of the same old forces of massive resistance that have always held Mississippi back and benight us still. But among the lessons we learned at Murrah is that it really is okay to go it alone and trust our own instincts regardless of the attitudes of the majority, and that decisions based on fear are always wrong."

Johnny credited the students for making integration work in Jackson in the seventies. "In places like Boston in 1974 and other northern urban areas the white population rioted, closed schools, shot into school busses and school buildings, and pitted their will against the federal courts with far more cataclysmic results," he wrote. "The story of integration of the public schools in those enlightened places is one of abject failure and embarrassment. But in a strange turnabout or trick of fate, here in the heart of Dixie the school administrators and parents were so out of their water that they left it to us to work it out, or not.

"One must remember that our 'leaders' in those days responded to court-ordered integration chiefly by seething at the federal courts and starting private academies, while others (including many top administrators at JPS) just gave up. But with the help of a few wise men and women like Principal Jim Merritt, Coaches Bob Stevens, Orsmond Jordan, Doug Clanton and Freddie Lee, our teachers like Mr. Barksdale, Ms. Revels, Ms. Canterbury, 'Magister' and a few others who should be remembered, we were urged in the right direction, and that was toward important goals and issues bigger than each other, and then toward each other to achieve them. We couldn't, and didn't, look to anyone else to make things work."

"Why didn't it work in the long run?" he asked. "Leaving aside for present purposes the core racism that continues to direct public affairs in Mississippi, several reasons appear obvious. It was too much too soon. A period of transition would have been invaluable in encouraging white people to stay. A statement of support for the public schools, perhaps encouraging white families to stay the course, would have been invaluable. Nothing of the sort happened, and that was a shame. By going for broke, the courts forced people to lock into their initial response—usually fight or flight . . . And then, when it was clear that integration was not working, creative plans to achieve a half-loaf or some change for the sake of balance would have been far superior to more of the same. Even today, the public education apparatus seems stuck with old approaches that have never changed anything as far as I can tell."

"Freedom of choice," as the early effort at desegregation was known, did not lead to integration, but, Johnny wrote, "For it to have worked there needed to be some degree of choice reserved to parents and their children; that would have caused more delay in achieving the goal of integration but it might have saved it for a longer run. Plus, the Jeffersonian concept of the neighborhood school was thrown down and trampled upon in our time. I never could get past the argument that driving students through several school districts closer to home to achieve a racial 'balance' was crazy, because it was crazy. Serious consideration and accommodation of these closely held principles of our democracy would have given it a fighting chance. It is enough to acknowledge now, forty years into the experiment, that the question of how to achieve desegregation of the public schools in the Deep South and preserve choice is still on the table."

Needless to say, Johnny's views—that the primary blame for the failure of integration rests with white people, and that we were all involved in some epic struggle—are his own. Myra Stevens Myrick, who was in Murrah's class of 1975, wrote in her questionnaire, "My political beliefs have definitely gotten more conservative as I have gotten older. Murrah only affected my attitude toward public education. I support public education, but I also support a parent who wants their child to have the best education available, whatever that is . . . I am glad race is no longer an issue. That is a good thing . . . good administrators, quality teachers, educating every child is important . . . The only thing I think might have worked back then was school choice. If all schools were evenly funded and evenly administered, then you should have had a choice where you went."

Richard Sanders wrote, "I enjoy exploring value sets and cultures. I cannot say it has had more than a modest positive affect on my support of affirmative action. I believe in welfare reform or 'work fare.' This story may be related. About twenty years after graduating from Murrah, I led part of a merger team, $11 billion purchase, of another company. While on one of my first trips to Kansas City, where the company being bought was located, my host took me to their president's cake-cutting. It was their president's birthday. In the room were two hundred or more leaders and managers in their company. I was shocked to notice that only two or three black people were in the room. This was in 1995. The majority of the rest were young white males. During the event, I asked my host what different people in the room did for the company.

Naturally I asked about one of the black gentlemen. 'He's the assistant product manager for product X,' he said. I thought, OK, that is a decent position. After asking about a few more folks, I circled back to the other black in the room. My host replied, 'Oh, that is the president's driver.' I, a Mississippian, then working for a German company in their New Jersey home office, was offended and embarrassed. I was also proud that our state had progressed and was decades ahead of this company. I was also appreciative that my office in N.J. was within a frisbee's throw of high level professionals from multiple nations. Upon reflection, maybe the [Murrah] experience impacted me more than I recognize. It is hard to determine."

In his essay, Mark Flanagan wrote, "I truly believe that my two years at Murrah High School made me a better person. The experience of being a minority continues to impress upon me to treat everyone equally. Prejudice is wasted energy."

During a group interview, Kip Ezelle said most whites—including our classmates—socialize with each other, not with black people. "I don't have any black friends," Kip said. "I have black acquaintances, but I don't have any that I'd call friends that I do things with. Do you?"

John Mixon, who was a year ahead of us, answered, "No."

Kip asked if any of the white students present entertained black friends in their homes. Johnny said no. Teena and John said yes. Kip then said that having been friends in high school had prepared us to interact more in the adult world, but that full integration—including our social lives—had evaded most of us. "My next door neighbor is black," he said. "Two doors up is black. I don't have any problem with that. That's not having friends. I'll stand out in the front yard and talk to the guy next door, discuss different things, but as far as being friends, no."

In her essay, Laura King Ashley wrote that integration failed in Jackson because the quality of education declined compared with private schools and public schools in the suburbs. "If equitable education was the true basis for the desegregation, forced at that time, in that regard failure occurred," she wrote. "I mean, unless it's one of those things that looks worse before it gets better—you know, on the downside for say, forty-one years, before positive results are seen. Look at our entire nation of education—our education system used to be the standard; now, so many other countries have left us in the shade. If forced desegregation in order to provide equitable education for all had succeeded, that would have been used as the standard to provide equitable education for all in other cities, other states, and elsewhere. Maybe the education is more equitably distributed to all students in Jackson, but is it better? I don't see it from where I am."

Lenda Taylor Brown wrote: "Murrah could have remained full of tradition but unless the white flight is willing to fly back to the city our public schools may remain off balance. Do not get me wrong, they are doing great things, but the voice is not there and it would be so much greater if the flight had not occurred. Again, I have to blame the ones who left. I do think today people are very prejudiced and we still have a very long way to go; not sure how long it may take for people not to hate and prejudge because of their differences. It is up to us to teach our children to not prejudge. How do we expect our children to go to college and then to the work force if they have been sheltered in an all-white perfect setting; sorry, but the real world is not that little box."

Adrienne Day said she has mixed feelings about recent court rulings ending efforts to achieve racial balance. "Now, there are no enforced laws that segregate the races and neighborhoods and schools can be more mixed racially," she wrote.

Adrienne taught at a predominately black elementary charter school in Oklahoma City, and said it was beset by gangs, drugs, and shootings in the neighborhood. "One of my students was tragically killed in a drive-by shooting into his house. I worked in this neighborhood every day, 9 1/2 months out of the year. Would I want my child to attend this school? Probably I would, because it was a good school where teachers and administrators worked diligently for quality education of the students." There is more to getting a full education than academics, she said.

Adrienne calls herself a liberal Democrat, "to the left of the late Ted Kennedy." She said of Murrah, "Perhaps this experience opened me to more possibilities than I realize. I became very interested in race relations in the U.S. and researched not only black/white relations, but Asian, Native Americans, and Hispanics. Unfortunately, race, ethnicity, and religious beliefs have put many at a disadvantage in this country. I have worked with low-income at-risk families of many races and ethnic backgrounds in teaching, with other jobs and places I have lived (Arizona, California, and Oklahoma). Disadvantaged (both economically and socially), disabled, alienated youth, struggling single parents, all need the help that society can muster. We are our brother's keeper. Some think it's not their problem, but I strongly feel it is everyone's concern. The place where I landed and have made my home is a university town in one of the most conservative states in the union. There are many nationalities, races, and religions represented here. I socialize with many Asian (Far East, Middle Eastern, Near Eastern), Native Americans, Hispanics from Mexico and South America, and Africans and African Americans. While they are in the minority, their presence is felt and seen in the community. This is one of the many reasons I enjoy living here. The diversity is stimulating and refreshing."

She continued, "I know many Mississippians that had an education that was more than academics, but learning human relation skills that have taken them far in making progress for Jackson and being forward-thinking ambassadors of Mississippi when they traveled beyond the state."

"What did I learn at Murrah and about the whole integration process in general? I learned to get along with others!" David Flanagan wrote. "I received the greatest social education ever. I learned that people are people and there are good black people and there are bad black people just like there are good white people and bad white people . . . So, for us, it worked."

Katie Barwick-Snell said she understands why some parents, black and white, want to insulate their children from crime and other unacceptable behavior. "I know how frightening it is to hear gunshots outside my mama's house in Broadmoor and not know whether to hit the ground," she said. "I was saddened to see her house sell for so little because her neighborhood is so impoverished. I hope that the time for Jackson to reinvent the city is slowly happening. I know that the societal changes that are occurring in the world today seem to have awakened many of the prejudiced feelings and hate that plagued the past . . . I believe that in America today, equal education for ALL children is what will save us in the future. As an educator and school volunteer I hope all of the Murrah Mustangs that were in school with me will help make a stand for a good and equal education for all and help make the world a better place for our children."

In his interview, Governor Winter said, "I try to take off my rose-colored glasses and be realistic. I doubt that we are going to significantly reverse what has already happened; the white flight has taken place in Jackson. Now what can happen, and what I hope will happen, is that as the inner city of Jackson develops the downtown neighborhoods—Belhaven, Fondren—we will attract enough progressive white citizens who will feel comfortable sending their children to public schools. But behind it all has to be the maintenance of an absolutely quality public school system, and that is happening in individual schools, but I'm not sure it's happening across the board in the public schools. I think Murrah has maintained good quality."

Joe Reiff, who was a year ahead of us, wondered in his essay how many of his white 1972 classmates who left Murrah for private school or early college did so truly voluntarily, and how many, had they been given a choice by their parents, would have stayed. In their sophomore yearbook, he said, there are 373 whites and 5 blacks pictured. By their senior year, there were 126 whites and 97 blacks. That, Reiff wrote, "means that of the white kids who started as Murrah sophomores in the fall of 1969, almost two-thirds of them left the public schools before high school graduation. The female numbers are even more revealing: There are 207 white sophomore girls pictured in the 1970 yearbook, and only 47 white senior girls in the 1972 yearbook, meaning that over three-fourths of the girls in our class left Murrah before senior year."

In short, Reiff wrote, "It is amazing to me how quickly so many white families abandoned Murrah High School. I have heard many stories of pressure put on white families in smaller Mississippi communities to send their kids to the new segregation academies, and I wonder about interactions on the northeast Jackson parent grapevine during that time.

"Many of the whites who stuck it out at Murrah resented Jackson Prep and the attitude reflected in its founding and existence: The idea that the old Murrah could be recreated at Prep," Reiff wrote. "We scornfully referred to Prep as 'Murrah across the River.' I suspect our anger was more complex than we realized. We scoffed at the elitism and racism reflected in the very existence of that school out east on Lakeland Drive, but we were probably a bit jealous, too—of what, I am not quite sure. I had no desire to be at Prep, and I know that was true for many of my white classmates. If I am honest, though, I must admit that the ninth-grade Joe Reiff would probably have wanted to be at Prep, still chasing that illusory membership in the inner circle of the northeast Jackson elite crowd and all the popularity and 'happiness' it promised. The twelfth-grade Joe Reiff was a little more self-aware—able to critique such desires and probably relieved to be free from the imagined tyranny of the old Murrah elite hierarchy. Perhaps the whites in my class who remained at Murrah were more able to be ourselves.

"We were also angry at the constellation of factors which had led to this state of affairs. Some of my classmates use the passive voice when speaking of this: We were 'split apart,' etc. But again, there was choice involved: Each family chose how to deal with the change, and too many of them deserted the public schools. So maybe the anger of some of us who stayed at Murrah centered on our unarticulated sense that so many of our white classmates (or their parents) made the wrong choice. Maybe we were saying, 'We stuck it out and are doing fine. Why couldn't you have done that?'"

Reflecting on his days at Murrah, Freddie Funches said, "Whatever you put in life is whatever you going to get out of it. And some peoples, you know, they had more interest in what was going on than other peoples did."

Freddie said he has lots of white friends, mostly through his church, which is integrated. "After church we go out to dinner. We go to each other's houses on birthdays. We get together or meet at whatever place you want to eat at on your birthday."

During Freddie's interview, Teena noted, "Y'all were transported to the white part of town from where you were. Did you feel funny going into places like . . . I think I specifically remember being in Poet's [restaurant and bar], and I had a date with a guy from Jackson Prep. I saw you in there. I went down there to say hey to you, and I gave you a hug and we danced a little bit. When I went back, my date was so mad, because he had never seen a white girl dance with a black guy."

Freddie: "That's what I was saying. That's what private school has done to some people. It separated their mind and everything away from what real life is all about. See, you didn't even think nothing separate about it, and I didn't think nothing separate about it either. We gave each other a chance and an opportunity and a change because that's what life was all about. It was all about changing and all about your attitude . . . That's why we are here today talking, because of the fact that you treated me like a human being. You treated me like I was somebody, you didn't prejudge me; you didn't judge me at all; you just knew that you had somebody in your eyesight and somebody in your life at that particular time that meant something to not only the school, but to each other, and that was the greatest thing that could've ever happened."

The class of 1973 "jumped a lot of obstacles that we didn't know we had to jump at that particular time, but we did it in stride," Freddie said. "We dealt with a lot of things that was given to us that we didn't ask for, but we dealt with it. We mended some bridges . . . we made it happen. And when we're coming back to class reunions and stuff—we had bigger classes as it started, but as the years went on, it kind of dwindled down, because that's what life was all about." People move on, he said; not everyone cares to revisit the past. But back at Murrah, it was real, he said. He recalled visiting in Charles Irby's family home in the exclusive Eastover neighborhood, and going with Charles to River Hills Tennis Club, where, he said, "People looking at me strange, like, what is going on? And [Charles] really grabbed that real quick because, you know, he was going to private school at that time. He come out of there." Charles had been among the private school students who returned to Murrah, in his case from Jackson Prep. "He came back," Freddie said. "Well, see, he told me one time, the thing that he had to realize in life, regardless of what you do or how you do it, you still had to deal with these certain peoples at a particular time." There was no sense in trying to isolate yourself, he said.

"Some people don't like change," Freddie said, "but you know what, that's a part of life. And that's the good thing about it, that we did give each other the opportunity to change." In the years since, he said, "they pretty much dropped the ball. And it's a sad situation that it happened, because we are here today as a living witness that it could work."

Appendix: Letter to the Classmates

TO: MURRAH HIGH SCHOOL, CLASSES 1972–75
FROM: Dr. Teena Freeman Horn & John Griffin "Johnny" Jones, Class of 1973
RE: LEGACIES FROM THE INTEGRATION OF MURRAH

In December of this year, we mark the fortieth anniversary of the extraordinary efforts to achieve maximum desegregation of the Jackson Public Schools by court order. If you went through it with us (we were in the ninth grade at Bailey), you will remember the great upheaval for African American and white students and their families that attended those efforts. It was a radical plan of desegregation, an intense social experiment, and one of the strangest and most phenomenal events of our youth. Those days are long gone, not just for us fiftysomethings but for our courts and our politicians and society in general, not to be repeated in our lifetimes.

But what did it all mean? Was the disruption of expectations we all had, African American and white, worth it given the success of the efforts to integrate Murrah? Being guinea pigs for the experiment in radical desegregation of the public schools has always joined us as actors in a potent historical moment. What did we learn from it?

We ask you to write a short memoir, or an essay, or whatever you wish to call it, that tells your personal story about how you, your family and friends reacted to the changes that came about in December 1969 and for the four or five years thereafter. Then we want you to address the legacies of that effort and how you feel about the experience from your present perspective some 40 years later. We thought it would be appropriate to the effort to add an epilogue reporting on what happened to you after Murrah, your education and vocation and family including children. When you have a completed draft, please give it a title and put your name under the title. Send the draft to Teena or Johnny, or both: [e-mails and addresses were listed here].

If you have no interest in doing this much work, we are enclosing a questionnaire which contains most of the areas we are trying to cover but in a shorter format. The answers to the questions should be sent to us with your identifying information. We ask you to *please* consider this proposal and pitch in with all of us who know that the only real answers come from the hearts of each individual who went through those days with us.

That's about as far as we have gotten in planning. I'm sure that if we've got enough participation Teena and I will edit the essays and responses and put everything together in a publishable product, if only for us. We do think that publishing companies such as the University Press of Mississippi will have keen interest in this kind of thing. We are unaware of any similar attempts to do something like this—which is why we decided to do it. We may prepare an article for submission to magazines utilizing what we have learned from each other's submissions, sort of a greatest hits album from all of us. Neither of us are writers (we're a dentist and a lawyer, a mom and a dad with eight children between them) or have any proprietary interest in doing this project alone. We will have no pride of authorship, and anybody else from our class who wants to get involved in this is more than welcome. We just want to see something like this done. We are trying to collect these within a month if possible.

If you have any questions or concerns, please e-mail them to us at the address given or send us a letter. We will probably use this MHS '73 website to communicate with everyone, so make sure you're signed up.

Thanks for considering this. The only people whose perspective on the huge questions of race and the desegregation efforts of our time will matter, at least to us, are our classmates. We ought to at least try and figure out how each other feel about what happened and why. That, in the end, is all this is about.

Thanks,
Teena and Johnny, '73

Questionnaire Sent to Classmates

MURRAH MEMORIES
or
WHAT DID INTEGRATION MEAN TO ALL OF US?

INSTRUCTIONS: If you choose not to do a personal memoir, please please take a little while and write down on a separate sheet of paper or e-mail your answers to these questions:

1. What years did you attend Murrah?

2. What other schools did you attend beginning in 1969 through graduation?

3. Were you "bussed" to any school, or crossed school district lines to reach an assigned school?

4. What was that experience like? How did it make you feel then and now?

5. What expectations did you have about your high school days before radical desegregation efforts began in December 1969?

6. Did your experience at Murrah meet, surpass or fail your expectations?

7. Generally, describe how you felt about your experience at Murrah at the time you attended. How do you feel about it now?

8. Were the steps that were taken to achieve integration worth the upheaval and/or inconvenience?

9. Describe how your experience at Murrah affected your views of life and your thinking as you entered adulthood. What impact does that experience still have on your worldview and your thinking and response to issues today?

10. Did you have friends of another race at Murrah? Describe the extent of that friendship (did you visit each other's homes; go to functions together; etc.). Did you remain friends after you left Murrah?

11. Do you now socialize with people of another race?

12. How did your experience at Murrah affect your approach to people of another race or related but tangential issues such as affirmative action and welfare reform?

13. Did you engage in any fights or conflicts with people of another race while you were at Murrah or at any time after December 1969? Did that make you suspicious or fearful of people of another race? Do you still feel that way?

14. Overall, what are your attitudes and beliefs now on the issue of desegregation of the public schools? Was your experience good or bad on the whole? Was it worth it?

15. Would you describe yourself as a conservative, moderate or liberal? If you care to answer, what political party do you believe offers the best overall chance for all the people—African American, white, Latino, Asian, etc.—in 2009: Republican, Democrat or Independent?

16. If you care to answer, how have your political beliefs changed over time since December 1969 to 2009? Did your experience at Murrah play a significant part in your political beliefs and attitudes?

17. Recent court rulings have basically ended efforts at achieving racial balance or a unitary school system in favor of neighborhood schools, holding that the whole question of "race" should have no impact on the decision-making by school administrators. Do you think that is a good thing or a bad thing?

18. How does that make you feel about what happened to us and our experiences together at Murrah?

Please e-mail your responses to [e-mails and addresses were listed here].

Index